# Europe Without Defense?
### (Pergamon Policy Studies-33)

# Pergamon Titles of Related Interest

**Blazynski**   *Flashpoint Poland*

**Cannizzo**   *The Gun Merchants: Politics and Policies of the Major Arms Suppliers*

**Dismukes/McConnell**   *Soviet Naval Diplomacy*

**Douglass**   *Soviet Military Strategy in Europe*

**Foreign Affairs**   *America and the World 1978*

**Hahn/Pfaltzgraff**   *Atlantic Community in Crisis: A Redefinition of the Transatlantic Relationship*

**Link/Feld**   *The New Nationalism: Implications for Transatlantic Relations*

PERGAMON
POLICY
STUDIES

# Europe Without Defense?

## 48 Hours That Could Change the Face of the World

### General Robert Close

**Pergamon Press**

NEW YORK • OXFORD • TORONTO • SYDNEY • FRANKFURT • PARIS

*Pergamon Press Offices:*

**U.S.A.**  Pergamon Press Inc., Maxwell House, Fairview Park, Elmsford, New York 10523, U.S.A.

**U.K.**  Pergamon Press Ltd., Headington Hill Hall, Oxford OX3 0BW, England

**CANADA**  Pergamon of Canada Ltd., 150 Consumers Road, Willowdale, Ontario M2J 1P9, Canada

**AUSTRALIA**  Pergamon Press (Aust) Pty. Ltd., P O Box 544, Potts Point, NSW 2011, Australia

**FRANCE**  Pergamon Press SARL, 24 rue des Ecoles, 75240 Paris, Cedex 05, France

**FEDERAL REPUBLIC OF GERMANY**  Pergamon Press GmbH, 6242 Kronberg/Taunus, Pferdstrasse 1, Federal Republic of Germany

Library of Congress Cataloging in Publication Data

Close, Robert.
    Europe without defense?

    (Pergamon policy studies)
    Translation of L'Europe sans défense?
    Bibliography:  p.
    Includes index.
    1. Europe—Defenses.  2. Military policy.
3. World politics—1945-    I. Title.
UA646.3.C5613    1979        355.03'304      79-4693
ISBN 0-08-023108-X

Printed in the United States of America

# Contents

# CONTENTS

# Foreword

In 1897, a Polish banker named I.S. Bloch wrote a book characterizing future conflict in Europe. The book, whose 1899 English edition was titled *Is War Impossible?*, proved an uncannily prescient forecast of the horrors of World War I. Bloch's postulation of protracted slaughter, laden with equally murderous consequences for Europe's social and economic fabric, encountered derision and scorn on the part of those few general staff officers on the Continent who bothered to read the book. The Russian General Dragomiroff denounced Bloch's views because they rejected the supremacy of the bayonet. Contemporary military wisdon in all European capitols—exemplified by the Schlieffen Plan and by the French Plan XVII—reflected a common persuasion that the coming war would be a short and comparatively bloodless affair whose outcome would be determined by offensive action.

Today, over three-quarters of a century later, General Robert Close has written a controversial book of perhaps no less foresight. *Europe without Defense?* certainly deserves a larger audience than *Is War Impossible?* ever received. In contrast to Bloch, General Close envisages a future war in Europe of such lightning brevity that Guderian's blitzkriegs of the 1940s assume the temperament of leisurely eighteenth-century campaigns. Specifically, General

Close believes that the Soviet Union and its Warsaw Pact allies could conquer Germany east of the Rhine within forty-eight hours. General Close further believes that such a war would not only overwhelm NATO's forward defenses and preclude effective tactical nuclear retaliation, but also—if attended by proper Soviet diplomatic preparation—would present NATO with a politically fatal *fait accompli* resolvable only through capitulation or strategic nuclear holocaust.

How is it that such a sorry state of affairs could exist after almost three decades of substantial, uninterrupted United States and Allied investment in the defense of Western Europe? The answer, Close argues, lies in Soviet attainment of strategic nuclear parity with the United States, coupled with a dramatic expansion in the Warsaw Pact's traditional superiority in nonnuclear forces. The combination of these two developments has diminished the utility of continued NATO reliance on nuclear weapons as a means of compensating for the conventional imbalance while at the same time widening that imbalance.

I believe that General Close is correct in identifying the disappearance of American strategic nuclear superiority in the late 1960s as the root of the present dilemma confronting Western Europe's defense today. For twenty years, NATO justifiably regarded United States strategic nuclear superiority as a credible means of deterring the Warsaw Pact from employing its preponderant conventional military power in Europe. Longstanding deficiencies in NATO's own conventional forces—maldeployment, insufficient equipment and ammunition, lack of common arms, poor command and control, and tardy reinforcement capabilities—were not viewed as critical weaknesses, since the principal role of the alliance's ground and tactical air forces was that of a trip wire designed to set the stage for devastating nuclear retaliation by the United States against the Warsaw Pact. However, the demise of United States strategic nuclear superiority has confronted NATO with the prospect, first addressed by De Gaulle in the mid-1960s, that America's nuclear guarantee of Western Europe's security may no longer be reliable.

The emergence of strategic nuclear parity has clearly diminished the willingness of both the United States and the Soviet Union to resort to all-out nuclear war in defense of anything less than their respective homelands. In doing so, parity has inflated the value of preparation for conflict below the nuclear threshold. Thus, had the erosion of the West's nuclear superiority been accompanied by a reinstatement of its conventional defenses to the point where they would be capable, without reliance on a nuclear "crutch," of defeating the Pact's nonnuclear forces, General Close would have had little reason to write this book. However, as Close convincingly argues, during the past decade the balance of conventional military power in Europe—always tenuous for NATO—has deteriorated even further. Soviet strategists may now be persuaded that a two-day march to the Rhine is militarily feasible and could be undertaken without undue risk of a strategic or tactical nuclear riposte from NATO.

It is one of the paradoxes of recent history that NATO today maintains far fewer men under arms than it did during the era of massive retaliation—a strategy which relegates nonnuclear forces to an almost perfunctory role. Since the late 1950s, NATO has devoted an even smaller percentage of its collective economic product to defense, and a growing proportion of what has been allocated to the military has been consumed by spiraling personnel costs. The result has been steadily contracting force levels and dwindling resources available for research and development, and for procurement of advanced weaponry.

In contrast, since its invasion of Czechoslovakia in 1968, the USSR has embarked upon a conventional military buildup in Europe unprecedented in peacetime since Hitler's rearmament of Germany in the 1930s. Soviet ground forces have been expanded and impressively modernized. Soviet tactical air power has been transformed from a purely defensive appendage of the Soviet army into a powerful, offensive air armada capable of carrying the air war into the deepest recesses of Western Europe. The Soviet navy, once little more than a coastal defense force, now challenges Western naval power around the world. Among the most disturbing fruits of the Soviet conventional military buildup has been the pronounced reduction in NATO's traditional margin of superiority in the principal technologies associated with land and tactical air warfare—a margin believed to be essential to compensate for NATO's numerical inferiority.

The implications of the Soviet buildup for NATO transcend changes in the quantitative military calculus. As Senator Dewey F. Bartlett and I concluded in "NATO and the New Soviet Threat," a report we presented to the Senate Armed Services Committee in January 1977, the simultaneous quantitative and qualitative expansion in Soviet military power deployed in Eastern Europe raises the specter of an invasion of Western Europe preceded by little or no warning. No longer dependent upon detectable reinforcement from the western military districts of the USSR *prior to launching an attack*, Soviet forces deployed in Eastern Europe today possess combat power sufficient to mount a major invasion with comparatively little observable preparation. For an alliance whose military effectiveness still hinges upon the time-consuming mobilization and redeployment of its typically less-ready and more dispersed military forces, the consequences of a surprise blitzkrieg could be catastrophic.

Admittedly, the "no-notice" invasion scenario depicted by General Close in the pages that follow, which is also the focus of my concern in "NATO and the New Soviet Threat," constitutes perhaps the worst of all military calamities that could befall NATO. Moreover, care must be taken not to extrapolate new Soviet capabilities into new Soviet intentions. However, the threat of a lightning-fast siezure of most of Germany deserves careful scrutiny precisely because it may represent the "best case" for Soviet military planners. Could NATO's military forces today halt a sudden Soviet blitzkrieg aimed at conquering Germany east of the Rhine? Even if granted sufficient warning of an impending attack, could the alliance's cumbersome political decision-making machinery provide its mili-

tary commanders timely authority to insure a rapid, coordinated, and comprehensive mobilization of Western Europe's defenses? General Close does not think
so, and I am inclined to share his pessimism.

General Close's proposals for resolving the problems of NATO's defense
beneath the nuclear threshold are as bold as his explanation of those problems.
Many of his proposals—increased standardization of arms, repositioning of
combat units to their assigned wartime positions, improved readiness, faster
mobilization and reinforcement procedures—parallel recommendations made by
me and Senator Bartlett, and by numerous other observers. The unassailable
logic of these measures and their obvious necessity undoubtedly account for the
new and heartening attention NATO is now paying to their translation into
reality. However, General Close's call for a new European defense structure, for
eventual construction of a credible European nuclear deterrent, and for a
creation of a "popular deterrent" in the form of a massive territorial antitank
militia is likely to stimulate controversy for some time to come.

No matter what the comments are about *Europe without Defense?*, there is no
doubt that it constitutes a major, serious work by a man whose appreciation of
the political, economic, and social context of Europe's defense decisions is no
less accute than his understanding of the new military realities afoot on that
continent. General Close's grim picture of those realities is no cause for refusing
to read on.

SAM NUNN
*Senator from Georgia*

# Acknowledgments

The publication of *Europe Without Defense?*, in its original French and also in translation, would not have been possible without many friends who have given me their support, encouragement, and advice at all stages. It is impossible to mention them all by name, but I trust that these words of recognition will show my appreciation to everyone concerned.

Special gratitude, however, must go to Major Yterbrouck and Major van Esch of the Belgian Army, whose War College thesis was of enormous help in establishing the chronological and operational details of the "surprise attack"; to Professor John Erickson of the defense studies department at the University of Edinburgh for his advice; to the research library of the NATO Defense College in Rome; to Mr. Goodhart who so willingly translated the book into English; and to Mrs. Ruth Prathafatakis and Mrs. Catherine Vitagliano and the NATO Defense College secretariat for their untiring devotion in producing the manuscript and endlessly checking the data.

I am also extremely grateful to Dr. Thomas A. Callaghan, Jr., of the Center for Strategic and International Studies at Georgetown University in Washington, D.C., for his contribution.

And finally, to those not mentioned, my sincere thanks.

Brussels
November 1978

# Introduction

The theme developed in this work is built around three fundamental ideas. The evolution of the geo-strategic force relations between the two superpowers, culminating in strategic nuclear parity between the United States and the Soviet Union, has created an entirely new situation which gives full value to the conventional forces. It lends credence to the assumption of a possible open conflict with Western Europe (and thus mastery of the Eurasian continent) as the stake. In this context the threat represented by the undoubted superiority of Soviet conventional forces in Central Europe is more formidable than that which in 1949 gave birth to the Atlantic Alliance.

At the same time, the erosion of the conventional forces of the partners of the Alliance has continued unceasingly for various economic, internal political, or psychological reasons under the reassuring symbol of détente, which announces an era of peace, absence of confrontation, and elimination of potential conflict. The firmly rooted belief of the West in the "ultima ratio" of the nuclear weapon, the automatism of the American commitment in favor of Europe, and the vainness of nuclear confrontation leaving the two adversaries bled white has contributed to this "demobilization of the minds" that throws the security of the West to the winds and relies on the presumed intentions of the adversary.

The Procrustean bed of exponential costs of personnel, of more and more sophisticated equipment, and of stagnant or regressive budgets, inevitably leads to a continuing diminution of fighting units. This alarming situation increases the risks of a conflict, since it represents a growing temptation to exploit the weakness of the adversary should a favorable moment arise.

Faithful to the main principles of a strategy based on offense, surprise, speed, and shock effect, the Soviets have the capability to launch a terrifying attack and, within forty-eight hours, to take possession of the territory of the Federal Republic of Germany from the iron curtain to the Rhine. This lightning strike, making full use of the third dimension of helicopters and airborne forces and of the subversive actions of thousands of agents infiltrated into the FRG, would prevent the use of tactical nuclear weapons. The rapidity of the action and the penetration deep into opposing forces, by close intermingling with the civilian population, make use of nuclear weapons illusory, since they would cause more loss to the civilian population than to the aggressor. Furthermore, it is doubtful whether the time required for making decisions would allow action to be taken before the surprise attack had reached its objectives, thus creating an irreversible situation which would indefinitely eliminate any hope of a politically united Europe, and would, for an indeterminate length of time, ensure Communist domination of Western Europe.

It is true that this scenario is not the only possible one and that the indirect strategy, backed by superiority of military power, is liable to deprive the West of any possibility of independent decision in accordance with the process commonly called "Finlandization."

In either case, the West would be guilty of losing sight of the basic requirements for its security, of wallowing in thoughtless tranquility, and of sanctioning a more and more pronounced imbalance in force relations resulting from the progressive decay of its military apparel.

Such is the main theme of the agrument which, after an examination of the evolutionary factors as well as of the constant factors in the complex game of international relations (chapter 1), deals with the evolution of the strategic concepts of the United States and the Soviet Union from 1945 to the present time (chapter 2).

These two chapters set the scene for the development of the study which, on the basis of an analysis of the vain attempts to build up a coherent European defense (chapter 3), stresses the "balkanization" of the Atlantic Alliance, a juxtaposition of outdated national defenses rather than a geometric center for integrated, effective, and rational action.

The defense policies of the United Kingdom, France, the Federal Republic of Germany, and of the other European members of the Alliance are reviewed in turn in chapters 4 through 7.

The specifically European problems, from continuing erosion of conventional forces under the combined action of economic pressure and internal politics to the absence of standardization which costs the Alliance between $6 and $10 billion a year, are examined in chapter 8.

Have we already reached a point of no return in which the vastness of the stakes involved, i.e. the mastery of the Eurasian continent, could incite the Soviets to attempt a lightning operation? The conditions for the success of such an undertaking, the political and strategic directives which would control its planning and preparation, are examined in a realistic context in chapter 9.

The chronological scenario for the operation, starting with the action of Soviet forces in Eastern Europe together with helicopter or airborne forces and infiltrated agents, is presented in detail, as are the future geo-strategic consequences which would result (Chapter 10).

Of course, it is a useless exercise to make a diagnosis without proposing adequate remedies. Starting with the fundamental idea that the national defenses of the small- or medium-sized powers are already out of date, the study envisages various remedial measures, political, military, economic, and psychological. These range from the establishment of bodies to coordinate European defense, inseparable from political union but at the same time respecting Atlantic solidarity, to the revitalization of the present strategy.

A "popular deterrent" must intervene as a fourth dimension and be equipped with appropriate means if it is desired that "European security" be something better than a meaningless expression (Chapter 11).

The lessons of the past, the unforeseeable reversals of international relations, and the fragility of a defense policy based on presumed intentions of the adversary rather than a balance of European forces all argue that a return to a less precarious situation is possible and achievable within a European context. It is in this context that we see (in chapter 12) the best guarantee for the peace and future of Europe.

# 1 Evolution of International Relations, 1945 to 1979

When looking at a fossilized shell in the pink rocks of Monte Lessini, whose history goes back more than 300 million years, one wonders about the validity of an analysis relating to thirty years of the present century. Some of us see the last three decades as a period of profound change and of substantial modification to the system of international relations which are liable to have a determining effect on an uncertain future. It may be true to say that the acceleration of events, technological progress, disappearance of the wartime and postwar political leaders, emergence of a new generation, the impact of economic phenomena—a whole group of actions and reactions of the complex system of inter-State relations—have transformed our view of international relations as they appeared immediately after the war. It is no less certain that these changes follow profound forces which are closely linked with permanent factors and which are undoubtedly the basis of the changing panorama.

This is why it is necessary to review events of the last thirty years within a more general framework, and take these essential and almost immutable principles into account before setting down the changing events which have altered the earlier international scene without profoundly affecting the causes of this evolution.

We shall examine the changes which have occurred from the strategic and political points of view in an attempt to show their clear interdependence. Europe's position in the world, and more particularly its position between the empires of the United States and the Soviet Union, will be discussed.

This chapter will therefore include sections on the permanent and changing aspects of foreign policy; important events of the last thirty years and the main changes in the strategic and political fields; and the position of Europe between the empires—from confrontation to coexistence.

From the beginning of time to the present, the foreign policies of the powers have been guided by two main principles, *security* and *expansion*.

Whether it is expressed as the Great Wall of China, the Roman "limes," the medieval fortified castles, Vauban's fortresses, the Maginot Line, or the ring of satellites protecting the Soviet Union, this elementary concern to protect the community or nation against aggression or hostile actions is found.

Alliance or neutrality was designed with a similar concern in mind. But the most significant symptom of the desire to insure security has always been the arms race, with the purposes of facing the potential enemy on a supposedly equal footing and preventing surprise by the enemy's technological lead.

The second principle, expansion, has always been with us. It involves the deep-seated biological instinct, thirst for discovery and adventure, religious proselytism, desire for conquest, and economic pressures which have determined the start of great invasions or migrations.

In any case, it seems that the technology of the moment has always imposed limits on expansion. As Grousset said, "What is gained in extent is lost in intensity . . . " Despite modern means of communication and the immediacy and ubiquity of information, the United States, and the Soviet Union have learned that everything is lost in overextending capabilities, whatever their vastness.

Nevertheless, there are two great trends which seem to be the basis for all historical evolution—the desire to establish united groupings and centralized empires, and the centrifugal movements based on a feeling of belonging. The first phenomenon explains the entire history of the Roman Empire, the conquests of Alexander the Great, Charlemagne, and Charles V, as well as the Napoleonic and Hitlerian conquests.

The resurgence of nationalism, the "balkanization" of empires, and the present trend toward decentralization and regionalization support the second tendency. In any case, it appears that the evolution will continue with its disregard for national frontiers, since present-day problems are no longer on the scale of the nation-state and can only be solved in a much wider frame. Before going beyond the stage of association to enter that of more or less advanced integration, there must either be a totalitarian regime with the necessary means of coercion (the Soviet imperium and the satellite states which are part of it) or a general consensus and adequate degree of homogeneity to bring about political union in Europe.

I have felt it necessary to set out these fundamental tendencies, often antagonistic, which seem to form an integral part of humanity's history before analyzing the factors affecting the foreign policy and strategies of the powers.

## THE PERMANENT FACTORS

Such factors as the continental or maritime nature of the country, the vulnerability of the frontiers, the fertility or aridity of the soil, the density of population, the length of coast lines, and access to the sea, are all permanent aspects affecting the foreign policy of powers. West Germany, cut off from a third of its territory and with a population density far higher than in the 1930s, is a prime example.

Recognition of the equality of the rights of all States, whatever their size, is a phenomenon of the twentieth century and is probably the final result of the leveling tendency foreseen by Alexis de Tocqueville as long ago as 1830.[1] This major trend is seen in all fields and is expressed as much in the movement for racial equality as for the equality of sexes. As a secondary consequence, the appreciable reduction in external manifestations of authority and hierarchy, be it education, the traditional role of parents, or military discipline, has occurred.

In the case of the structure of international relations, there is some similarity with the oligarchic society before the 1789 revolution and the international society of the nineteenth century when there were only a few major decision-making powers on the one hand, and on the other, the "small States" whose opinions on an international scale were considered insignificant.

In our century, this principle of domination by the major powers has been attacked, and the opposing principle, equality of the States (set out in the preamble to the Charter of the United Nations), has appeared. There is an analogy between recognition of this principle and the achievement of one man/one vote for the masses. Although reservations must be made about the decision-making power and the intervention by the major powers in the affairs of the world, it is quite clear that in the voting procedure of the General Assembly of the United Nations, each nation has an identical vote. The recognition of equality of rights *should* enable major groupings to be established—not by force, but by a general consensus since each participating member can make its point of view heard.

The unity of any major grouping is only feasible under two types of organization, the imperial or authoritarian system which assumes the subordination of all other desires, or the federal system under mutual agreement and discipline.[2]

The political Europe of the future has not yet been able to overcome completely this "great power" idea which permeated the international relations of the last century and the first half of the present century, although all the working methods of "international democracy" are already in existence. We might think of Ferrero's comment about "a new legitimacy opposing the concepts of the last century with equality of rights."

## THE CHANGING FACTORS

It is appropriate to group the changing factors under five main headings: political, social, economic, technological, and strategic. However, there is no rigid distinction between each of these, and any one of them can affect or be dependent on the others.

## The Political Aspect

The most striking political feature is the shrinkage of the planet and the arrival of "cosmic thought" in the sense predicted by Teilhard de Chardin. The instantaneous and omnipresent nature of communication has made politics international in scope. Despite differences of race, language, and religion, the individual can be instantaneously informed of what is going on in any part of the world. None of the medium-sized powers of Europe is big enough to play a world role, and this has been confirmed by successive dialogues between the United States and the Soviet Union when the fate of the world has been at stake.

*The increasing number of States* is also a new phenomenon and is the result of decolonization and the awakening of national sentiments, particularly the desire for greater equality. During the last century five or six powers, all European, decided world policy. Today, one hundred and fifty states are theoretically entitled to a part in the decision-making.

*The changeover from bipolarity to multipolarity* is another fundamental change of these last thirty years. The economic rebirth of Europe and Japan, and the role of China (with demographic power and membership in the nuclear club) are the salient features that have radically changed the chessboard of international relations. However, we must not see these changes as an upheaval. The United States and the Soviet Union are alone able to combine *all* the factors of power, including their unrivaled, thermonuclear capabilities.

The growing role of the *Third World* or *developing countries* must be discussed. The split between the rich and poor nations has been less apparent in recent years and will continue to be so because of the energy crisis and the growing dependence of the developed countries on those holding the basic raw materials. But a new gap is now developing between the countries of the Third World that have basic energy resources and those that do not. The poorest countries will become poorer still, which means that in the near future, we cannot hope for a more equitable distribution of wealth or surpluses.

## The Social Aspect

*The population explosion* seems to be one of the most alarming phenomena of the century. If the present growth rate continues, the total population will reach seven billion in the year 2000 with an average increase of seventy million each year (the world population was estimated at 3.9 billion in 1974). The balance between resources and population could be comprised and make Malthus's forecasts very applicable. In any case, it is clear that population growth will weigh heavily on the international relations of the future and will widen the gap between the developed and well-endowed countries and all the others for whom the problem of hunger arises daily.

At the Bucharest Conference of August 1970 attended by 5,000 delegates from 130 countries, it was already possible to see how widely divergent the opinions of the two groups were. One group concentrated on population limitation by contraception, family planning, and sterilization and the other on better distribution of the riches of the planet. At the Conference, the Soviet Union maintained that it is imperialism and not population growth which is the major obstacle to Third World development. There appears to be no possible agreement between the two opposing viewpoints, but it is important that this crucial question has been examined at a world meeting.

All of the industrialized countries have, generally speaking, undergone a radical change of social order because of the shift of agricultural labor to industry or the services, together with a considerable increase in tertiary activities. This is an irreversible phenomenon that has developed to different degrees in various countries.

An examination of the table of most recent statistics of population distribution lists the agricultural population as 4.1 percent in the United States, 3 percent in the United Kingdom, and 3.9 percent in Belgium; while it is 17.4 percent in Italy, 34.1 percent in Greece, and 63.4 percent in Turkey.[3] Beforehand, four-fifths of the population worked on the land before the industrial revolutions. This phenomenon, the shift away from the land, has led to a redistribution of political and social forces. Traditionally tied to the land because he was bound to the soil by the problems of production and by a permanent concern for his livestock and harvests, the peasant was a normally stationary element whose horizons were limited to his land. The conversion of a large proportion of the rural masses to an urban proletariat resulted in wider horizons, greater mobility, and more contacts. A striking example is the movement of the emigrant worker (such as the Yugoslav or Turkish "Gastarbeiter") in the German Federal Republic. The peasant masses were more sensitive than others to the defense of the soil, and made up a greater proportion of the armed forces.

From the international point of view, we should note that the Soviet Union, although its rural population is diminishing each year, still has a high percentage of agricultural population.

## The Role of Youth and the Generation Conflict

The rapid succession of events is a demonstration of an infinitely more perceptible evolution than was the case in past centuries. Then, changes were slow and hardly felt; now they occur within a generation. Youth now has economic power it did not have; it is influenced by the mass media, while the parental role in the education of children has been reduced. By the time he is eight years old, the American child will have watched television for 8,000 hours and by the time he is an adolescent of 16, he will have spent an average of almost 16,000 hours in front of the screen. What parents can devote such a large proportion of time to the education of their children? We must surely give proper value to the influence of these means of thought diffusion.

All this is also reflected in a feeling of disaffection for military service (conscription), a reduction of patriotism, and growing internationalism and cosmopolitanism.

We must not underestimate the role of students and young intellectuals in our analysis of social change. They have always formed minority groups and now their role is becoming more and more important (Japan, Hungary, and May 1968 in France), fanned by the works of Marcuse, McLuhan, and others. Their influence will surely be felt in a variety of directions depending on whether it occurs in the countries of the Third World, in Europe, or the countries of the East.

In the Third World, the main trend will probably be toward the arousal of nationalist sentiments, the accentuation of racial conflict, frustration against the industrialized world, and the consequent development of some degree of xenophobia. In Europe, youth generally favor leftist tendencies, are inclined to support disarmament, the suppression of conscription, and a change in the consumer society. They are receptive to generous, but not always realistic, ideas and rise up against the old order without necessarily proposing new, more effective, and achievable alternatives.

This movement is to be found in almost all countries of Western Europe. Its consequence is the rejection of, or indifference to, the problems of defense and security. The granting of political rights to young people at the age of eighteen gives them a new importance as a determining factor in elections. It is therefore logical to assume that the themes defended by the young will be taken more and more into consideration by governments and politicians, since a new generation of politicians, with no direct links with the last World War, is coming to power and is less sensitive to the lessons of the past.[4]

In the Soviet Union, but particularly in the countries of Eastern Europe, the activities of young people and students could lead to attempts at liberalization and a more humane kind of socialism. Actions of this kind, if they exceed a certain threshold, will come up against ruthless repression because they open to question the very basis of the regime.

### The Decisive Influence of the Mass Media

The press, radio, and television have probably changed the face of the world and of a major proportion of humanity, and have thus created a feeling of belonging and of community. The instantaneous broadcasting of an event does away with distance and frontiers, and creates a new dimension in the problems of the world.

Through the mass media, the various themes of propaganda can reach a previously undreamt of audience, a phenomenon which will grow further when telecommunications satellites are put into orbit and allow any part of the world to be reached directly. The preferred instrument of psychological warfare, of conditioning, intoxicating, and arousing crowds, modern mass media technique brings a new factor to international relations and enables public opinion to be mobilized as part of the political apparatus.

### Periodic Migratory Movements

An underestimation may have been made of the importance of the periodic migrations of tourism and the development of means of communication, and individual or group transport.

Every year, millions of human beings travel thousands of miles from their normal environment and establish a wide variety of new contacts, discovering other regions and adding a new factor to the economy of the countries visited. Mechanization is the basis for this growing phenomenon. It might almost be considered a substitute for the great migrations of the past and it is even possible that it may be responsible for the birth of a European conscience. Despite its extent, this "transhumance" is still limited by individual standards of living and only concerns the developed peoples not subjected to travel restrictions. It seems certain that it will grow in the future because it is linked to the development of living standards and freedom of movement. It may contribute to the maintenance of peace since it is a factor in the establishment of international contacts at the level of populations rather than government leaders. It is worth noting that there are severe restrictions which limit the flow of peoples of Eastern Europe, the Soviet Union, and China, not only because of lack of resources for the individual but as a result of deliberate government policy aimed at limiting exchanges among ordinary people.

## The Economic Aspect

Since the nineteenth century, the industrial revolution linked with technological progress has altered the familiar way of life. Massive production must involve the search for outlets that can now be found on a world scale because of advances in transport. The conquest of markets or, conversely, the protection of newly growing industries, leads to an imperialist policy or to national economic self-sufficiency. But during the second half of this century, it has become apparent that the medium-sized powers are no longer capable of maintaining an economy which can extend beyond national frontiers. The gigantic investments needed for developing unexploited areas, for the search for new sources of energy, and for new projects require increased international cooperation, real solidarity, and pooling of knowledge. They also call for a widening of markets and the appearance of transnational companies capable of influencing the actions of governments and guiding the conduct of international relations in a precise but often hidden manner.

Present-day Europe is establishing itself on the basis of these premises. The European Coal and Steel Community and the Common Market meet the require- ment of a continually expanding society for increased productivity, for division of work, and for wider outlets. But the so-called consumer society is vulnerable in more than one way. The uncontrolled use of natural resources is liable to compromise a fragile ideological balance, and the industrialized countries are becoming aware of their dependence on the energy-producing countries, par- ticularly the oil-producers of the Middle East. The energy crisis of 1973 is a clear demonstration of how this affected Europe and Japan who are dependent on outside sources for seventy to eighty percent of their oil supplies. This is causing a considerable change in consumer-producer relations, whose most immediate consequence is a vast transfer of income. The consequences are not limited to a financial phenomenon. Oil is used as a political weapon and brings out the differences of view of the Atlantic allies and the lack of cohesion of a particular- ly weak Europe.

From another point of view, the economic factor *is* bringing the Soviet Union and the United States closer together in the pursuit of common interests, for example the development of Siberia and the search for new outlets and the implementation of industrial resources on a continental scale.

The monetary field is no longer a stranger to crises of confidence in inter- national relations. The declaration of the nonconvertibility of the dollar, the absence of a common European monetary policy, and the weakness of certain currencies are tangible signs of the growing hold of economic and monetary factors on present-day international relations. In the final analysis, a general crisis, giving rise to social troubles, strikes, and trade disputes, might alter the general balance by undermining existing structures, weakening the authority of governments, and substituting new systems claiming different ideologies.

## The Technological and Scientific Factor

The technological and scientific progress achieved has been enormous and is part of man's growing mastery of his environment. There now exists an insatiable desire to master and dominate nature to improve the quality and the length of human life, and to conquer and use all sources of energy.

The space race is only one aspect of this development. Putting artificial satellites into orbit now enables us to think of covering the planet with telecommunications networks, achieving more accurate weather forecasting, and acquiring more knowledge of interplanetary space. This technological evolution has brought with it a unifying factor. GARP (Global Atmospheric Research Program), dispatched from Dakar in August 1974, included the use of dozens of weather ships and fifteen laboratory aircraft, and involved the cooperation of scientists from many parts of the world with the aim of improving long-term weather forecasting. Satellite photography gives a new dimension to the military intelligence system, particularly the siting of new weapons or the redeployment of opposing armed forces. But the vital factor in scientific development lies in the use of nuclear energy and its military applications. For the first time in the history of mankind, *man now has the possibility of causing the destruction of the species.* From the twenty kiloton bombs used at Hiroshima and Nagasaki to the multiheaded megaton missiles of American and Soviet arsenals, developments have been decisive and are liable to ensure the destruction of our planet or (at the very least) to create radioactivity conditions that would seriously compromise future generations. According to the most serious statistical estimates, in the first few days of such a conflict, twenty-three percent of the population and sixty percent of heavy industry in America would be destroyed as compared to fifteen and seventy-five percent on the Soviet side. This prospect has probably caused revision of Soviet ideas about the inevitability of conflict and is the origin of peaceful coexistence as defined by the Twentieth Congress.

Two observations on technological progress are worth stressing: The amount of scientific research needed to bring a new development into service requires such enormous investment that it is no longer within the capacity of small- or medium-sized powers and therefore assumes large-scale international cooperation. Scientific discoveries applicable to the military field have permitted nuclear weapons to be miniaturized and thus used tactically. The possibilities of detection and of electronic jamming have increased, but they have resulted in infinitely shorter reaction and decision times.

We have reached the stage when the solution of outstanding problems by means of *international settlement* appears to be the only way in which we can prevent self-destruction of civilization. The continuous development of science could in the long run have unforeseeable repercussions on political systems which still maintain considerable limitations on individual liberty. Scientific discoveries in the widest variety of fields, and pure and objective research demand emancipation of the mind and the possibility of constructive criticism.

It is hardly possible to have a division between science and political realities, open to view on one side, and facing restriction and blind acceptance of established order on the other. The intellectual movement in the Soviet Union, the views expressed by a Sakharov or a Solzhenitsyn, bear witness to an awakening of conscience and a desire for greater freedom among the Soviet intelligentsia. The maintenance of the present structures in the East through restriction or intimidation will not be able to continue indefinitely.

## The Strategic Factor

Examination of the changes which have taken place in scientific and technological fields leads us to the study of changes in the strategic field. The most decisive factor of the last thirty years is the *strategic arms race and the achievement of nuclear parity between the Soviet Union and the United States.* The recent SALT II agreements put this state of affairs into concrete form but it is worthwhile to retrace the phases of this competition which has continued throughout three decades, and may spread to other countries if there is no end to nuclear proliferation.

What are the consequences of the growing parity? They are various and sometimes contradictory. At first sight it may be considered that the balance achieved in the strategic nuclear field is a favorable factor for the relaxation of tension. Reassured by its potential (which from now on is the equal of that of the United States) and confident of a second strike capability which now makes it secure from preemptive attack, the Soviet Union appears ready to create a new climate in international relations and to avoid friction with the West. The visible sign of this change of approach appears to be the pursuit of peaceful coexistence and a real effort to reduce tension in Europe.

However, "semi-nuclear parity bring immobility with it and makes a fallacious argument of any guarantee of the nuclear umbrella for third-party countries."[5] Conventional forces regain all their importance and, since the Soviet Union has a crushing superiority in this field, the potential threat against Western Europe is more formidable than ever.

Another beneficial consequence is that the halting or reduction of the strategic arms race should enable the considerable resources previously devoted to it to be diverted to other ends and should allow cooperation in peaceful research. Less optimistic people see in parity the possibility for the Soviet Union to improve its conventional forces—particularly its navy—still further, both qualitatively and quantitatively, and at the same time to increase its influence throughout the world.

As will be seen, the consequences of thermonuclear parity may be interpreted in different ways. It does seem that, whatever the importance of the first step, it must be followed by others in order to achieve a real lessening of tension and a less precarious balance of power. Adequate control must be established on both sides; a proportional reduction of the conventional forces facing each other across the iron curtain should take place on a fair basis without compromising the minimum security of the parties involved.

Above all, a climate of relative confidence must go hand in hand with the practical measures. It seems essential, however, *not* to separate the strategic problems of intercontinental missiles and thermonuclear projectiles from those concerning the imbalance of conventional forces and, in consequence, the immediate security of Western Europe.

This general discussion leads to some fundamental conclusions. The deep-seated *aspirations* of States remain unchanged; security and expansion are always the basis of foreign policies. *The means of action* have reached unthought of dimensions. Destructive power, instantaneous communications, and the range of intercontinental missiles all combine to give an armed confrontation between East and West a worldwide character whose consequences might prove incalculable.

The mass media are the ideal vehicle for the ideological struggle and for the psychological conditioning of the masses on a previously unheard of scale.

*The new structure of industrialized societies*, the trends of Western youth, and an appreciable relaxation of authority at various levels make the Western world more vulnerable than before and bring with them a diminished perception of the necessity for security. But the East, through its authoritarian and centralizing regime, is in the immediate future better equipped to achieve success in the extension of its area of influence and its ideology. It is capable of forging an unparalleled tool of power by directing its intellectual and material resources in a particular direction without regard for raising the standard of living and the welfare of its population.

*Technological progress*, along with the immense increase in destructive power, has considerably diminished warning and decision times. They were reduced to a few days at the beginning of the Second World War, and in the present era of strategic missiles, mechanized armies, and supersonic aircraft, they must be counted in hours or even minutes.

It is against this background that the last thirty years separating us from the end of the Second World War have passed. Characterized by the cold war and then by peaceful coexistence, they have seen no direct confrontation between the rival empires. The growing interdependence of the peoples of the world and the "balance of terror" led to the belief that a new international order might arrive which would favor the era of peace that both sides were claiming.

Yet the hopes founded on détente and the Helsinki Conference have been disappointing. Two rival ideologies are facing each other; one of them continues to build up a formidable military apparatus, the other is relaxing efforts and putting all its hopes in the relaxation of tension as the moral imperative for avoiding the worst. Despite increased exchanges and verbal declarations to a complacent ear in the West, the fear of a possible conflict, and the insecurity resulting from the disproportion of forces are coming to the fore again. Between two adversaries, Western Europe is trying to establish its identity through its economic power, culture, the common roots of its civilization, the dynamism of its industry, and its external relations.

Politically, however, Western Europe's influence is feeble and it is forced to fall into line with the strategic decisions made between the superpowers. In defense and security, the Europeans are accustomed "to a dependence which no longer surprises them."[6] As Henry Kissinger said when he was secretary of state, "No nation can remain great if it leaves its safety to the mercy or the good will of others. . . ." "Foreign policy must be based on realities and not on rhetoric."[7]

What are the realities of the present day and what has been the evolution of the last thirty years which has resulted in a lessened credibility in the automatic intervention of the American nuclear arsenal and in a disturbing imbalance of conventional forces in Europe?

Almost a quarter of a century ago, and with a surprising sense of premonition, André Fontaine wrote the following: "The crushing atomic superiority for the moment compensates for the very clear superiority of the Soviet bloc in troops and conventional weapons. The armies stationed in Western Europe must however be reinforced:

(1) in case of conflict, to force the Red Armies to concentrate, thus furnishing the strategic air forces with the targets without which the atomic weapons would in the long run be of little use;

(2) to reestablish the balance with the conventional forces of the Soviet bloc, the day when the latter catches up in the nuclear field and when it may be tempted to stake its all, taking the initial advantages of an overwhelming attack."[8]

André Fontaine's prophetic vision has been corroborated. This is what we shall try to show in Chapter 2 in an analysis of the evolution of the strategies and the means of action of the two rival empires.

# **2** 1945 to the Present Day: Atomic Monopoly to Nuclear Parity

Between 1945 and the present time, the geo-strategic balance has been profoundly altered. It is not really possible to understand the present or future problems without tracing the changes in the balance of forces from the end of the Second World War to the present time. It would also be a mistake to consider only military strategy. A strategic view of the world must necessarily include the political, economic, social, and psychological fields of actions.

We have already made many references to the main changes which have appeared in these various fields. This is why we shall now do no more than give a broad outline of the events which have appreciably changed the political and economic strategies of the United States and the USSR, while making a more detailed examination of the evolution of military capabilities at the strategic and tactical nuclear weapons level and at the level of conventional forces (an essential factor in the so-called flexible or graduated response strategy officially adopted by the Atlantic Alliance since 1967).

In conclusion, a critical analysis of present strategy is necessary, and this will naturally allow us to make a diagnosis.

## EVOLUTION AT THE POLITICAL, ECONOMIC, AND TECHNOLOGICAL LEVELS

It is a truism to say that our world is characterized by profound change. That changes are occurring at a high rate is part of the phenomenon of the acceleration of history, which is often barely perceptible to those living with the day-to-day events, but more obvious to those who make the effort to see things in a different perspective. These cumulative changes were mentioned by President Nixon in 1971 in his annual message on the foreign policy of the United States delivered before Congress.[1] Within the framework of this study, it may be interesting to examine the six points mentioned by Nixon and then to fit them into the present context.

Nixon's first point concerned *the reappearance of Western Europe and Japan as international centers of power.* Implicitly, it could be understood that this refers more to "civil" power (based on economic vitality, advanced technology, and stable social organization) than to military power. His second point dealt with *the emergence of new States* whose influences make themselves felt in the new international order.

*The change in the Communist challenge* was the third topic in the foreign policy message. The Sino-Soviet ideological conflict, the end of the Stalin era and the proclamation of "peaceful coexistence," and the prelude to détente all were the main factors in this reassessment of the Communist challenge. Another point of Nixon's policy report, to be discussed here later, concerned *the achievement of strategic parity between the Soviet Union and the United States.*

Then the foreign policy discussion mentioned *the end of bi-polarity and the fluidity of a new era in multilateral diplomacy.* What did President Nixon mean when he used these terms? He was probably thinking about the apparent disappearance of an abrupt cleavage between East and West, and about the interlacing of preferential relations in the diplomatic, economic, cultural, and technological fields. Perhaps he was also referring to the appreciable impairment of United States/European relations, characterized by partially hidden antagonisms in economic and financial fields, and misgivings about the disproportionate weight of a super-powerful ally in an ill-matched coalition. In any case it is certain that he was not thinking about the Manichean vision of the world of the 1950s or of the paroxysm of the cold war.

Nixon's last point, *world problems*, dealt with the results of technological development and other changes in society. Here we have to stress the interdependence and complexity of international relations in the face of the challenges of tomorrow, which disregard frontiers and endanger the future of the human race. Can we propose free democratic choice, new international or authoritarian order in the likeness of the rival ideology as the answers? The debate remains open.

I shall now try to answer three questions. Is it true that bi-polarity has given place to a multipolar system? How can the internal and external policies of the two opposing blocs be summed up? Are we entering an era of "destabilization," or shall we manage to promote an international order based on tacit or intentional acceptance of the "rules of the game"?

## Bi- or Multipolarity?

Although it is clear that the world scene is no longer exclusively dominated by the superpowers, it is no less true that by their geographic, demographic, and economic dimensions, their technological resources and their nuclear arsenals, they are the only ones with sufficient weight to have a determinative influence on the major problems of the world.

This acknowledgment of these facts is confirmed by the worldwide role assumed in parallel by the United States and the Soviet Union. The SALT agreements on the limitation of strategic nuclear weapons, the de facto recognition of the influence of the USSR in Eastern Europe hallowed by the Helsinki Conference, the modus vivendi established in the Middle East, and the technical and economic aid (the supply of wheat is probably one of the most spectacular aspects), are perhaps the outward signs of the "détente." But they are also the tangible results of a tacit agreement between the superpowers to avoid exacerbation of tensions liable to develop into a direct confrontation.

In the face of these vast problems, divided Europe has only played a modest part and its political weight is minor.

Despite its enormous demographic potential, China has little weight in the economic and technological fields. Its nuclear potential is still only a minute fraction of that of the superpowers and, as a result, it is not in a position to play a decisive role under present circumstances.

It is true, however, that the situation of the two blocs has undergone major changes since the end of the Second World War.

## Evolution of the American Position

When the North Atlantic Treaty was signed, the United States was the uncontested leader of the West. Europe was digging itself out of its ruins and the Soviet threat associated with an aggressively expansionist policy, or assumed to be such, made American protection a de facto necessity.

The American omnipotence was based upon three sound foundations—a military hegemony dependent on an absolute monopoly of atomic weapons; an uncontested economic supremacy; and unrivaled financial power.

At the present time, these three factors have changed profoundly. The nuclear balance between the United States and the Soviet Union has been established over the years. Although the American "nuclear umbrella" still remains in some eyes the sole guarantee of the very existence of Europe, New York has become just as vulnerable to the atomic exchange as London, Paris, or Moscow. The dollar has lost its sovereignty. American gold reserves have fallen to less than $12 billion and, collectively, Western Europe holds more than double that amount (see Table 2.1).

*Table 2.1.* Gold Reserves: United States and Western Europe

| | |
|---|---|
| United States | $11.91 billion |
| *Western Europe:* | |
| France | 4.352 |
| Federal Republic of Germany | 5.076 |
| United Kingdom | 0.954 |
| Belgium | 1.822 |
| Netherlands | 2.344 |
| Italy | 3.558 |
| Spain | 0.625 |
| Portugal | 1.391 |
| Denmark | 0.083 |
| Norway | 0.046 |
| Sweden | 0.255 |
| Finland | 0.039 |
| Switzerland | 3.544 |
| Austria | 0.901 |
| Greece | 0.161 |
| Turkey | 0.156 |
| Ireland | 0.020 |
| | TOTAL  $25.327 billion |

Source: *International Financial Statistics, June 1978* (IMF); data furnished by the Credit Communal de Belgique.

The economic balance has been reestablished. American technological advance is still uncontestable and continues to progress; but Western Europe and Japan have managed practically to equal and even surpass the United States in overall production.

These fundamental changes have had a marked influence on relations between the United States and the Soviet Union, and also with Europe.

At the time of Truman's election in 1948, the American commitment to Europe was considered assured, and the defense of the Western World against external and internal Communist pressure was apparently an established fact. Twenty-eight years later, the American electorate was wondering about the validity of the global role of the United States. Dr. Kissinger's foreign policy had been superseded. The newly perceived role of the United States found its roots in the feeling that the United States had embarked on a world policy which was no longer within its capability.

The "Wilson syndrome," that periodic oscillation between the crusader spirit and isolationism, is not a new phenomenon. It seems to be more accentuated now, after the Vietnam experience, the weakening of the executive resulting from Watergate, and the internal problems of the United States resulting from the energy crisis and the consequences of a marked recession.

As the London *Times* stressed in an editorial of February 23, 1976 titled "America's Policy Vacuum," the result has been a partial paralysis in American foreign policy which probably facilitated Soviet penetration into Angola. Whatever the facts may be, future prospects for American/Soviet relations might take three different forms.[2] There could be a *renewal of antagonism towards the Soviet Union and its allies*, thus breaking off the SALT negotiations and starting a new strategic arms race. Western Europe would be invited to make a considerable increase in its defense effort, in default of which it would have to envisage a reduction in American forces stationed in Europe. The conventional forces would be reinforced; Japan would be encouraged to develop its military power, including a nuclear capability; and considerable improvement in relations with the People's Republic of China would be recommended.

Of course, the United States could *pursue a policy of moderation towards the Soviet Union*. Those in favor of this policy rely on the fact that, in terms of world peace, there is no alternative to negotiation with the USSR. The end of détente would bring about a return to the cold war and an increased probability of nuclear conflict. Adequate defense based on cooperation between the United States and Europe must be maintained, but the accent would be put on political and economic power rather than on military superiority. Another possibility is a *retreat by the United States in the defense of the Western hemisphere*. This is the modern version of the "American fortress" philosophy. It assumes an abandonment of the world imperial role and the reduction of external agreements, leading to a gradual diminution of the American commitment to Europe while maintaining existing links between the United States and those European members of the Atlantic Alliance desiring to retain American strategic protection. Under these circumstances, these nations would have to bear the major part of the burden of the necessary conventional forces for the defense of the European continent. The power of the United States would be concentrated in North America and in the two oceans, but no longer in the Mediterranean basin, the China Sea, or the Indian Ocean. Priority would be given to economic and political influence.

What is the present state of relations with Europe? The uncontested leader-

ship of the United States, a product of the outcome of the Second World War, has
been progressively questioned while Europe has been making progress toward
renewed economic good health and political awakening. Over the years a dual
phenomenon has appeared. On the American side, despite repeated statements
that a strong and united Europe would strengthen the solidarity of the Atlantic
Alliance, it appears that facts have not always matched declared intentions.
Paradoxically, it can be observed that Europe's inability to unite justifies the
American feeling about giving it a "regional" role and favors the maintenance of
the de facto leadership while a certain impatience or indifference is shown about
the shilly-shallying and Byzantine discussions that hamper the process of European unification on the European side.[3] A clearer awareness of the role a united
Europe might play is associated with superficial reactions when the weight of the
transatlantic ally makes itself felt to an unduly high degree. But, on the other
hand, the ideas about union and "power policy" are only timidly shown for fear
of precipitating American disengagement and losing the "strategic nuclear protection." The emergence of "Euro-communism" in France and Italy is creating
an additional problem and is liable to reopen the whole question of the very
organization of the Alliance and the definition of its tasks.

At this point in the analysis an American choice appears necessary. Either
maintain a divided Europe incapable of contributing effectively to the security
of the West or produce an absolutely clear statement of desire to deal on an
equal footing with a politically adult Europe ready to take its destiny in hand,
i.e., to ensure its own defense, *in close cooperation with its transatlantic partner.*

This second option would probably appreciably alter the relations between
partners of equal size. It would have the merit of clearing the horizon, of
eliminating the burden of the United States's unduly heavy weight in the
Alliance, and of putting the accent on European determination to defend, with
the United States, their common values.

In order to escape from the deadlock, it is up to the Europeans to make a
decision about their future destiny and to throw out their selfish and outdated
nationalism in favor of action enabling them to speak "with a single voice."

At the present time, Europeans have doubts and grievances with regard to the
United States. The Vietnam war was certainly no encouragement for regaining
confidence. Its logical outcome, the decision to suspend convertibility of the
dollar because the war was being financed without a correlative increased burden
on the American taxpayer, put an end to the Bretton Woods agreement.
Monetary instability and inflation were the result, with their unsettling effect on
interstate relations. Finally, the superpower dialogue made some people fear an
American-Soviet condominium, settling world problems without paying particular attention to European interests. As Alain said, "I don't want to be ignored."
This profound truth is perhaps at the root of some European reticence to
commit themselves unconditionally to follow in the footsteps of their ally and
de facto protector.

## The Soviet Union and the Continuity of
## its World Strategic Aims

The foreign policy of the Soviet Union, like that of all the other powers, is closely linked with geo-strategic factors—its continental and Eurasian position; the vulnerability and length of its frontiers; its lack of access to the open seas; and the ethnic mosaic of its widely varied component states.

On the basis of the fundamental data, it is easy to find in the present Soviet policy a repetition of the traditional tendencies of Tsarist policy and a certain continuity in the pursuit of outside objectives.[4] A *new* factor in the Soviet Union's foreign policy stems from the Communist ideology and the prominent role the USSR has reserved for itself as the world vehicle for Marxist-Leninist theories and as the "home country of socialism." We shall make a detailed analysis of these various characteristics before going on to examine the evolution of Soviet post-Second World War foreign policy. The conclusions reached will allow us to make a prudent extrapolation to establish the main lines of Soviet policy in the immediate future and to make assumptions about future events.

The Continental and Eurasian Character
of the Soviet Union

Examination of a map of Eurasia is significant. Western Europe and the "little Asian cape" seem almost ridiculous in comparison with the vast continental mass of the USSR straddling Europe and Asia, extending six million square kilometers from Kamchatka to the Elbe. Expansion has taken place westward, with a view to establishing an opening toward the Baltic and the Mediterranean, and eastward toward the steppes of Siberia.

The appearance of Russia on the European scene is of relatively recent origin. If we disregard the conflicts with Sweden and the Turks of the seventeenth and eighteenth centuries, it is only after 1815 and the Napoleonic campaigns that Russia really became a European power as a result of the role played by Alexander I in the organization of a European order and the Holy Alliance. From then on Russian influence in Europe was to have various fortunes but was never to be relaxed. Before 1918 its European frontiers included Finland, the Baltic countries, Poland, and Bessarabia. A marked withdrawal eastward of Russian territory occurred after the 1918 Treaty of Brest-Litovsk when it lost all the above-mentioned territories plus the Ukraine and Belorussia which were to rejoin the union in 1922.

The German-Soviet Pact of August 23, 1939 enabled it to reconquer—for a short time—the territories abandoned in 1918. Its present frontiers, as established since 1945, correspond closely to those of before 1918, with the exception of Finland and the Königsberg area. On the other hand, by means of the so-called satellite states, its area of influence includes all Eastern Europe as far as the Elbe and the meridian of longitude 12° West.

Because of its territories east of the Urals, the Soviet Union is also an Asiatic power. This double character is of paramount importance for a foreign policy which *avoids at all costs engagement on two fronts, to the west and in the Far East*. This continuous concern is found throughout the history of the last century. After the Crimean War, interest in the Balkans gave way to expansion in the East. But after the Russo-Japanese War and the defeat of 1905, its attention was directed once again to the Balkan Peninsula since it had been countered by Japan in the Far East and halted in its expansion toward the Indies by the Convention of August 1907. During the Second World War, it was to succeed on a single front by avoiding engagement with Japan. At the present time, Russia's ideological conflict with China is forcing it to adopt a more flexible policy on the European front where détente has taken the place of confrontation. Even so, it still maintains three-quarters of its armed forces facing Western Europe.

### The Length and Vulnerability of the Soviet Union's Frontiers

The vast size of the territory results in a major security problem. To the west, the frontiers extend 18,000 km. without any effective natural barrier; to the east, they run for 45,000 km., of which 10,000 are common with China.

From the beginning of its history, Russia has been attacked from the east and the west, by the Mongol hordes, the Swedes, and the Turks. But more traumatic still must be the memory of the three invasions of Russian soil which threatened its very vitals or resulted in considerable territorial losses. In 1812, Napoleon penetrated to the heart of Russia and took possession of Moscow; in 1917, the Germans forced a humiliating defeat of the Russians which led to the Treaty of Brest-Litovsk and the loss of a quarter of its territory and three-quarters of its iron and coal mines. In 1941 there was a new invasion by Hitler's troops, who reached within a few kilometers of Moscow and in 1942 reached the Volga and the foothills of the Caucasus. The results of the war were very painful. Losses amounted to 20 million dead, half of them civilians, and to enormous material damage (7,000 km. of railways out of use; 70,000 built-up areas destroyed).

It is necessary to remember these events in order to understand the almost morbid concern for security shown by the Russians, demonstrated by the "capitalist encirclement" started by Stalin, and whose echoes are still felt. All this has led to an obsession about seeing sufficient power re-established in the West to threaten Russian territory once again, whether it be a reunited, economically and militarily strong Germany or a united Europe, over which this same Germany would establish leadership. From this fear also stems the absolute barrier against the independent possession or manufacture of atomic weapons by the German Federal Republic and the support given for all plans for the neutralization of Central Europe. In summary, in the West the Soviet Union comes up against the Westerners. There are two opposing concepts of the world, two ways of seeing relations between societies and individuals. As long ago as 1918 Lenin said that their existence alongside each other for a prolonged period was unthinkable.

In the East, there is a potential threat from a mass of 920 million people whose government is hostile, both politically and ideologically. The reality of the present, as well as the bitter lessons of the past, partially explain Russian maintenance of the most powerful army in the world, and the constant improvement of its conventional forces.

### The Pursuit of Access to the Open Seas

Imprisoned by the Baltic and the Black Seas, Russia has always tried to obtain openings towards the Atlantic and the Mediterranean. The reconquest of the Baltic States and the annexation of Kaliningrad (formerly Königsberg) have considerably improved its position in the Baltic. To the south, despite Stalin's requests at Potsdam and Yalta, it did not succeed in having the terms of the Montreux Convention altered to ensure the free passage of its fleet through the Straits, the aim of Russian policy since the Treaty of Ankiar-Skelessi in 1833 or the Isvolsky Project in 1908.[5]

It is not surprising that Stalin, following the policy of the Tsars, had asked for control of the Dardanelles, the cession of a city in northeastern Turkey, a port city of Iran, as well as a mandate in Libya. Although these requests were rejected, it has not prevented the Soviet Union from pursuing another objective —sharing the mastery of the seas. This new trend means that the Soviet Union is a maritime power exercising its influence in all the seas of the world, but in particular in the Indian Ocean, the Persian Gulf, and the Mediterranean.

### Russia's Ethnic Mosaic

Comprising more than 100 different ethnic groups whose Moslem communities account for 30 million people, the population of the Soviet Union has always needed a strongly centralized authority. This fundamental characteristic explains the need for an authoritarian regime, and the roles of secret police, the Party, and the army.

But since the Soviet Union has extended its area of influence to Eastern Europe, the problem of internal security has taken on new dimensions and it is significant that the Soviet Union's only direct armed interventions have been against satellite states. Any attempts at secession, liberalization, or excessive independence are liable to spread throughout the whole. Such a possibility would fundamentally compromise the defensive strategy of the Soviet Union and the security represented by the barrier of satellite states. Of course, the contagion of liberalization might spread throughout the Soviet Union and shake the structure of the regime. An appreciable reduction of Soviet authority over the satellites would constitute a considerable loss of prestige and might reopen the question of its leadership of the world Communist movement, already questioned by China.

The importance of the stake is, therefore, that the Soviet Union has never hesitated to apply harsh reprisals against any attempt upon its hegemony. The events of Berlin and Poland in 1953, the brutal repression of the Hungarian revolt in 1956, and the invasion of Czechoslovakia and its subjugation in 1968, are some examples illustrating the principle and show a certain continuity with the Tsarist regime.[6]

The Soviet Union maintains excessive numbers of armed forces. It is within these that a mixing of the ethnic groups is achieved, and indoctrination is carried out, teaching faith in the Marxist-Leninist ideology and the Soviet fatherland.

The possibility of deep splits or even a process of disintegration cannot, however, be absolutely discarded. As George Kennan said, "The state of the satellite area today, and particularly of Poland, is neither fish nor fowl, neither complete Stalinist domination nor real independence. Things cannot be expected to remain this way for long."[7] In this case, it is possible that the Soviet leaders will look for an external diversion. Such an attitude is a constant factor of history and has been practiced on many occasions with success. Internal cohesion would be strengthened by the specter of a peripheral threat; repression against deviationists would be justified because of remote controlled subversion from abroad.[8]

Such a situation would, according to Sonnenfeld, be the most "destabilizing" possible and could lead to a local or generalized confrontation or to preventive action. It is on this basis that the theory bearing his name was born, and implicitly recognized the permanent influence of the Soviet Union over Eastern Europe unless there is direct or indirect intervention on the part of the United States.

After an interval of more than a century, we find ourselves faced with a situation strangely similar to that prevailing at the time of Palmerston and Tsarist Russia. Safeguarding the European balance was the essential aim, and the nationalist aspirations of the Hungarians and Poles met with nothing but indifference since Great Britain wanted to prevent the unleashing of a general war. At the present time, the two superpowers consider the territories of their allies as spheres of influence in which any intervention by the opposing side would be considered intolerable.

### Détente and its Interpretation

Faced with three crucial and permanent problems, i.e. long-term economic development, technological innovations, and its agricultural situation, the Soviet Union could choose between two opposing options—either withdrawal upon itself and the solution of the problems by its own means or cooperation between East and West. The first of these has been chosen on two occasions, the first by Stalin after the NEP era when it was decided to build up socialism in a single country, and the second when participation in the Marshall Plan was refused and rigorous control over the satellite countries was tightened.

On the other hand, Brezhnev's choices follow the second option. The acceleration of economic development as a result of technological contributions from the West and the agreements relating to the delivery of millions of tons of cereals were paid for by certain political concessions. These have been argued step by step since they carry unforeseeable risks to the cohesion of the system itself. It has also been necessary to reconcile détente with the pursuit of the proselytism movement abroad. In this respect, the Soviet leaders have not allowed any ambiguity to remain. "Peaceful coexistence" in no way means ideological coexistence any more than the abandonment of the attempts to alter the force relationships of the world by means other than war.

The diminution of tension brings to the countries of Western Europe the danger of a relaxation of the effort to ensure collective security. A less apparent threat and appeasing proclamations go hand in hand toward removing the feeling of need for unpopular defense expenditures. The East is aware of this phenomenon, which plays into its hands by increasing the imbalance of forces. As we shall see later, the societies of Eastern Europe, despite the process of détente, but thanks to control of information, are continuously pursuing their defense effort.

It therefore appears that détente remains an unstable phenomenon even if both sides agree on its necessity. In order to remain viable, it assumes the maintenance of the balance. Any weakening of the West could lead to encroachments on the part of the Soviet Union and its allies who are skillful at exploiting any weakness, as has been demonstrated by the events in Angola.

After this general look at the political and economic factors of the American and Soviet strategies, it is time to go on to the analysis of the changes in their military strategies.

## FROM THE AMERICAN ATOMIC MONOPOLY TO MUTUALLY ASSURED DESTRUCTION ("MAD")

The day the Hiroshima flash announced the arrival of the nuclear era, both anguish and hope escaped from Pandora's box. All speculations about the foreseeable future of mankind bear this dual stamp. Unlimited development and the survival of the species are the two aspects of an unprecedented "mutation" in human history.

The nuclear arms race has been the result of this constant effort to maintain an adequate balance and avoid the risk of annihilation by maintaining a residual reprisal capability aimed at preventing the unleashing of a reciprocal holocaust. It has been marked by technological breakthroughs which have profoundly changed prevailing strategies, whether they are the increase in range of intercontinental missiles or, on the contrary, the miniaturization of nuclear weapons.

I shall make a distinction, perhaps in rather too arbitrary a fashion, between the three main phases of this constant competition for the achievement and maintenance of the strategic balance. The first is the period of the *American nuclear monopoly* covering a dozen years from the end of the Second World War to about 1955. The second, from 1955 to the Cuban crisis in 1962, is that of *American superiority*. The third, from 1962 to the present day, is characterized by the *continued erosion, both quantitative and qualitative, of the American lead* and the achievement of parity, or essential equivalence, between the United States and the Soviet Union.

Examination of each period will relate not only to the nuclear force relationship, but also to that of conventional forces and their air, land, and sea components since they also constitute the instrument of global strategy. The change of strategies from one period to another will be accompanied by a brief commentary relating to the implications of these changes for the Atlantic partners—the United States and the European members—and then for the Soviet Union.

## The American Nuclear Monopoly

During the first phase, the United States was the only nuclear power. This was the time of Admiral Radford's massive reprisals strategy, associated with the Truman Doctrine and the containment policy of John Foster Dulles. The Prague coup and the Berlin blockade found the West in a state of total political and military unpreparedness.

At the end of the war, the United Kingdom and the United States had undertaken the withdrawal and demobilization of their forces stationed in Europe. At the time of Germany's surrender, American forces numbered 3,100,000 men on the continent, and a year later, 319,000. The British forces in Europe were reduced from 1,300,000 to less than 500,000.[9] The Soviet Union had meanwhile neither reduced its occupation forces, nor disarmed. It was as a result of this situation of imbalance that a start was made on joint defense in the form of an international organization without precedent.

Looking back, however, we may wonder about the motives which incited the Soviet Union to maintain such huge conventional forces facing an almost powerless Europe. Were they the pursuit of an expansionist policy or concern to balance the American nuclear monopoly by a superiority of conventional forces in order to "hold Europe hostage" to prevent a nuclear attack against which it would have been powerless? We are reduced to conjecture about this, but the feeling of the moment was that there was a monolithic threat which called for immediate measures to reestablish European security.

The commitment of the United States also is without precedent. Twice, in 1917 and in 1941, America has intervened in Europe to put an end to domination of the continent by a hegemonic power. Tardy interventions that had only been able to restore the balance at the cost of considerable sacrifice were possible because external events had catalyzed public opinion and succeeded in sweeping away the misgivings of the noninterventionists. (It is worth remembering that when the conquest of Europe by Hitler was a fait accompli, eighty-two percent of American public opinion was against any form of direct intervention. It needed the shock of Pearl Harbor to give President Roosevelt a free hand.)

The signing of the North Atlantic Treaty hallows the community of interests between Europe and North America with a view to preventing any further encroachment westward by the Soviet Union. The resources available for this policy are an American nuclear arsenal, whose vehicle is the S.A.C. or Strategic Air Command, and the progressively built-up conventional forces whose essential role is that of an alarm bell. It is the trip-wire strategy, the aim of the conventional forces to prevent the fait accompli, to measure the extent of the attack, and to act as a detonator of massive reprisals aimed at destroying the vital centers of the aggressor by nuclear attack.

The slenderness of the Alliance's forces is compensated by the destructive capability of the American arsenal, and thus the idea of deterrence, i.e. the prevention of open conflict, is born. But it quickly becomes apparent that the technological progress of the Soviet Union will enable it to make good its backwardness. The first A-bomb was tested as long ago as 1949 and in August 1953 the first explosion of a Soviet H-bomb took place. The American monopoly was coming to an end.

## The Period of American Technological Superiority and its Strategic Consequences (From 1955 to the Cuban Crisis of 1962)

Two major events took place during this period. On the American side, the reduction in power and miniaturization of nuclear weapons enabled them to be used tactically; on the Soviet side, the launching of the first "Sputnik" on October 4, 1957, heralded the era of intercontinental ballistic missiles and put an end to the invulnerability of the American land mass. These two events together led to a reexamination of the massive reprisal strategy and to its replacement by the so-called flexible or graduated response strategy.

The reasons result from established facts. The continued growth of the respective nuclear capabilities no longer allowed a straightforward strategy, whose full scale implementation would lead to a nuclear confrontation and reciprocal destruction, to be considered valid. This is because, for the first time, the American continent was within the range of Soviet intercontinental missiles. It therefore seemed essential to develop a less rigid strategy which would adjust the response to the threat and to envisage a whole range of possibilities between purely conventional warfare and the strategic nuclear exchange.

It was during the famous speech at Ann Arbor that the new strategy was brought out into the open. Already, Maxwell Taylor's work *The Uncertain Trumpet* had aroused worldwide interest, since it stressed the weaknesses and shortcomings of the strategy of the time.

But it was not sufficient to draw up a new strategy; the means for its implementation had to be made available. As we have seen, because of technological progress a whole range of tactical nuclear weapons was developed. The first was the atomic gun, the strike aircraft carrying nuclear explosives (initially for the F-104G and then capable of being used with a large variety of aircraft) usable tactically in various theaters of operation. Then came missiles, either surface-to-air like the "Nike," or surface-to-surface, like the Honest John, the Pershing, or the Lance. Then there was the Sergeant, and finally the atomic mine or A.D.M. (Atomic Demolition Munition).

This technological upheaval was to have two major consequences—the supply of tactical nuclear weapons to the allies of the United States, members of NATO;[10] and the development of a new strategic doctrine and tactical procedures which, if not revolutionary, were very different from the traditional methods of conventional warfare.

In view of the importance of these changes, a few words of explanation are necessary. The European members of the Alliance were progressively equipped with the new weapons. The personnel for using them, whether air or land forces, and the launching equipment or vehicles were national. The warheads were American and the depots were guarded by mixed detachments supplied by the United States and the user nation. On the other hand, their effective use depended on a decision at the highest level by the country holding the supreme weapon, i.e. the president of the United States himself.

It immediately became apparent that the deterrent value of the tactical nuclear weapon depended essentially on the credibility of the American commitment to begin with and then on making the decision quickly enough. Another factor of change resulted from the fact that these weapons would necessarily have to be used in Europe with the resulting consequences for the territories where the tactical nuclear exchange would occur.

The development of new tactics which take the effects of nuclear weapons into account follows two different lines, one relating to the procedure for use and the other for use in different situations. A detailed analysis of these two aspects lies outside the framework of this study. I shall therefore do no more than indicate the main ideas of them and stress certain weaknesses. As we have seen, the decision on use is made at the supreme level and no delegation of authority to the military commanders responsible for implementation is permitted. In view of their confidential and conjectural character, information about restrictions on use is limited and uncertain. It seems, however, that the country holding the weapons, as well as the country where they would be used, is likely to have a right of control over their actual use. Whatever the case may be, a consultation procedure is provided for, and, despite optimistic statements, it is logical to think that there will be a relatively long time before the decision to use the weapons is made. Are these delays reconcilable with the speed of modern operations and the surprise and shock effect sought by the adversary? There are many such crucial problems, and we shall have to come back to them.

As regards actual tactical use, this has been put to the test "in abstracto" in an impressive number of maneuvers with and without troops, war games, and theoretical studies. The conclusions reached are that the use of tactical nuclear weapons assumes the a priori dispersal of both the attacker and the defender. Paradoxically, the effects of a "medium-sized" tactical weapon (of the Hiroshima or Nagasaki type) on a dispersed adversary appear to be negligible. The two most effective and apparently paradoxical means of protection are burying (bunkers, casemates, or individual holes in the ground) and armor plate, which confirms the chances of survival and the effectiveness of battle tanks and armored personnel carriers. Close contact between forces—friend and enemy— prohibit the use of tactical nuclear weapons by one or the other party because of the extent of the destruction radius.

On the offensive, the practice of infiltration, particularly at night, makes the use of tactical nuclear weapons impossible. On the defensive, inflexible and static dispositions appear to be out of the question. In both cases, mobility is essential in order to change speedily from dispersed dispositions to concentration of forces. The use of the tactical nuclear weapon assumes two "sine qua non" conditions—the existence of a *worthwhile target*, i.e. a sufficiently large and concentrated formation to justify the use of an atomic weapon of appropriate power; and a certain *permanence* of the target in time in order to permit its identification, its pinpointing, the transmission of the necessary data, and the final engagement with tactical nuclear weapons.

It results from all this that there are two essential prior conditions for the use of tactical nuclear weapons. There is the need to force the adversary to establish a worthwhile target and therefore to concentrate, which will only occur as a result of the dual action of firm and solidly established resistance and the use of natural or artificial obstacles. It is also necessary to obtain a speedy decision to use the weapon, bearing in mind the mobility and fluidity of modern operations and the high speed of armored formations.

These restrictions have appeared over a period of years; they have become still more imperative since the Soviet Union has also considerably developed its tactical nuclear arsenal.

Let us bring this long but necessary digression to an end with a final but vital observation on the validity of the present strategy. If the adversary breaks the continuity of the front by achieving a major and sudden breakthrough and succeeds in establishing it in depth similar to the "Schwerpunkt" and "aufrollen" used by the German forces during the 1940 campaign, the use of tactical nuclear weapons becomes extremely hazardous, if not unthinkable. Indeed, the adversary would have strategically achieved that "close contact" with the civilian populations which, from the tactical point of view, prohibits the use of atomic weapons.

How can their use be justified in as densely a populated area as the Ruhr against four, five, or six Soviet divisions which have succeeded in establishing themselves there?[11] All of this argument does not finally and unequivocally dispose of the flexible response strategy. It does force us to wonder about the conditions for its implementation and its credibility as a major deterrence factor. As we have seen, the present strategy is above all a strategy for the prevention of conflict. The arsenal of the available forces must be sufficiently imposing and diversified to discourage the adversary from attempting an action whose anticipated advantage would not be commensurate with the risk incurred.

If the deterrent fails, we must be capable of defending ourselves with conventional forces alone in order to assess the extent of the aggression, to contain it if possible, and to delay the use of nuclear weapons as long as possible. This is the ultimate recourse if the imbalance of forces makes defeat inevitable. It is here that we find the ideas of "nuclear threshold," "pause," and "escalation." The greater the conventional resistence capability, the higher the nuclear threshold; the converse is obviously true, and, in the worst case of almost instantaneous collapse of the conventional forces, the nuclear weapon would have to be used almost immediately. This course may force a suspension of operations by proving to the enemy our determination to take things to the extreme if necessary, and to proceed in stages as far as the strategic nuclear exchange.

Let us note in passing that this idea of "pause" could be no more than a twinkling of the eye, and nobody is capable of foreseeing the rate and intensity of the spiral leading from tactical nuclear weapons to the hundredfold more powerful strategic missiles. All this assumes sufficient conventional forces to force the adversary to mount a major operation, to be capable of offering a resistance so that the time required to bring tactical nuclear weapons into use is not overtaken by events, and finally to contribute to a rational use of the latter if they should prove necessary.

For political, economic, or psychological reasons, the members of the Alliance have never mounted the necessary conventional forces for implementing the graduated response strategy. To begin with, the West saw in the tactical nuclear weapon and its uncontested superiority an adequate compensation for its marked weakness in conventional forces. As we shall see in our study of subsequent developments, the imbalance in conventional forces has never ceased to grow to the detriment of the West, and the tactical nuclear arsenal of the Warsaw Pact is now nearly equal to that of the West. Times have changed, and we are justified in questioning the validity of a strategic concept whose very foundations have been shaken to this degree.

Whatever may be the means and methods of application, the profound changes which have taken place in the strategic concept have aroused doubts about its credibility. A whole school of thought, particularly French in inspiration, has stressed the fragility of a security whose sole guarantee depends on the truism of the automatic intervention of the United States. This brings us back to the debate about the problem of the decision of choice. Compromises have been found, starting with the Nuclear Planning Group of NPG, which have five permanent members (Germany, Italy, the United Kingdom, the United States, and Canada) and others on an alternating basis. This initiative has not completely dispelled European doubts. Questions remain about who can guarantee nuclear commitment despite the presence of American troops in Europe, about where the escalation will end, and whether the decisions will be made in sufficient time before the achievement of the "fait accompli" which would place Europe in a situation of deadlock. There are many questions without answers involving the security of a Europe totally dependent on its transatlantic partner for its defense.

During this same period, from 1955 to 1962, a fundamental change took place in the foreign policy of the Soviet Union. Its influence was to extend to other continents, and the advent of Khrushchev was to see the beginning of the Soviet commitment worldwide. The initial successes were achieved without major difficulty, but they were followed by a systematic policy during the following period only at the zenith of détente and at the time of the rocketing rise in power of the Soviet navy.[12]

For that to begin, another striking event was needed—the Cuban crisis. It was certain that the United States would find it very difficult to accept the establishment of Soviet missiles within direct range of the North American continent. We all know the sequence of events and how the crisis was solved, putting an end to a direct confrontation whose consequences could have been catastrophic. But the Soviets were to draw two major lessons from this, being aware from then on that it was always necessary to possess the means to pursue a policy. The first lesson was that it was necessary to achieve *nuclear parity at strategic levels* at all costs; the second was the *priority development of a maritime force* adequate for supporting their global expansion.

It was during the third phase, from 1962 to the present day, that these two aims were pursued and achieved.

## From American Superiority to Nuclear Equivalence

### The Striking Political Events

The period under consideration most definitely bears the hallmark of the emergence of the Soviet Union as a world power with imperial aspirations. The indirect strategy of world influence was served by the achievement of strategic nuclear power with the United States, the building up of a naval power without precedent in the history of Tsarist Russia, and the climate of détente, the master card of Brezhnev's policy (what Richard Löwenthal calls "a new 'forward' Soviet policy," May 1976, "Has Détente Failed?", p. 55).

At the same time, centrifugal movements appeared in the two blocs. In the West, they were catalyzed by the Vietnam war, the successive tensions in the

Middle East, and the Energy crisis, which made Europe aware of its vulnerability and its dependence on others for its basic supplies. The withdrawal of France from the integrated military organization of the Alliance, the Greco-Turkish dispute following the events in Cyrpus, the social revolution in Portugal and its African disengagement, the emergence of "Euro-Communisms" and the prospect of access to power by the Italian Communist Party are all alarming symptoms facing the cohesion of an Atlantic Alliance. Split between the traditional system of an organization wasting away because of its own success, and a new structure based on partnership between a united and strong Europe and the North American continent, the West has not yet been able to find a reasonable balance between dependence and complete self-sufficiency.

The resurgence of national egotisms, a climate of "demobilization of minds" encouraged by the euphoria of détente, the impact of the energy crisis, and the inability to advance the development of a united Europe all create an atmosphere of uncertainty and unacknowledged weakness which seriously compromises the security of Europe.

The Eastern bloc has not escaped similar polycentrist phenomena which reached a peak in August 1968, at the time of the Prague "Spring" uprising and the Czechoslovak crisis. The Soviet Union could not tolerate a secession with such serious consequences from both the strategic and the ideological standpoints. The vain attempts to bring a socialist client, dedicated to the heresy of a pluralist and more liberal system, back into the ranks was followed purely and simply by force and the invasion of Czechoslovakian territory. This brutal repression brought order back to the socialist camp, although it was a considerable—but temporary—blow to the policy of détente.

The West, alerted for once, did not take long to relax its effort, tempted by the long-term prospects of economic, technological, and cultural cooperation, the herald of an era of unadulterated peace. This led to the preliminary meetings for the Conference on Security and Cooperation in Europe (CSCE). The West, in exchange for increased freedom of movement of people and ideas, undertook to furnish the Soviet Union with economic and technological contributions needed for the development of Soviet industry and agriculture as well as the exploitation of its vast natural resources.

At the same time, the SALT negotiations between the two superpowers and the MBFR talks with a view to reducing tension and the disparities of forces in Central Europe, were being continued with varying degrees of success. We shall come back to these, but it has been necessary to fill in the political background before starting on the accompanying evolution of strategic capabilities.

Externally, we have already referred to the American disengagement from Southeast Asia, the epiphenomenon of a more pronounced withdrawal into the North American continent.

On the Soviet side, two major events must be mentioned in conclusion since they may have a profound influence on the next few decades. On the one hand, there is the possibility of the *exacerbation of the Sino-Soviet dispute* resulting both from deep ideological differences and old but still active territorial claims. On the other hand, *Soviet penetration in Africa*, by its skillful policy to support both the Angolan national movement and Ethiopia, is drawing the maximum advantage from the division of the West, the void following the Portuguese withdrawal, and the weakness of the foreign policy of the United States which is torn between a controversial executive and a reticent Congress. The May 1978 events in Shaba are no more than an epiphenomenon of a vast undertaking to destabilize the African continent by taking maximum advantage of local rivalries and the lack of cohesion of Western foreign policies.

**Strategic Developments**

Backed by a centralist totalitarian power capable of mobilizing all the energies of the system for the achievement of its priority objectives, the Soviet Union worked unceasingly towards a triple aim. Its goals were real nuclear parity with the United States, both qualitative and quantitative, endorsing its status as superpower, and justifying dialogue between partners of equal sizes; marked superiority in conventional air and land forces, thus hallowing its dominating position on the Eurasian continent; and the establishment of a powerful navy putting the Soviet Union militarily at a level close to the United States and constituting the major instrument for a world policy of presence and influence.

Let us briefly examine these three objectives. *Recognition of nuclear parity at the strategic level* stems directly from the "Strategic Arms Limitation Talks," better known by the initials as SALT. These talks are bilateral but the United States has kept its allies informed of the progress of the negotiations.

"Everything indicates common acceptance of the idea that nuclear stability is based on the invulnerability of forces and the vulnerability of populations, kept as reciprocal hostages."[13]

A quantitative limitation on intercontinental missiles has been agreed to, but the agreement is silent about the qualitative improvements and, in particular, the multiple nuclear heads of MIRVs (Multiple Independent Re-entry Vehicles) as well as megaton power (see Fig. 2.1).

The number of antimissile missiles (or ABMs) and the areas in which they are deployed (two per country) is strictly limited. At present, the Soviet Union has 1,594 intercontinental missiles (ICBMs) against the 1,054 of the United States; 160 strategic bombers against 400; 3,442 missiles with nuclear warheads against 6,794; and 73 missile-launching submarines against 41. A detailed table of the strategic forces facing each other is shown in Appendix A. At this stage it may seem illusory to talk of numerical parity in view of the diversification of means and the "overkill" capability. This is why the official vocabulary has accepted the expression "essential equivalence" or, more recently, "mutual assured destruction" or "MAD" and this is an entire program in itself.

**Strategic
nuclear            Weapon
potentials         systems**

ICBM Land-based
intercontinental missiles

MRBM Medium range ballistic
missiles

SLBM Sea-launched ballistic
missiles

Strategic bombers

Medium range bombers

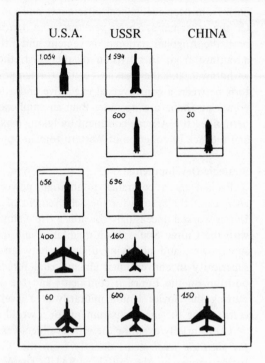

Weapon
systems

MRBM Medium range ballistic
missiles

SLBM Sea-launched ballistic
missiles

Medium range bombers

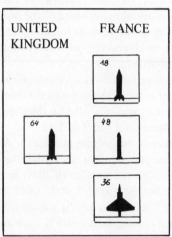

*Fig. 2.1.* Extract from White Paper 1975-76
of the Federal Republic of Germany.

## Technological Developments and Their Impact
## on the Nuclear Strategic Balance

It was foreseen that the Soviets would quickly master the technique of multiple warheads, or MIRVs, and would attempt to overcome their quality gap. This was achieved by means of only a few years of intensive trials with the introduction of the SS-16, SS-17, SS-18, and SS-19 missiles. Finally, the combination SS-20 (*mobile*, intermediate range) and SS-16 (intercontinental range) gave a new dimension to this problem by combining mobility with range. Similar progress has been apparent in the field of strategic submarines. Two systems have been tested, the SS-NX-17 (solid fuel missile) and the SS-NX-18, both of them equipped with multiple warheads.

On the *American side*, the introduction of the Trident weapons system has enabled the range to be increased to 7,200 km. The first strategic submarines of this type should come into service in 1979 and the program should be completed in 1984.

Above all, it is the "cruise missile" which has introduced a new factor into the interminable SALT negotiations and has deferred their conclusion. The cruise missile is a small folding-wing aircraft weighing about 1,000 kg. which can be launched just as easily from a land vehicle, a submarine, or a cargo aircraft. Its range varies from about 1,000 to 4,000 km. depending on the weight carried. Thanks to its very low altitude navigation, it is secure from detection by radar.

Furthermore, its accuracy is exceptional since a radar altimeter enables it to follow the terrain and variations in altitude until it reaches its target where its error should be no more than 30 m. at a range of 4,000 km. In addition, it need not travel in a straight line like the ballistic missiles, but may follow a roundabout route so that the enemy is unaware of the target being attacked until the last moment and thus unable to sound the alert. The cruise missile may be fitted either with a conventional head, equivalent to 240 kg. of explosives, or with a nuclear head of at least 200 kilotons (ten times the power of the Hiroshima bomb). The Soviet Union protested strongly against the introduction of this missile and demanded that transfer of the technology to the European NATO allies be prohibited.

On the other hand, the appearance of the Soviet "Backfire" in 1974, with a maximum radius of action of 7,500 km., increases the vulnerability of the American continent, although the Soviets refuse to include it in the category of strategic weapons. In 1976, some 60 aircraft of this type had been counted and a figure of 250 Backfires is expected by 1985.

### THE "NEUTRON BOMB"

Few new weapons have unleashed such a virulent psychological campaign, such bitter criticisms, or such impassioned controversy as the enhanced radiation bomb, much better known to the masses as the "N bomb" or "neutron bomb."

Herein lies an alarming phenomenon which most deeply affects the reactions of public opinion when the cataclysm of a nuclear war is involved. These reactions are often emotional but are of such a nature as to have a profound effect, through their extent and permanence, on strategic trends.

Paradoxically, when President Carter made the decision on April 7, 1978 not to start production of the bomb, extensive strata of European and American public opinion contested the soundness of that decision. They saw in it fresh proof that the "credibility" of an American nuclear response was becoming smaller and smaller and that the imbalance between East and West was accentuating. Accordingly, it is worth making an unbiased analysis of the extent of the various arguments.

*Technologically*, it is well known that all nuclear weapons are noteworthy for their mechanical, thermal, and radioactive effects. The neutron bomb is designed for the near complete disappearance of the mechanical and thermal effects and an increase in the radioactive effects. Broadly speaking, the latter are ten times greater for a power ten times less than that of a "conventional" nuclear weapon. The first American studies on this project go back to 1958 and were organized by the congressional Joint Atomic Energy Committee. It was assessed as "an infinitely more effective tactical weapon than all other weapons at present in service," as we shall see.

*Militarily*, the massive emission of neutrons denies fortifications and armor a considerable portion of their protective power and thus enables tank crews to be put out of action to a previously unknown degree. For the West, this represents the considerable advantage of being able to check the mass of Soviet armor whose three to one superiority constitutes one of the most serious threats to the security of Europe. *Strategically*, the weapon is capable of giving a new credibility to the strategy of flexible response. "Through its capability of destroying the armor-protected aggression troops of the potential enemy, while minimizing damage to populations and property, this weapon offered a new chance to the defense. Being on the border line between conventional and nuclear, it lowered the threshold of use and thus enabled the enemy conventional superiority to be compensated for; in the graduation of the response, it respresented a further barrier, before reaching the culmination, to the Manichean absurdity of the all or nothing of the deterrence of the sixties which has been rendered out of date by technological developments."[14] Furthermore, the neutron bomb relieved much of the distress of the crucial problem of the catastrophic devastation of the territory of the Federal Republic, the inevitable battlefield of a future conflict.

Psychologically, the magnifying effect of press bulletins, the skillful campaign conducted by the Soviets, and the support of the European Communist Parties, have provoked emotional reactions without realization of the real problem. They went as far as talking about a "capitalist" weapon destroying men but sparing property, of a "diabolical invention," of going to the extreme in destructive devices. Against this propaganda it may be said that the development of the

Soviet SS-20s, which can carry warheads of the order of a megaton, produced no reaction in public opinion, whereas the devastating effects of a nuclear missile of this power had absolutely no comparison with those of the neutron bomb. The argument used by Mr. Brzezinski also seems to be pertinent: "If the neutron bomb were deployed in West Europe right now and someone were to suggest replacing it with a big, high-yield nuclear weapon causing ten times more destruction, he would be shouted out in every European parliament."

It seems certain to conclude that the decision to produce the neutron bomb would have had the effect of strengthening the credibility of the strategy in force at present. In other words, it would increase the *deterrence*, and the imbalance of forces between East and West could be reduced without accelerating the arms race to the extreme.

We have already stressed the danger of confusion between *deterrence* and *defense*. In my opinion, the neutron bomb is subject to the same constraints in use as all the other nuclear weapons. Its implementation presupposes the prepositioning of allied units and a homogeneous and coordinated defense. It is difficult to imagine it in a fluid situation, in sudden encounters, in extremely mobile operations, or in case of strategic and tactical surprise.

Finally, its use still remains subject to the supreme decision of the president of the United States. There thus remains a margin of uncertainty about its commitment on behalf of the defense of Europe.

In this context, President Carter's decision to suspend its production without any parallel concession on the Soviet side has not strengthened the confidence of Europeans in the nuclear guarantee by the United States, nor in the role of its president to make full use of it on behalf of Europe.

The rapid review of the strategic arms race between the two superpowers demonstrates to us the differing viewpoints of the Americans and the Europeans toward vital interests and the threat facing respective continents. As has been remarkably and clearly expressed by Marc Geneste: "The growing capability of the Soviets in strategic nuclear weapons has concentrated more and more the attention of the United States on the air space and, for the Americans, the 'Blue Line of the Vosges' is the stratosphere."[15]

Two observations are necessary at the end of this examination. The balance of forces at strategic nuclear level has now been achieved and officially recognized; and the two superpowers are working more and more in concert and this has "had a marked effect on the credibility of the American protection of Europe."[16]

As General Beaufre has said in his work "Stratégeie pour demain," this could lead to "a reciprocal paralysis of the two strategic nuclear systems."

What is the situation in this respect? This is what we shall see in our examination of the second objective.

## Marked Superiority in Conventional
## Air and Land Forces

As we have seen, hegemony of numbers has been a constant factor in Soviet strategy. Confirmation and accentuation of this trend in the past few years, i.e. at the very heart of the so-called détente period, create a particularly alarming situation since in itself it brings in factors of destabilization, uncertainty, and potential peril. Since 1960, Soviet military forces have risen from 3 million men to 4.4 million, i.e. double the U.S. forces. From 1968 to 1976, the United States forces decreased by 1 million men (James Schlesinger, *Fortune*, January 1976).

The quantitative assessment of the imbalance of conventional forces is too well known for us to need to discuss it in detail.[17] We should, however, remember that out of the 166 divisions maintained by the Soviet Union, 43 are deployed against China, and 123, i.e. three-quarters, are facing the NATO forces.[18]

On the northern and southern flanks of the Alliance there is an alarming disparity of forces facing each other (see Fig. 2.2). This imbalance is still more apparent in the vital Central Europe region where 58 Warsaw Pact divisions oppose 27 NATO divisions. These figures become significant when we compare the number of tanks (19,000 Soviet against 6,100 on the NATO side) and the aircraft (2,460 tactical fighter aircraft against 1,700 in the West). If we now consider the dynamics of the development, we reach conclusions which are, at the very least, alarming. From 1968 to 1974, troop numbers in the Soviet mechanized divisions rose from 11,000 to 14,000, i.e. an increase of 22 percent; and in the tank divisions from 9,000 to 11,000, i.e. 19 percent more.[19] From 1970 to 1975, the number of tanks per division increased by 41 percent from 188 to 266 and those of the multibarrel rocket launchers rose from 220 to 700. Whereas there were 13,650 Soviet tanks in 1970, their numbers are now about 19,000.

We are thus justified in questioning the contradiction between the declared intentions of détente and the intense and continuous military effort which confers on the Soviet Union such a superiority in conventional forces "that it appears to be in a position to win a non-nuclear war against Western Europe."[20]

At the end of this brief analysis, it is fair to be rather skeptical about the happy end of the MBFR negotiations which opened in Vienna in October 1972 relating to the mutual reduction of conventional forces and weapons. It is difficult to imagine that the Soviets will subscribe to the "common level" requested by the West, thus deliberately losing all the diplomatic or military advantages conferred on them by their supremacy in conventional forces. Some optimists who refuse to face facts justify this crushing Soviet superiority as a concern to maintain the cohesion of the "imperium" and to cut short any attempt at rebellion or uprising on the part of the satellites. This is a weak and craven argument if we consider the disproportion of the forces facing each other.

Without lingering over this, we must consider the validity of the explanation when we move on to examine the third objective of Soviet strategy.

### The Building of a World-Scale Naval Power

Admiral Sergei Gorshkov is generally recognized as the architect of the extraordinary expansion of the Soviet naval fleet. It was after Cuba that he became "admiral of the fleet" and succeeded, in ten years, in transforming the Soviet Union into a top-level naval power, making its presence felt in all the seas of the world. In numbers of ships, NATO still has a certain margin of superiority, but this relative advantage loses its apparent significance when it is examined in a geo-strategic concept. The Alliance, and particularly Europe, depends on sea lines of communication for eighty percent of its essential supplies, energy in particular. This is not the case with the Soviet Union which is a continental and self-sufficient power. The most serious threat is constituted by the submarine fleet whose sixty-seven conventional vessels are equipped with missiles, and whose seventy-three strategic nuclear submarines are capable of hitting any point on the North American continent. Note that their number has practically doubled in seven years, from thirty-eight in 1968 to seventy-three in 1975.[21]

From the qualitative point of view, the Soviet fleet is the equal of, or surpasses, its American counterpart. Its ships are more modern, its unity of action stems from its central command and from its standardized equipment and logistics. The training and professional ability of its crews are in no way inferior to those of the NATO fleets. This is an estimate confirmed by the evidence of American naval authorities, either the commander of the Sixth Fleet or Admiral Zumwalt, the previous chief of United States naval operations.

Certainly the Soviet Union has a considerable inferiority in aircraft carriers and embarked aircraft. But the construction of two ships of this kind, one of which (the "Kiev") is now operational and the other operational in the near future, indicates that it plans to remedy its backwardness in this field.

We may wonder about the real causes of an expansion of Soviet naval power at such a rapid rate. I see three major reasons. They are to establish for all time the superpower status of the Soviet Union, from now on the equal partner of the United States in sharing world responsibilities; to forge the preferential instrument, both flexible and powerful, for supporting the USSR's policy of presence and influence on a world scale and more particularly with respect to the Third World; and to create a potential and permanent threat to the sea lines of communication of the Alliance and Europe, and possibly to apply diplomatic blackmail, taking advantage of the vulnerability of the West and its dependence on others for energy resources and raw materials.

In retrospect, we may be surprised at the rapidity with which the USSR has been able to achieve these three objectives *simultaneously*. A few figures will make it easier to understand the vastness of the task completed within such a short time. In 1965, the USSR had 224 intercontinental missiles (ICBMs). Ten years later, this number had reached 1,618. Battle tanks, for all theaters of operation, rose from 30,500 to 42,000, and tactical aircraft from 3,250 to 5,350. This quantitative expansion went hand in hand with remarkable qualitative improvements.

The growing gap between the military equipment production capacities of the United States and the USSR is justifiably alarming those responsible for the military policy of the United States. General George S. Brown, former chairman of the Joint Chiefs of Staff Committee, has quoted the following figures. Since 1962, the Soviets have built more than 1,300 ships against 300 by the United States during the same period. In the last five years, the Soviets have produced about 15,000 tanks against our 2,100; 20,000 armored personnel carriers compared with out 7,900; 6,750 artillery pieces against 1,350; and about 4,600 tactical aircraft against 3,000.[27]

Since 1965, intercontinental missiles have risen from 244 to more than 1,600, and strategic nuclear submarines from 29 to 73. In manpower, during the same period, the increase has been almost a million men. In short, comments General Brown, present Soviet military power exceeds ours by more than two to one. He concludes by asking, "Can the American people still ignore this evolution and base our defense on hopes rather than facts?"

Continued progress in building up an unprecedented military power has been subject to no checks, despite technological backwardness in some civilian sectors, an economic situation branded with instability, an acute crisis in the agricultural sector, and above all a standard of living far inferior to that of the West.

It is an alarming sign that the Soviets have continued, without any relaxation, to give absolute priority to the instruments of power and to their external protection without any real concession to improvement of the consumer economy, and without any rearrangement of its budgetary choices to help an unsteady economy.

Has the West interpreted all this correctly? It is doubtful. In any case, it is time to open the eyes of a European public opinion which is still the prisoner of outdated slogans and remarkably unwilling to accept the analysis and lucid interpretation of concrete facts which run counter to its hope. They must recognize that the automatism of the protection assured by the "American atomic umbrella" is far short of being guaranteed. It has served as a facile pretext for the European refusal to insure its own security, but it will only apply if there is agreement to make the necessary effort. The myth that the quantitative imbalance is compensated for by the superior quality of our equipment should be stacked in the storehouse of outdated equipment. The subtle distinction between *intentions* and *capabilities* which have given rise to interminable controversy obscures the real issues.

The building up of adequate facilities is a catalyst and authorizes modified policy for use and strategy. In other words, the possibilities are inseparable from the long-term intentions. To think otherwise would be to deny any logic in the unbelievable expense which has been the principal factor in the construction of the tool. My conclusion will discuss the reality of the potential threat, considered by most as infinitely less tangible and less formidable than that with which we were faced at the dawn of the Alliance.

### The Worldwide and Diversified Nature
### of the Present Threat

After almost thirty years of the Atlantic Alliance, and as a result of the evolution of political and military strategies associated with circumstantial events, the potential threat facing Western Europe is more diversified, more insidious and probably more formidable than was the case at the birth of the Alliance.

At that time, Stalin's expansionist aims, supported by conventional armed forces superior to those of an anemic Europe, appeared to be an admitted fact. Comparison between the past and the present leads me to think—and this may appear paradoxical—that we perhaps wrongly blame Stalin for ambitious aims which were not in conformity with the realities of the situation. Were the threat of the "rush of Soviet tanks" towards the Atlantic coasts and the conquest of the "little Asian cape" without firing a shot no more than illusions resulting from fear and insecurity? Certainly, the autocrat of the Kremlin had the means available for such a policy. But the atomic monopoly of the United States was an effective counterweight to any desire for a "coup de force." Attempting it would have been courting the certain destruction of the Russian cities, already sorely tried during the war, and the buildup of socialism and its founder country. There are other arguments which relate to the personality of Stalin himself. Having been a witness to the First World War and the territorial amputation undergone by Tsarist Russia, his first aim was to recover the lost territories and to guard against any future aggression. From that stems the creation of a ring of bugger states whose obedience to Moscow guaranteed their protective function.

"The intangible territory collected together by the Tsars and conquered 'in the name of Communism' by Lenin, and the solid buffer zone won during general sorties, of which it must be known how to take advantage, are already difficult enough to safeguard, to manage, and to keep afloat."[2 3]

There is nothing more traditional and conventional than this defense in depth based on conventional forces which are considerably superior to those of the adversary. Let us remember also that the development of the Balkans into areas of influence is very much along the lines of a continental policy of dominance of Europe.[2 4] This may explain Stalin's reticence about giving open support to the

Greek communists or encouraging Tito in Yugoslavia. It may also have stemmed from his fear of overextension at a time when all the country's energies had to be mobilized to raise the ruins and rebuild the Soviet economy from scratch.

Finally, Stalin's totalitarian system was partly based on the idea of "capitalist encirclement" and the potential danger of the resurgence of a strong and unified Germany. In my opinion, his views at the time were more directed toward *security* than toward *expansion*.

There were changes with Khruschev, who introduced a new era. The advent of nuclear weapons enabled him to abandon Austria and Finland and to put himself forward as the apostle of peace. This facilitated Russia's penetration into the Middle East and Asia. It was at that time that links were established with India, Syria, and Egypt. It was on completion of this policy of world expansion that the Cuban crisis broke. The latter showed the Soviet leaders that they did not yet have the means for such a policy, and that from then on all their efforts would be directed towards the achievement of nuclear parity and the building of a powerful fleet. This was to be the work of Brezhnev who, under cover of détente, was unceasingly to pursue these two objectives, while at the same time continuing to improve the conventional forces both quantitatively and qualitatively. The expansion phase is still in progress and its latest episodes have been the penetration into Angola and Ethiopia, the very heart of the African continent.

Is this a short-lived adventure or a platform aimed at increased influence in that part of the world? The future will tell. But there are two major facts to be remembered. The counterweight of the American nuclear monopoly, or at the very least its superiority, is from now on failing to compensate for the considerable superiority of the Soviets in conventional forces. The development of Russian naval power adds a new dimension to the strategic confrontation and stresses the vulnerability of Europe, threatened along its vital lines of sea communications. The logic of the reasoning therefore leads to the conclusion that the present threat is more formidable and more diversified than that which burdened the West in 1949.

The official recognition of the area of influence in Eastern Europe was a major success of the Helsinki CSCE. The security reflex is from now on giving way to the pursuit of expansionism, even if it is carried out at a measured tread and in prudent fashion.

The result might be an open conflict which would lead to the Sovietization of Europe or indirect pressures resulting in the "Finlandization" of the Europeans, or in severe restrictions on their freedom of decision. We shall refer later to possible scenarios.

In the face of this situation, Europe must become aware of its dependence and its vulnerability. In former times, attempts were made to create a European political entity and a European defense as guarantors of the security of the West. In the following chapters we will retrace the history of the efforts and failures,

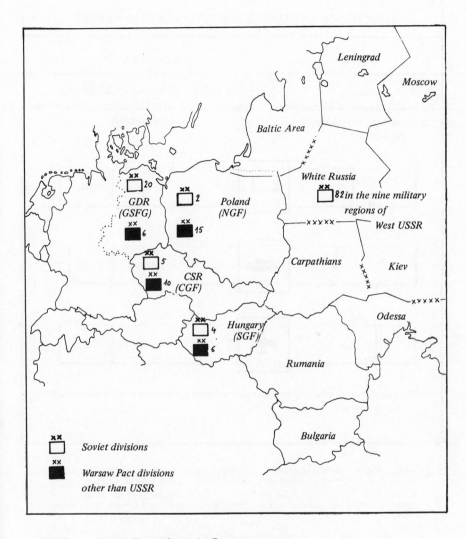

GSFG = Soviet Group forces in Germany
NGF = Northern Group forces
CGF = Central Group forces
SGF = Southern Group forces

*Fig. 2.2.* Deployment of Warsaw Pact land forces facing the Central Europe Region.

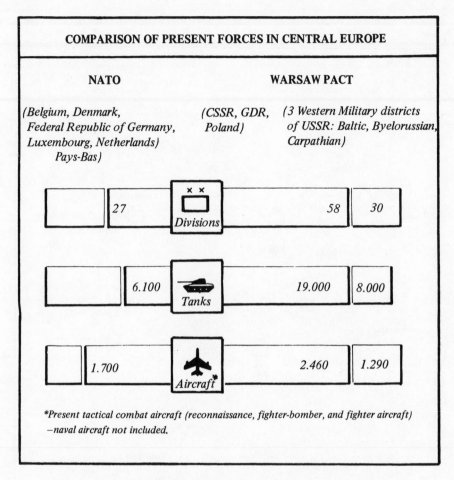

**COMPARISON OF PRESENT FORCES IN CENTRAL EUROPE**

| NATO | | WARSAW PACT | |
|---|---|---|---|
| *(Belgium, Denmark, Federal Republic of Germany, Luxembourg, Netherlands) Pays-Bas)* | | *(CSSR, GDR, Poland)* | *(3 Western Military districts of USSR: Baltic, Byelorussian, Carpathian)* |

*\*Present tactical combat aircraft (reconnaissance, fighter-bomber, and fighter aircraft) —naval aircraft not included.*

-NOTE: NATO: forces provided by Belgium, Canada, Denmark, Federal Republic of Germany, Luxembourg, Netherlands, United Kingdom, and United States.

Warsaw Pact: divisions provided by C.S.S.R., G.D.R., Poland, and the Soviet stationed forces, plus the forces in the three Western Military Districts of the Soviet Union.

Fig. 2.3. Extract from Western European Union
Assembly Document 663.

follow the evolution of national defense efforts within the Alliance, and examine the bilateral or multilateral agreements aimed at widening the narrow base of the nation-states. We shall try to answer the fundamental question of what Europe has become, and what Europe has achieved during the long evolution of worldwide strategies and the means of action of the two rival empires.

# 3 The European Defense Community: Lessons of Failure

More than a quarter of a century ago on August 30, 1954, the French National Assembly, refusing to consider the draft approval of the treaty establishing the European Defense Community, put a final stop to the first attempt at integrating the European forces with a view to ensuring the security of a group similar in size to the superpowers, and to opening the way for the political unity of Europe.

This chapter will mainly discuss the birth of this unprecedented attempt which has no apparent future; the circumstances of the time; the institutional arrangements of the treaty; the arguments supporting the attitudes of its adversaries and its partisans; and the lessons which may be drawn from it.

This study is not solely of historical interest. If we put aside from the old debate the circumstantial events, the fever of nationalistic passions, and the impact of a war whose wounds were still fresh, and if we consider the evolution of international politics since that date and the new data of the world chessboard, we may be able to find today (like yesterday) essential principles and fundamental ideas whose validity may be of assistance in building the future to the extent to which we already accept the idea that a political Europe is developing and that its mandatory corollary assumes the establishment of European defense.

## ORIGIN AND CIRCUMSTANCES

The birth of the EDC results from a dual impulse—the desire to build up Europe by transferring specific sectors to a supranational European body from the sovereignty of the states and the desire to forge a defense tool capable of facing the threat of Soviet expansionism encouraged by the political void created in Central Europe by the defeat of Germany. In addition to these fundamental factors, there is a contributory element of considerable importance. *The fear of uncontrolled German rearmament* could at a future date have led to new European oppositions relating to the disastrous experience just undergone.

Let us recall in a few words the successive stages from the end of the war to May 27, 1952—the date of the signature in Paris of the treaty setting up the EDC—during which the idea of common defense (European and then Atlantic) was born and developed. After the defeat of Germany in May 1945, Europe was so anemic that it was practically struck off the political map. Its economy was at the end of its tether, the defeat of Germany had created a dangerous void in the middle of Europe since the Allies were demobilizing their forces, whereas the Russians were maintaining a large proportion of their forces and encouraging the creation of strictly obedient regimes in Eastern Europe. The Prague coup d'état of February 24, 1948 made the West understand the imminence of the danger and the precarious state of their security. As long ago as March 17, 1948, a treaty of mutual assistance was signed in Brussels between Belgium, France, the United Kingdom, the Grand Duchy of Luxembourg, and the Netherlands. But the later participation of the United States and Canada[1] considerably widened its field of action and, on April 4, 1949, led to the North Atlantic treaty to which other nations (Denmark, Iceland, Italy, Norway and Portugal) also adhered. The German problem was not solved as a result and it was to become the central theme of all future negotiations.

This problem has three components. First, the United States desire, expressed in New York in September 1950 by Mr. Dean Acheson, to use the economic and demographic potential of the Federal Republic of Germany (established on September 15, 1949) in the defense of its own territory and, as a result, to participate in the defense effort of the Western world. The second is the prior condition imposed by Germany of the recognition of the principle of equal rights and nondiscrimination (defended by Chancellor Adenauer and Mr. von Brentano among others). The third was the French position, vehemently hostile to German rearmament (as expressed in debate at the National Assembly in September 1950 which adopted the Pleven Plan on the EDC by 313 votes to 225 but affirmed "its desire not to allow the recreation of a German Army and Staff").

Finally, the Korean war, which started in 1950, probably acted as a catalyst for the progress of the negotiations which were about to start. In September 1950, the majority of the NATO Council supported Dean Acheson's proposals and accepted the principle of the participation of the FRG in the defense of Western Europe, despite the objections of the French representative, Robert Schuman. On October 24, 1950, the chairman of the council, Mr. René Pleven, placed before the National Assembly an organization plan for the European Defense Community to which Germany would supply its contribution. The plan provided for "the complete fusion of the human and material elements," "under a single, political and military authority." The military budget was common and a European armaments and equipment program was planned. From the very beginning, two main principles were advanced (*integration* and *supranationality*), which were later to be the subjects of passionate discussions.

In this form, the plan was approved by the National Assembly by 343 to 225 and the Atlantic Council was informed of it at its meeting of September 16 to 18, 1950 in New York. The question was sent back to the military committee and the council of deputies. A little later, on November 24, 1950, Robert Schuman, minister of foreign affairs, put the French plan before the consultative assembly of the Council of Europe at Strasbourg. In particular, he said: "The States must resign themselves to giving up a part of their sovereignty in order to form a collective authority in which they would participate, but to which they would be subordinate in advance. In actual fact, this meant a minister or a European defense high commissioner under the control of a committee of ministers representing all the participating countries. This body was to have the responsibility for the recruitment, training and maintenance of the European armies. It was to manage the common defense budget and, if necessary, was to report on this management to a common inter-parliamentary assembly" (quoted from Mr. André de Smet, *La Communauté Européene de Defense*). The Assembly of the Council of Europe approved the plan with the exception of the German Social Democrats and the British Labour Party.

In its resolution of December 18, 1950, the Atlantic Council meeting in Brussels instructed the three occupying powers to study the French plan in consultation with the government of the Federal Republic. From then on, parallel negotiations were to take place: in Bonn (Petersberg), between the three Allied high commissioners with a view to studying the conditions for German participation within the framework laid down by the Atlantic Council, and others in Paris, at government level and on invitation from the French government, in order to study the arrangements for the organization and functioning of a European army including German forces.

The Petersberg Conference ended on June 4, 1951 and recognized that Germany should have equal rights in the defense community, a principle which was to be solemnly confirmed by the three allies on September 14, 1951 in New York. The Paris Conference opened on February 15, 1951 and was attended by Germany, Belgium, Italy, and Luxembourg, as well as France, as effective members, and the other NATO countries were present as observers (the Netherlands was to become an effective member on October 8, 1951).

The Pleven Plan was described at the meeting by Robert Schuman and work continued for a year with three suspensions during the meetings of the Atlantic Council in Ottawa, Rome, and Lisbon. But the French idea rallied new partisans of considerable importance. General Eisenhower supported it in July and August 1951, and in September 1951 Mr. Acheson also supported the plan for a European army (Tripartite Declaration of September 14, 1951). During this time, the work of the Paris Conference continued and succeeded in reconciling the differing points of view in a text published on February 1, 1952 by the French foreign minister.

On the eve of the meeting of the Atlantic Council in Lisbon on February 19, 1952, the French National Assembly was consulted and once again let it be known that it opposed the reestablishment of a German army and staff. Finally the Atlantic Council, at its new meeting on February 20 to 25, 1952, ratified the French plan stating that a European Defense Community *"would strengthen the common defense of the Atlantic area, enabling a closer association to be achieved between the countries of Western Europe and would satisfy the needs and guarantees of security."*[2] (My emphasis.)

The European Army was to consist of 43 groups of about 13,000 men, the basic unit being the army corps, and the air force was to consist of 75 aircraft. The institutions would include a council, an assembly, and a commissariat. The contracting parties mutually guaranteed each other against any aggression.

From then on, there was nothing to prevent the final drafting of the treaty which was initialled on May 9, 1952 by the representatives of the six participating nations and signed at the Quai d'Orsay on May 27, 1952 by the foreign ministers of Germany, Belgium, France, Italy, Luxembourg, and the Netherlands. Beforehand, on May 26, 1952, the contractual agreements were signed in Bonn between Federal Germany and the three occupying powers, reestablishing German sovereignty subject to certain guarantees to the Allies.

Before reviewing the controversies which divided opinion and finally resulted in rejection of the treaty, it is appropriate to examine its main arrangements and its general principles.

## ANALYTICAL STUDY OF THE TREATY: GENERAL PRINCIPLES AND INSTITUTIONS

It would be tedious to go into the detail of all the arrangements of the treaty, a bulky and complex document of 132 articles with 17 annexed protocols reflecting both the difficulty of the negotiations as well as the more and more obvious French reticence on the subject.

It is sufficient to stress the fundamental principles to analyze its institutions, and to give information on some basic military arrangements (financial and economic), and finally to discuss the general philosophy which we feel is still valid in the present context.

## The Fundamental Principles

There are four principles. They include the supranational character (Art. 1), the exclusively defensive character (Art. 2), nondiscrimination between the member states (Art. 6), and integration (Arts. 2, 9, 15, 68, 69, 70).

The *supranational character* results from Article 1 which provides for common institutions, armed forces, and budgets. It is however tempered by the existence of the Council, the real political leadership of the EDC made up by the representatives of the member states, as we shall see under the "institutions." in any case, there is no question that the signatories accepted a limited transfer of their sovereignty in the vital area of defense.

The *defensive character* clearly stated in Article 2, paragraph 3 states that: "any armed aggression against any one of the member states in Europe or against the European defense forces would be considered an attack directed against all the member states. The member states and the European defense forces will bring to the state or states being attacked aid and assistance by all the means within their power, military or other." The wording of this last paragraph of Art. 2 seems more restrictive than Art. 5 of the North Atlantic Treaty, which states: "each of them, in the exercise of the right of individual or collective self-defense recognized by article 51 of the Charter of the United Nations, will assist the Party or Parties so attacked by taking forthwith, individually and in concert with the other Parties, *such action as it deems necessary, including the use of armed force*, to restore and maintain security of the North Atlantic area." (My emphasis.)

We should add that cooperation and joint defense with NATO are expressly mentioned in paragraph 2 of Art. 2 (" . . . by taking part in the defense of the West within the framework of the North Atlantic Treaty") and in Art. 5 ("the Community shall work in close cooperation with the North Atlantic Treaty Organization"). Additional protocols[3] further strengthen these arrangements and state them unambiguously. Mutual consultations and joint discussions are provided for between the North Atlantic Council and the Council of the EDC as regards their common objectives; an exchange of information and permanent contact will exist between the commissariats of the EDC and of NATO.

Finally, Article 18 expressly states: "In time of war, the competent Supreme Commander who is responsible to the North Atlantic Treaty Organization shall exercise over the forces referred to above the full powers and responsibilities as Supreme Commander conferred upon him by his mandate." Article 6 refers to *nondiscrimination between the member states*. We should observe, however, that Art. 107, paragraph 4.a., introduced a factual inequality—accepted by Germany —forbidding the production of atomic weapons "in strategically exposed areas."

*Integration* is mentioned in several articles. It stops at the basic unit and was clearly introduced mainly as a guarantee against German rearmament and in certain places in the name of greater efficiency. This principle was the subject of violent criticisms on the part of the adversaries of the treaty and, paradoxically, in France where it initially found its warmest partisans.

## The Institutions of the Community

There are four bodies which comply with the classic conception of the separation of power. We shall examine them in a different order which corresponds to the listing in Article 8, paragraph 1, and probably also in order of relative importance.

### The Council

The Council is composed of a representative of the governments of the six (Art. 40), and meets as often as necessary and at least once every three months (Art. 41).

The Council is the real political authority of the community and its general task is to "harmonize the activities of the Commissariat with the policies of the Governments of the Member States" (Art. 39). The ambivalent nature of this body is immediately apparent. It is indeed composed of *national* ministers representing the interests of their governments, but, at the same time, it is the essential element and the high political authority of an institution whose supranational character is that of states.

"Being both national ministers and supranational administrators, they must be able to reconcile the interests of their respective States and the development of the EDC."[4] The Council decides unanimously when it gives directives to the Commissariat or on questions having a political influence. In other cases, agreements or decisions, unanimity gives way to a two-thirds majority. A weighing system gives three votes to Germany, France, and Italy, two to the Netherlands and Belgium, and one to Luxembourg. General rules lay down the method of voting whenever the Council is consulted, makes decisions, or gives approvals. The variety of methods of voting depending on the political importance of the matter involved again demonstrates the concern to reconcile the interests of the national states with the harmonious functioning of a supranational institution.

### The Assembly

The Assembly is identical to that provided for by the ECSC treaty (Arts. 20 and 21), with the addition of three representatives from the Federal Republic of Germany, France, and Italy (Art. 33).

The Assembly holds an annual session, the duration of which may not exceed one month, and it meets as a matter of routine on the last Tuesday in October. It exercises democratic control over the functioning of the Community and may give its opinion on the management of the Commissariat by a motion of censure carried by a two-thirds majority. It may also alter or reject the budget. One of the most important points about the Assembly is set out in Art. 38 of the Treaty which gives it the power to *establish a future European political community*. This was intended to correct one of the weaknesses of the Treaty—the constitution of a European, integrated, and supranational army before the establishment of a European political authority. Art. 38 stresses the provisional nature of the EDC organization later to become one of the elements in a subsequent federal or confederal structure, based on the principle of the separation of power and having a two-chamber system of representation.

The Assembly was to submit its proposals to the Council within six months. These were then to be transmitted to the governments of the member states, which within three months would convene a conference to consider them.

### The Commissariat

This is in fact the ministry of European defense in collegiate form. It consists of nine members appointed for six years, chosen for their general qualifications (Art. 20). The supranational character of the Commissariat is particularly stressed in paragraph 2 of the same article 20. ("In the performance of their duties, the members of the Commissariat shall neither ask nor receive instructions from any governments. They shall refrain from any action inconsistent with the supranational character of their duties.")

Generally speaking, the Commissariat is subject to the directives of the Council, without however being under its direct control. It makes decisions and recommendations and expresses opinions on majority vote of its members present. The quorum is fixed at five members present and at least four votes are required for a majority decision (Art. 23). Its competence includes powers of nomination, management, and intervention in financial and legal matters. In military matters in particular, it prepares and executes joint weapons, equipment, supply, and infrastructure programs for the European forces and makes contracts.

This arrangement was probably made to face the crucial problem of standardization which would automatically have been solved in case of application of the treaty.

### The Court

The Court's structure is the same as that of the European Coal and Steel Community. Its authority is extensive since it is the Council of State (setting aside decisions), judge of facts, and appeals board at the same time.

## The Military, Financial, and Economic
## Provisions of the Treaty

Parts III, IV, and V deal with these provisions in detail. We shall only mention briefly the principles relating to the integration of the European forces and the financial management of the community. The economic provisions are worthy of closer study since they encounter an as yet unsolved problem.

The basic unit of the land forces is the single nationality element. With a strength of 13,000 men, it is subordinate to a higher integrated échelon, the army corps, which consists of three or four elements and integrated logistical support and tactical maintenance units. The basic unit of the air forces is the half brigade of 75 aircraft; integration takes place at the tactical air command level. The naval forces, the troops needed for the defense of overseas territories, and the forces destined for certain international commissions are excluded from the European armies. The police forces remain national.

*The principle of the same period of active duty* for personnel recruited by conscription is set out in Art. 72. The Commissariat has considerable responsibilities: organization and management, the territorial location of the Atlantic forces, training, mobilization plans, the administration of personnel and equipment. The common budget for the European army is prepared by the Commissariat. The Council takes a unanimous decision about the total amount of the budget and the contributions of each member state. It is, however, in the economic area that the responsibilities of the Commissariat take on a new aspect as regards defense.

Indeed, the common armaments, equipment, supply and infrastructure programs for the European forces are prepared and carried out by the Commissariat in consultation with the governments. Under the same conditions, it prepares a common scientific and technological research program in the military field and enters into contracts after calling for tenders on as wide a basis as possible and without consideration of nationality. Finally, Art. 107 states that the production, import, or export of war material shall be forbidden, except where authorization is granted by the Commissariat.

These major provisions met the criterion of standardization of equipment on the basis of interoperability, i.e. for maximum efficiency in use. Cooperation in scientific and technological research matters and common production programs avoided duplication and ensured a vast market resulting in a lowering of the cost of manufacture. From then on, as regards defense, there was to be an economic homogeneous grouping of similar size to avoid dispersion of effort, large numbers of different types of the same equipment, and uncertainty of outlets. None of these actually took place and it is only twenty-five years later that the problem was to arise again in acute form.

## REACTION, OPPOSITION, AND ABANDONMENT

The first signs of an opposition, which was to grow steadily, appeared in October 1952.[5] From that date until the treaty was rejected on August 30, 1954, the partisans and adversaries of the European Defense Community argued with each other on behalf of the construction of Europe, or national sovereignty, in discussions which were often violent and in which the business of criticism was just as powerful as the explosions of passions sometimes hiding the real meaning of the argument.

In all probability the time was not ripe. The rearmament of a Germany whose economy was in full expansion, with its foreboding of future hegemony, the badly healed wounds left by the Second World War, the considerable costs of overseas campaigns, the chronic instability of the political system of the Fourth Republic, the absence of the United Kingdom, and finally the individualism and chauvinism of the French who were jealous of their prerogatives as regards national sovereignty explain (if they do not always justify) the profound motives of the adversaries of the treaty.

Let us now take a look at some of their arguments. The fear of a *German hegemony* within a Europe in which France, engaged as it was in overseas campaigns, would not carry its weight from both the military and economic points of view. The FRG produces 120 million tons of coal against 55 in France (the Saar excluded from both sides); 15 million tons of steel against 9. On the basis of 100 in 1936, its production index has risen in the last months of each year from 39 in 1947, two years after capitulation, to 72, then to 98, 130, 140, 167, and 170 at the end of 1953; whereas it never exceeded 153 (basis 100 in 1939) in France and it was 150 at the beginning of 1954. Integration therefore cannot but be unfavorable to Germany's neighbor (Jules Moch, *Alerte!* Paris-Laffont, 1954).

Other motives were *the abandonment of an essential prerogative of national sovereignty*, made more sensitive by the abstention of the United Kingdom which was favorable to the treaty but resolved in no way to participate in it; *the absence of a European political authority* which would have had to procede and not follow the establishment of a European army, cut by the very fact of any moral and political justification; and *the complexity of the provisions of the treaty*, a potential source of allocation conflicts, a generator of inefficiency in case of crisis and, marked by the brand of "stateless technocratism." Other points were *the factual subordination to the United States* and to the American strategy through the supreme commander of allied forces in Europe and by the weight of the contribution of the United States, the only holders of the decisive weapon and resources on the scale of an empire; and *the radical and even brutal nature of the "changes" envisaged*, in the area of integration and supranationality in a less technical context than that of the ECSC and infinitely more susceptible to violent or passionate reactions. These were the essential factors providing more and more violent opposition to the EDC treaty.

They had already substantially been listed by General de Gaulle at his press conference of February 25, 1953 in an indictment whose validity, pertinence, and objectivity do not always appear to be up to the level of the debate and the importance of the stake involved. It is perhaps worth quoting some selected extracts since their contents still, twenty-six years later, provide fuel for present-day arguments, even though some arguments have not stood up to the test of time and the march of history. Here is what General de Gaulle was saying at the time.

In order to provide a good measurement of the "value" of the project, if it may so be called, let us observe that it is based on four statements none of which is true. First it is said: it is a question of making a European army. However the proposed army is absolutely not this. It is also said: it is a question of ensuring for France a powerful American competition without compromising its independence.

However, the treaty makes us subordinate to American strategy without in any way guaranteeing that France would be defended. Again it is said: it is a question of the Six of establishing supra-national institutions which can be responsible for joint defense, particularly ours. However, these institutions by their very nature and their organisation would be absolutely unable by themselves to ensure this defense. Finally, it is said: it is a question of preventing Germany from rebuilding its military power. However, other than this open mistrust of a partner with whom we pretend to cooperate, demonstrating by itself the absurdity of the co-operation, it is absolutely wrong that the European army treaty is to re-arm the Germans without at the same time re-arming Germany. It is on the other hand very clear that this treaty, combined with the present American policy, is leading directly to the military and political hegemony of the Reich in Europe.

The first five arguments already mentioned are to be found in this preamble. De Gaulle goes on. "For there to be a European army, that is the army of Europe, Europe must first exist as a political, economic, financial, administrative and above all moral entity . . ." "and so that, if the need arises, millions of men are willing to die for it." (The Army is only the instrument of a policy; without this it is useless to create a European force.) "However, this so-called European army which the treaty claims to establish, is handed over for use, organically, automatically, and solely to the Commander-in-Chief Atlantic, that is calling a spade a spade, to the American Commander-in-Chief in Europe which makes one of the tools of the American strategy." (This shows the dependence and subordination of Europe to the United States.) "Once the treaty is ratified, France will be able to claim to have foreign relations but no longer a foreign policy." (Abdication of prerogatives of national sovereignty.)

As regards the institutions: " Part II sets out a vast array of provisions from which must be artificially created a technocracy which, having neither bases, credit or responsibilities, appears in 50 articles to have to play above the terrible realities of the defense of nations a role similar to that of an angel who on old pictures blows the trumpet of the last judgement in the sky." (Beyond a picturesque reference to the frescoes of the Sistine Chapel, there is to be found in this a direct criticism of the complexity and clumsiness of the institutional provisions.)

Finally, the General takes up the problem of a future German hegemony and without beating about the bush states: "I repeat that in the mixing of the French element and the German element, as provided for in the Treaty, it is the German element which will necessarily take the upper end."

What do the supporters of the European army answer to this? The main points of the rebuttal appear in a thirty-page booklet under the signature of Henry Frenay.[6] In addition, the extent of the criticisms against the EDC are objectively examined by Guy de Carmoy.[7] The following is a brief analysis of these two papers.

Europe starts, like the United States started, where the States hand over part of their sovereignty to a joint power. The community feeling is always born of absolute necessity and sometimes of constraint. The abdication of France and subordination to the American commander-in-chief are more illusory than real. The Supreme Commander is, in time of peace as in time of war, subject to the directives of the Atlantic Council, a permanent body where France has a right of veto.

Whether or not there is a European army, would in no way alter the risk of a German hegemony, if Germany proves numerically and industrially superior to France. Under this assumption—and if there is a danger—is it preferable that Germany should have its own national army rather than be integrated within the EDC? The evolution of the modern world and particularly of military techniques has meant that real sovereignty has escaped us. The EDC Treaty will give the peoples associated with it the possibility of recovering it; however, its rejection would be a new victory for nationalism and probably mean the defeat of European unity. The bases of the problem of security are altered by the evolution of weapons techniques. Modern weapons are only available to Europe if a defense community develops a single program for weapons manufacture within the framework of a large market. Only then will the European countries recover a military sovereignty at present solely possessed by the American and Soviet empires. Finally, France may want to protect itself against Germany but "there is little risk of one day seeing a re-armed Germany invade its Western neighbours. The age of national wars came to an end with the century of the empires." (Mr. Maurice Duverger, Le Monde, November 8, 1952.)

These were the opposing arguments. In the last part of this chapter, we shall examine their validity, going back a quarter of a century during which the

Atlantic Alliance has been built up and evolved with various fortunes.

We all know what happened to the EDC treaty. Although it was ratified by the German, Netherlands, Belgian, and Luxembourg Parliaments, the treaty was submitted by Mr. Mendes-France, the chairman of the French Council, to the National Assembly which refused to discuss it on August 30, 1954 thus automatically setting the seal of failure on the European Defense Community.

## AN EVALUATION OF THE EDC
## AND THE LESSONS OF A FAILURE

The rejection of the EDC by the National Assembly was an extremely heavy blow to the process of European unification. The broadening of the Brussels Pact was a palliative enabling Germany to participate in the defense of Europe. The "Paris Agreements" reestablished West Germany's full sovereignty, broadened the Brussels Pact which took the name of "Western European Union" from then on (including the Federal Republic and Italy), and raised the question of the entry of Germany to NATO. The United Kingdom undertook to maintain in Europe the four divisions already there and the necessary tactical air forces.

The Protocol of October 23, 1954 dealt with the accession of the Federal Republic to NATO and the establishment of German sovereignty. All the aggreements came into force on May 5, 1955. From May 9 to 11 the Atlantic Council met in Paris and the Federal Republic was officially represented there.

We shall now present the balance sheet of these five years of effort, of various bargainings, discussions, and arguments. Certainly West Germany now participates in the defense of Europe and its contribution, although limited by the Paris Agreements, will be one of the most important of the Atlantic Alliance. Furthermore, Great Britain undertook to maintain its forces on the continent and the establishment of the Western European union opened the way for consultations and possible future military cooperation.

But the two fundamental principles which were the basis of the EDC treaty, *supranationality* and *integration*, were from then on a dead letter. The Alliance was to be little more than a juxtaposition of national defenses with American weight decisive. What remained of the arguments of the opponents was little in reality other than the satisfaction of having conceded nothing as regards national sovereignties. On the other hand, German rearmament, even under the symbol of the Alliance, had become effective and American preponderance in the face of a divided Europe, stemmed from the logic of things.

What the adversaries of the treaty had not foreseen was the importance of the economic factor, which as the years went by was to weigh more and more heavily on the budgets of the lesser powers who were from then on incapable of getting hold of the strategic weapons of the nuclear age whose cost and complexity were no longer within their means. What they had also not realized was the enormous waste resulting from duplication of efforts both in research and development, and in the production of modern weapons. It is what the promoters of the European Defense Community had wanted to avoid and this is clearly shown here in the preamble of the treaty which lucidly defines the advantages expected of joint and integrated defense and the hopes it raises for the future of a political Europe.

> Determined ... to contribute to the maintenance of peace, more particularly by ensuring the defense of Western Europe, against all forms of aggression in close collaboration with organizations having the same purpose;
>
> Considering the fullest possible integration to the extent compatible with military necessities of the human and material elements of their defense forces assembled within a supranational European organization to be the best means for the attainment of this aim with the necessary speed and efficiency;
>
> Convinced that *such integration will lead to the most rational and economic use of their countries' resources, in particular through the establishment of a common budget and common armaments programmes*; ... Recognizing that this is a new and essential step towards the creation of a united Europe;
>
> Have resolved to set up a European Defense Community. ...

All that is just as true now as it was then, although the circumstances of the moment have evolved to a very considerable degree. Indeed, the enlarged community now includes the United Kingdom; the fear of the German hegemony leading to new fratricidal struggles can reasonably be dismissed; and the age of overseas wars seems to have ended with the completion of decolonization.

On the other hand, the problem of European defense remains in its entirety, and any national solution has to be excluded a priori under the pressure of economic facts and the factual hegemony of the superpowers.

## The Lessons of a Failure

The rejection of the treaty setting up the European Defense Community brought the process of European unification to an abrupt halt. It is difficult for a political Europe to be conceived if the essential attributes of sovereignty, and foreign and defense policies are separated from it. For more than twenty-five years, no real attempt has been made to restate the problem whose very mention seems to be banished from European conversations. Such was the traumatic effect of the failure of 1954 and it is very true that new efforts towards a common European defense policy should take the lessons of the past into account.

The authors of the treaty probably wanted to go too fast and too far. What they planned was a complete change but they underestimated the strength of nationalist sentiments and their deep roots.

Things have evolved. The real achievements of the Europe of the Six and then of the Nine have clarified the idea that the construction of Europe is not only Utopian, but that defense is a difficult area, a bastion of national sovereignty. Any new undertaking must develop gradually and probably by separate sectors taking into account pragmatic data rather than grand principles.

It will probably be impossible a priori to consider a return to overall supranationality. Temperaments capable of sparing national susceptibilities must be found and the experience of the functioning of the EEC may prove particularly useful. Possible sollutions and the ways of achieving them will be examined later but the unhappy experience of the EDC will not have been entirely negative. Many practical provisions are still valid today, perhaps more so than when the treaty was conceived.

Moreover, we cannot allow a second failure to occur since this time it would be disastrous. The spirit of initiative and faith in the future of Europe must be tempered by a wariness which experience has made necessary.

Let us return to the period immediately following the rejection and abandonment of the European Defense Community. Returned to their national concerns, under the umbrella of the Atlantic Alliance, we shall discuss how the defense policies of the main European members of the Alliance (the United Kingdom, France, and the Federal Republic of Germany) were to evolve.

# 4 The Defense Policy of the United Kingdom: The Shift Toward Europe

In the face of the upheaval in technologies, the enormous increase in fire power, and the staggering rise in costs, the defense policy of the United Kingdom (like that of other European countries) has undergone a complete change. Was it a race to become a superpower or the maintenance of the traditional markets of the empire; strategic mobility or permanent bases; independent or integrated nuclear policy? The answers were not easy, but they probably stemmed from a more fundamental choice, the abandonment of the "high seas" to offer a helping hand to Europe at a time when narrow nationalisms seemed to be giving way to the community idea.

It may be said that British defense policy fits in with two striking phenomena of this century, the first noteworthy for the long process of decolonization and the political awakening of the countries of the Third World, and the second remarkable for the building of the great economic and technological communities on the scale of the United States, the Soviet Union, or Europe. In addition, it is impossible to understand the evolution of the United Kingdom's defense policy over the last twenty years without considering what has happened during the same period in the political and particularly the economic fields. The alarming situation of the economy, the continuing erosion of the pound, and the almost chronic deficit in the balance of payments have all played a decisive role in the trends of defense. The great change took place during the years 1967 to 1968 when the Labour government started far-reaching reforms and undertook the "East of Suez" withdrawal, deliberately sacrificing imperial policy to European rapprochement. Despite the severe cuts in the budget and the massive reductions in the personnel of the three armed forces, the trend toward reductions has continued because of a precarious economic situation, a situation which moreover does not yet seem to be on the road to recovery.

After a brief reminder of the United Kingdom's commitments towards the Alliance and Europe, we shall review the steps taken by Labour at the time it came to power in 1964, the main events which have characterized the reign of the Labour government, and the political consequences they imply. The British nuclear force will be the subject of a particular study; and the cooperation agreements within the European framework, and future trends will complete this broad survey of British defense policy.

## BRITISH DEFENSE POLICY
## UNDER THE CONSERVATIVE PARTY

It is outside the framework of this study to carry out a detailed analysis of the characteristics of British defense policy during the long period in which the Conservatives remained in power. It is however worth stressing the main aspects, particularly those affecting the British position with regard to Europe. The United Kingdom came out of the Second World War victorious but exhausted. It bore the weight of responsibilities both on the continent and in the world through its direct links with the members of the Commonwealth.

It favored the European Union movement whose aspirations were clearly stated by Winston Churchill in his Zurich speech on September 19, 1946: "We must build a kind of United States of Europe. . . . The first step in the recreation of the European family must be a partnership between France and Germany. . . . Great Britain, the British Commonwealth of Nations, mighty America, and I trust Soviet Russia—for then indeed all would be well—must be the friends and sponsors of the new Europe and must champion its right to live and shine."[1]

The stage was set from the very beginning. There was sympathy for Europe and its initial steps, but no inclination to be part of it. "We are with you but not of you."

Indeed, at that time the United Kingdom was at the point of intersection of three circles—the Commonwealth of which it was the leader; the community of the Anglo-Saxon people under its special relationship with the United States, cemented by the war, language, and institutions; and finally Europe, of which it was one of the principal States.

But centrifugal forces were already becoming apparent within the Commonwealth. Canada was coordinating its air defense with the United States; and Australia and New Zealand were not relying on an England no longer able to ensure the protection of all its associates. There remained the special relationship with the United States. But the latter, aware of its strength and its continental weight, was not ready to sacrifice its independence of decision to partnership with the United Kingdom.

Was the United Kingdom ready to commit itself to Europe? The reply was unequivocably given by Anthony Eden in his speech in the United States on January 11, 1952.

> If you force a nation to adopt a manner of conduct which runs contrary to its instinct, you weaken or you may destroy the main force of its action. . . . I refer to the frequent suggestions that the United Kingdom should join a federation of continental Europe. It is a thing we feel to the very marrow of our bones that we cannot do . . . since the United Kingdom and its interests extend far beyond the European continent. Our thoughts go beyond the seas to the many communities towards which our people have a share in all the corners of the world. This is our life without which we would be nothing more than a few million people living in an island alongside Europe.[2]

Obviously, the time was not yet ripe.

In the defense field, the United Kingdom was like France a co-signatory of the Treaties of Dunkirk, Bussels, and Washington. The military commitments it undertook on the continent were the image of those undertaken by the United States and were to become institutionalized after the failure of the European Defense Community. Its aversion to becoming a full member of the EDC was moreover one of the reasons for France's refusal to ratify the treaty, despite the constant support it had always given to this vast undertaking.[3]

British forces were to be maintained on the continent as long as there was a threat to Western Europe and to the European Defense Community. On a decision by the supreme commander, these same forces could be included in European formations, and vice versa. The closest cooperation was envisaged between the future community and the United Kingdom. After the failure of the treaty, Eden thought of using the expedient of the Treaty of Brussels to include Germany and Italy in it.[4]

This is what happened on September 18, 1954 when the British government invited eight countries to attend a meeting which took place ten days later in Paris. The Western European Union was born, and the British initiative had enabled the worst to be avoided.

The United Kingdom's commitment specified the maintenance on the continent of the forces assigned to SACEUR (Supreme Allied Commander in Europe), i.e. four divisions and the tactical air force. (Cmnd. 9289, p. 18.)

Exception clauses provided, however, that in the case of "an acute overseas crisis" or "abnormal pressure on the United Kingdom's external finances," the level of British participation could be subject to review. Indeed, this clause was invoked in February 1957 in a request to the council of ministers of the Western European Union for the withdrawal of one third of the British forces stationed in Germany. This step should be linked with the decision announced in the 1957 White Paper on Defense to do away with conscription in the United Kingdom.

The troop numbers of the British Army on the Rhine (B.A.O.R.) were reduced in consequence from 77,000 to 64,000 in 1957 to 1958, and from 64,000 to 55,000 the following year. During this same period the tactical air force was reduced by half. This same 1957 White Paper announced the birth of the British nuclear force: "The United Kingdom must possess an appreciable element of nuclear deterrence power for itself."

Under the Nassau Agreements of December 21, 1962, this force (V bombers and Polaris) was to be assigned to NATO except if "supreme national interests were involved."

Before the arrival of the socialists in power, the state of the British defense policy can be summarized. It included a firm commitment in Europe within the framework of the Atlantic Alliance; maintenance of the global obligations of the United Kingdom in the rest of the world; the preferential relations with the United States which took precedence over European rapprochement in the hope of a world diarchy and of imperial responsibilities; development of the British nuclear force (but the strategy for its use remained uncertain and ill-defined until its inclusion in the integrated system of the Alliance).

But the pressure of the economic factor never ceased to grow and the United Kingdom became aware that its ambitions were no longer compatible with its means and that decisive choices involving inevitable sacrifices were imminent. It was to be the task of the Labour Government to convert the realities of the time into hard facts.


## THE GREAT CHANGE AND THE DIFFICULT CHOICES
## OF THE LABOR GOVERNMENT

After thirteen years of opposition, which the Labor Party called the "Conservative mess," October 1964 saw Labor back in power with an extremely slender majority. The economic and financial situation was bad. The state of the pound was precarious and the battle of prices and salaries was still indecisive, the increases in both contrasting with an almost stagnant productivity.

After the spring dissolution of parliament in March 1966, Labor returned to power with a majority of 100 and from then on seemed assured of being able to take the necessary rehabilitation measures. Externally, the world role of the United Kingdom was considerably reduced by the de facto recognition of the

American-Soviet diarchy. The unending Vietnam initiatives and the slackening of the links between the White House and Downing Street went hand in hand with the crumbling of a Commonwealth policy and the presence east of Suez. It was in this tense situation and this precarious balance that a series of factors arose in 1967 which had been difficult to foresee[5] and which was to precipitate the crisis and drive the Wilson government into the devaluation of sterling and drastic reductions in defense. The real causes of this alarming situation were, to begin with, the cost of two world wars from which the United Kingdom came out appreciably poorer than the countries it had conquered.

Then, "the time-honoured habit of the English to spend more than they earn which did not have any serious consequences as long as they were at the center of an Empire working for them. Unfortunately the Empire had disappeared but the habit has remained. Finally, trade union demands were weighing heavily on the cost of production, backed up by anti-economic practices aimed at ensuring full employment." (Order Paper 3371 of November 21, 1967.)

Accordingly, faced with the most serious financial situation (a deficit of £800 million left to them by the Tory administration), the Labor government had to undertake long-term measures to reestablish British external credit while at the same time applying massive cuts in state expenditure and particularly in the defense budget. This cutting down to size was to be one of the main points of the Labor program, along with disengagement, the precursor of the abandonment of world politics.

The medium-term aim was the reduction of the defense budget from 7.2 to 6 percent of the GNP. We only have to remember that the present percentage is less than 5 percent of the GNP to see what has been happening. This concern for *quantitative* economies (reduction of defense expenditures in absolute terms) as well as *qualitative* (stopping the outflow of foreign currency) constituted, and still constitutes at present, the main aspect of British defense policy. Considering the triple aspect of resources (missions, means available, and the vital necessity to limit availabilities as a result of a reduced percentage of GNP), the secretary of state for defense had to act simultaneously on the two other terms of the trinomial, i.e. missions, the international commitments of the United Kingdom, and the means available to the three forces. The substantial reduction in available means mainly affected the weapons systems of the air force and navy and the reduction in troop numbers as regards the army (reserve and active service forces) and the other two services.

The TSR 2 program, aimed at developing a British multi-role aircraft (tactical-strike-reconnaissance), had already swallowed up a considerable number of millions of pounds (195 to be exact) when it was decided to abandon it. There is no doubt that the Plowden Report was the origin of this decision since it stressed that the United Kingdom no longer had the means available, by itself, to build aircraft or guided weapons involving both costly and extremely complex development. Mr. Healey claimed that the abandonment of the TSR 2 enabled a saving of £700 million to be made.

Other programs also abandoned were the P 1154 (which had already cost £21 million) and the HS 681. As regards the navy, it had to accept the medium-term cancellation of aircraft carriers (H.M.S. Hermes, Eagle, Victorious, and Ark Royal). The net savings resulting from this operation amounted to £500 million spread over ten years.

Finally, regarding the army, "the reduction in troop numbers" resulted in the removal of 75,000 men by 1975 (the RAF lost 13,600 men and the navy 8,600, i.e. 10.9 and 8.8 percent of their respective numbers).

*The change in missions,* announced as long ago as 1966 in the "Statement on Defense Estimates," was only to be made absolutely clear in July 1967 after visits to Southeast Asia by Mr. Bowden and Mr. Healey, the secretaries of state for the commonwealth and defense. From then on, it was the "potential military capability" which was to take the place of the "permanent presence."

In Europe, the almost unconditional faith in the principle of the Atlantic Alliance was reaffirmed on many occasions. But the strategy in force at the time was attacked by the secretary of state for defense who considered it hopelessly out of date.

It goes without saying that such a drastic review brought about certain upheavals which were little tempered by spreading the reforms over a period of years.

From the matériel point of view (re-siting of units, infrastructure, accommodation), from the social point of view (excess of personnel, compensation, and retraining measures), and the morale point of view (the reason for the existence of the forces, motivation, and encouragement of recruiting to the all-professional armed forces) a large number of problems arose. They were reasonably solved through long-term planning as much as through empiricism and the practical common sense of the British.

Starting with the known premises, i.e. the alarming economic and financial situation of the United Kingdom and of the trend towards European unification which was beginning to make itself clear at the time, it seems advisable to review the choices facing Her Majesty's government and to examine the consequences of the possible options.

When Labor came to power, British defense policy consisted of three main components: the nuclear deterrent; participation in the defense of Europe; and the imperial policy and world responsibilities. Sacrificing the first of these, in the context of a future grand Europe including the United Kingdom, would have meant definite recognition of the supremacy and leadership of France, from then on the sole holder of nuclear power within an enlarged community. Renouncing the second, or reducing European commitments below a certain acceptable limit, would have meant compromising the chances of negotiation with the Europe of the Six and accepting a German hegemony in the central Europe theater.

There remained the third, i.e. the end of the policy of presence east of Suez, the loosening of the traditional links with the nations of the Commonwealth or with traditional allies, and the resigned acceptance of the alignment of the United Kingdom among the medium-sized powers. But this third choice, however painful it may have appeared, fitted in with the trend of history—the long march towards decolonization, the awakening of nationalism in the countries of the Third World, and their increased political independence.

Governing means choosing and it seems that initially a policy of half measures was considered satisfactory, sacrificing nothing essential. However, changes in circumstances and the increasing pressure of facts acted as catalyzers for difficult decisions.

## THE BRITISH DETERRENT FORCE

It is indeed possible that the real reason for the creation of a nuclear force in the United Kingdom stems from the traumatic souvenirs of 1940. The British Government probably remembered the dark days when, defeated on the continent, England found itself alone without allies, forced to rely on its own resources. Possession of the nuclear weapon—"ultima ratio regum"—would permit avoidance of such situations. Accordingly, it was normal that the Conservative government should embark on a nuclear weapons program, greatly facilitated by cooperation with the United States and the common experience gained during the war (the Hyde Park Agreement in 1944 between Roosevelt and Churchill providing for full cooperation between the American and British governments in the development of the fission material needed for civilian and military applications after the cessation of hostilities).

We should remember that the first British A-bomb exploded in 1952 and the H-bomb in 1957. To begin with, the vehicle for Great Britain's strategic nuclear power was a bomber command consisting of two groups of 15 to 16 squadrons of V bombers[6] and a total of about 120 strategic jet aircraft, plus reconnaissance aircraft, flight refuellers, and other supporting units.

The bomber command mission, which initially consisted exclusively of high level bombing attacks with the Blue Steel thermonuclear missile or conventional bombs, was altered in mid-1964 to include low level missions below the enemy radar screen.

Bomber command absorbed about ten percent of the total defense budget, but this figure decreased to two percent as the deterrent was transferred to the Polaris submarine fleet which, in 1968, became the sole vehicle for British deterrent force. It consists of four submarines—the Resolution, the Renown, the Repulse, and the Revenge. It was irreverently compared to "a chick-pea on the top of a mountain" at the time when Wilson, the leader of the opposition, said on January 16, 1964: " . . . For the United Kingdom and France, the only advantage of a small submarine force equipped with nuclear weapons would be

the doubtful consolation of giving us a posthumous revenge—without doubt
devastating but not morally decisive—after our countries and the mass of our
populations had been struck off the map."[7] And further on: " . . . I believe we
will need an expanding naval construction program. How are we going to
finance it? From the savings achieved by stopping the ruinous expenditure on a
nuclear programme inspired only by political considerations."[8] In actual fact,
once in power, the Prime Minister did not sacrifice the nuclear program but
continued its development, reducing the total number of submarines initially
planned from five to four.

The Faslane base cost £45 million; the total cost of a Renown class submarine, from the day the keel was laid to when it becomes operational, is £52
million. Purchases in the United States for the Polaris program up to the end of
1957 amounted to $193 million. The cost of the Royal Navy Polaris School was,
at the time, £7,500,000.[9]

## The Arguments of the Opposition

When in 1967 the Prime Minister decided not to replace the A3 missiles of the
British Polaris with the multiple-headed Poseidon—a replacement whose cost was
estimated at $150 million per submarine—the deterrence file was reopened by
the Opposition and its validity was questioned.

What justification can we have for the existence of a force which does not
even insure the protection of purely British interests? Indeed, the Nassau
agreements, concluded in 1962 between Kennedy and Macmillan, stated that the
British strategic nuclear force was assigned to NATO (internationalization of the
deterrent) and that "except where H.M. Government may decide that supreme
national interests are at stake, these British forces will be used for the purposes
of international defense of the Western Alliance in all circumstances."

Accordingly, these same opponents commented about the use of exhausting
ourselves in a hopeless race in order to maintain the operational capability of our
four submarines when "we are no longer in the big league and can never be
again."[10]

The development of international events, the admission of the United Kingdom
to the European Communities, and the future prospects of a European defense
policy all probably had the effect of disarming the opposition and proving the
political value of a deterrent force, even a reduced one.

The possibility of a joint Franco-British venture was probably missed in 1962
at the time of the de Gaulle-Macmillan meeting. Another chance might have
occurred a relatively short time later, but the decisions could not be deferred
indefinitely in view of technological breakthroughs and the different characteristics of each of the deterrent forces.

After coming to the fore again in 1969 and 1970 (Alain Poher, Pompidou, Chaban-Delmas, Heath, Strauss) this question seems subsequently to have been relegated to the dusty files and has never since been the subject of precise political approaches.

In any case, the United Kingdom still has its own deterrent force which, although integrated with NATO, is a major political trump card in the establishment of a European Defense policy.

## THE UNITED KINGDOM AND EUROPE: FAILURES AND SUCCESSES IN INTERNATIONAL ARMS PRODUCTION

The triple allegiance of the United Kingdom—the Commonwealth, the United States, and Europe—has long been reflected in its defense policy, and also in its *arms production*.

Immediately after the last war, it was one of the largest exporters of military and aeronautical equipment. Its *production range*, like that of the United States or Russia, covered all fields from the tactical to the strategic. Finally, as we have seen, it was the first European power to lay the foundations for a national nuclear weapons program as well as for the production of the necessary vehicles, strategic bombers, and intermediate range missiles.

Over the years, however, this privileged situation was gradually eroded by various factors. The most important of these was probably the *growing economic tension* stemming from the incompatibility of ambitions on a world scale and the resources of a medium-sized power; the blaze of nationalisms and the *progress towards decolonization* which rendered the maintenance of distant and widely dispersed garrisons useless; and the *exponential growth of costs* and the rate of technical progress which limited choice and obliged selective priorities to be established.

The original features of the British armaments industry and their implications reveal a *wide variety of programs* and an inevitable dissipation of investment on research and development. *The absence of long-term priorities* and the large number of targets resulted in uncertainty, either as a result of changes in government policy, or for purely financial reasons. *The marked tendency towards national and independent production* gave rise to even more serious consequences, a certain reticence about production under license, probably in order not to overload a markedly negative balance of payments; and domestic development to meet purely British specifications. The example of the FV-432, an armored personnel carrier, is striking in this respect. Its cost was double that of its American equivalent, the M-113 ($50,000 against $25,000), and it was strictly limited to the British market. (C.J.E. Harlow, *The European Armaments Base: A Survey* [London: International Institute of Strategic Studies, 1967.])

In 1965, the report by the Plowden Committee officially recognized the incompatibility between the traditional concept of a world role by the United Kingdom and the actual resources available for it. Amalgamation of firms, allocation and specialization of effort, research into mass production to spread investment, looking for bigger markets to keep pace with greater and greater initial investments became the imperatives militating in favor of international cooperation.

Furthermore, the prohibitive costs of some modern weapons systems prevented purely national production; accordingly, common requirements had to be defined and associations had to be made with one or more partners to undertake the joint development of projects after sharing out the tasks.

## The Failure of the Anglo-French Variable Geometry Aircraft

The United Kingdom started on the variable geometry aircraft as long ago as 1965 when Labour decided to cancel the TSR 2 program, despite considerable opposition. It was then that the United Kingdom announced its intention of acquiring American F-111s. But almost immediately afterwards, it became apparent that the F-111s did not alone meet all the requirements of the R.A.F. Many of these would have to be met by a substitute aircraft not paid for in dollars.

The "VG" or "variable geometry" idea was born and became the A.F.V.G. (Anglo-French variable geometry), when the agreement in principle for its joint construction was signed with France on May 17, 1965. The project had mixed fortunes and, in July 1967, France (for purely financial reasons) gave up the joint construction of the AFVG.

The causes of this dismal failure were the pressures of the enormous increase in research and development costs as well as the difficulty of reconciling different specifications, and the British desire for a long-range strike and reconnaissance aircraft as opposed to the French support for a supersonic fighter for use in Europe. It was possible to avoid the escalation of costs for a dead loss of £2,500,000. In France, Dessault "went it alone" and continued the development of the Mirage G.

In the United Kingdom, new attempts were made at international cooperation, this time on a wider basis, giving rise to the birth of the MRCA (Multi-Role Combat Aircraft) project. The agreement on the development phase was signed on May 14, 1965 and the Panavia Company was formed jointly by the British Aircraft Corporation, Messerschmitt-Bölkow, and Fiat. Independent of the obvious advantage of international cooperation, particularly in the sharing of research and development costs, the project gave rise to other savings (logistics, training, nonduplication of prototype tests) and opened up vast prospects for building a European aircraft industry. The turnover of the whole European aerospace industry was estimated at some £6,000 million from 1969 to 1974, 34 percent of which was devoted to two projects alone, the MRCA and the Concorde (Flight International, December 11, 1969).

Other bilateral and multilateral projects have been successfully developed. We shall mention only the most important of these—the Anglo-French Jaguar, a tactical and training aircraft whose construction was decided on May 17, 1965 and is a joint Bac/Bréguet project; the Franco-British agreement on helicopter construction (Lynx, Puma and Gazelle) relating to 200 French Sud 330, 700 Sud 340, and 600 Westland WG 13 helicopters with a total value of £230 million in ten years; the Martel (AJ 168) air-to-ground guided missile; the FH 70 and SP 70 medium artillery weapons developed jointly with Germany and Italy; and the Belgo-British coproduction of the CVRT family of light armored vehicles, in production since 1973.

But all these projects lie very much below a real system of European cooperation with a vast world market and the resulting standardization of equipment. This is why the United Kingdom has never ceased to encourage the Eurogroup—which Mr. Healey had brought to the fore in 1968—in order to extend its authority and to make it a real European forum.

The British proposals of 1974 led to a wide consensus among ministers of defense at the meetings of the Eurogroup in June and December, 1964 about undertaking a joint and far-reaching study of national equipment plans with the aim of achieving much wider cooperation. If this idea were to become effective, the United Kingdom would find it of obvious *economic interest.* The establishment of a European armaments agency would probably guarantee it a market compatible with its advanced technology and its dominating position in the aircraft industry, while enabling it to spread its research and development costs by freeing it, because of its very existence, from automatic recourse to the American market.

In conclusion, we may say that through the considerable financial effort devoted to research and development,[11] giving a definite advantage in the technological field; through the range of its equipment; and through the importance of its aerospace and electronics industries, the United Kingdom is in a leading position in the European armaments industry. The United Kingdom was, for a long time, reticent about cooperation aggreements but it has changed its policy over the last ten years, demonstrating more flexibility in the establishment of specifications and is concerned with increasing the number of bilateral or multilateral attempts to widen its market, reduce its production costs, and associate itself more and more closely with Europe.

## RESULTS: 1967 TO 1977

Having come to the end of our study of the essential components of British defense policy, we feel it necessary to draw up a table of the results of a ten-year period of reviews, which, if they have not been agonizing, have at least been radical and have made the United Kingdom shift from a world policy to a European one.

Political objectives, impacts on the forces, constant economic pressures, and future trends, are the main fields of our analysis. From 1967 to the present time, the European trend of the British defense policy has become established and has been constantly reaffirmed in successive White Papers. "A closer European defense identity within NATO, which was welcomed by President Nixon at the meeting of NATO Ministers in Washington in April last year, will thus greatly strengthen the military security of Europe. It will give an impetus to the developing political unity of Western Europe."[12]

*The political interest*, resulting from a strengthening of the British position within NATO, enabled it at the same time to counterbalance the de facto Franco-German dyarchy in Europe. Progressively freed of its world commitments, Great Britain started concentrating the resources available to the United Kingdom and built up a combined force of strategic reserves. One of the tasks entrusted to it was "if available in general war, to reinforce the European theatre ground forces."[13]

Directed toward one or other flank of the Alliance, with a preferred option for the northern flank, the strategic reserves put the United Kingdom in a unique situation among its European partners. Initially composed of a mobile force with land and air components, an airborne force and an amphibious force, it has not withstood the deterioration of the economic situation and the resulting cuts in the budget.[14]

The United Kingdom's mobile force lost two out of three airborne brigades, the United Kingdom's joint airborne task force which had consisted of two parachute battalions and a transport capability of five Hercules squadrons was abandoned, while the amphibious force was reduced from four commando groups to three and lost a squadron of helicopters and a commando ship.

That is what happened to the strategic reserves, but the ebb tide did not spare the other forces. The army was reduced from 197,000 men on April 1, 1967 to 180,000 in 1974 and future reductions will bring its numbers down to 155,000 (including 6,000 Ghurkas) by April 1978.[15] However, in August 1978 the British minister of defense announced that 4,000 men were to be recruited to strengthen the armed forces.[16] Half of this number are destined for the British Army of the Rhine (AOR) which includes three divisions totaling 55,000 men. These measures have been taken within the framework of the NATO long-term defense program and agree with the spirit of President Carter's initiative aimed at strengthening the conventional component of Europe's defense.

As regards the air force, there are two consequences of the overseas disengagement. They are the abandonment of the strategic role in order to become almost entirely a European-style tactical support force; and a possibility of harmonizing the characteristics of the aircraft required by the United Kingdom with those of its European partners by avoiding differences in specifications between missions overseas and the European theater.

Manpower, which had been 120,000 in 1967, fell to 100,000 in 1974 and will be further contracted by 18 percent, bringing it to 82,000 by April 1979.[17] If we remember that the RAF had a total of 6,338 aircraft in 1952, 2,341 ten years later, and less than 2,000 at present, we can get a good idea of the trend of this reverse evolution.

The navy has also been severely cut. The suppression of the aircraft carriers has been considered by "Jane's Fighting Ships" (1968-69 edition) as damaging to the maintenance of minimum security. Furthermore, the concentration of resources within the home fleet has led to the end of the permanent presence of the navy in the Mediterranean at a time when the naval strategy of the USSR is becoming clear and when the threat to the southern flank of NATO is growing.

Manpower which was 96,000 in 1967, was reduced to 79,000 in 1974, and will fall to 74,000 in 1979. This is how far the United Kingdom is from Lord Fisher's policy at the beginning of this century, and we may wonder, without undue irony, whether the proud motto "Britannia rules the waves" is not completely outdated.

This *reversal* is due to the impossibility of a nation, which is no longer a top-ranking power, to developed balanced, powerful, and multipurpose forces in the face of the rise in nuclear power, the escalation of costs, and the enormous investments involved. Other factors are the end of the Empire, the feeling that a third battle of the Atlantic would be technically almost hopeless, confidence in the strategic resources and power of the United States, and the apathy or indifference of the public. Still more, it is *the pressure of economic factors* which determines the road taken by defense. *"The voice is that of the Secretary of State but the will, as usual, is that of the Treasury."*

The British government has, moreover, recognized this in terms devoid of any ambiguity: "For many years, the annual growth rate has been barely more than half that of France or the Federal Republic of Germany. The economic situation is at present more serious than at any time during the past 25 years."

It is also appropriate to compare the defense burden with that borne by its main European allies. The United Kingdom's defense expenditures in 1974 absorbed 5.8 percent of the gross national product, against 3.8 percent for France and 4.1 percent for Germany. Accordingly, the aim is to reduce the percentage of GNP devoted to defense to 4.5 percent in ten years, i.e. an overall saving of £47,000 million in ten years (at 1974 prices).

Let us discuss the future trends in the face of this apparently irreversible situation. Backed by long tradition, by front rank technology supported by considerable resources, and having available a range of equipment which could probably be better adapted to actual requirements, the United Kingdom is clearly oriented toward Europe and desires the creation of a European system with wide market outlets permitting standardization of equipment. The "Europeanization" of NATO has, in only a few years, made remarkable progress in responsible British circles. It could not be otherwise if there is a desire to maintain an adequate defense capability in the face of the continued growth of the military potential of the Soviet Union, the economic and social realities of the time, and the de facto parity achieved by the superpowers at strategic nuclear level. The only possible solution is to strengthen the European bastion of the Alliance. Ever pragmatic, the British believe it is desirable to show proof of this in the field of arms production and standardization, and also (and above all) in the harmonization of tactical doctrines and equipment specifications.[18] This is certainly a long-term process, but one to which the pressure of facts demands an urgent solution.

The possession of an independent nuclear force, although it is integrated into NATO, represents a major political advantage and could be the basis of a European deterrent force. The prospects for such an undertaking are analyzed in another part of this study. The realignment of British defense policy has closely followed the fundamental changes in foreign policy and the essential political choices. In the immediate future, it seems certain that it is *in Europe* that the destiny of Great Britain lies and that it is there that it will find its true vocation.

# 5 The Defense Policy of France: The Return to Nationalism

The successive trends of French defense policy reflect the profound opposition of the convinced partisans of nationalism, the full sovereignty of France and, accordingly, independence of strategic decisions and those who see in the European and Atlantic edifice the only possible solution for guaranteeing individual and collective security.

A major problem was to be grafted onto this, that of the possession of the ultimate weapon, previously the sole prerogative of the great empires, the symbol of the regained independence and the necessary instrument for foreign policy at great power level. Contingent events were to play an appreciable—and sometimes determining—role in the decisive choices which were to imprint its present characteristics on French defense policy and were to provoke the evolution from a declared Atlanticism towards a retreat within an uncompromising nationalism.

*The process of decolonization* was probably the basis for this evolution. It profoundly divided the French, weakened the military position of France in Europe, underlined the more and more marked disagreement with the United States and, after precipitating the fall of the Fourth Republic, opened the way for General de Gaulle and his clear-cut concepts of national independence. The *failure of the European Defense Community* marked the nadir of the European edifice and a marking time of more than a quarter of a century in any large-scale effort to associate defense policies with it. The long march towards *French nuclear self-sufficiency* was, as a corollary, to have the effect of widening the gap between the United States and France in the matter of different strategies because the growing weight of the American contribution to the Atlantic Alliance was to be less and less well accepted by the head of the Fifth Republic. The *personality of General de Gaulle* was to put a very distinct seal on French defense policy and would progressively withdraw it from the Atlantic system without however clearly taking a stand on a strictly European option.

The influence, prestige, and continuity of the views of the head of state enabled an end to be put on the traumatic experience of the war in Algeria, but were to be used toward the most intransigent nationalism culminating in the withdrawal of France from the integrated military organization, and the evacuation of the inter-allied bases and headquarters. It may thus be seen how different the defense policies of the Fourth and the Fifth Republics were. This is why we shall examine in succession their essential aims, methods, and achievements. It would however be wrong to imagine that this split occurred suddenly, that a clear break appeared with the fall of the Fourth Republic and the arrival of de Gaulle. Under the Fourth Republic it was already possible to see the harbingers of reborn nationalism and it was under this nationalism that the decision was taken to manufacture a French nuclear weapon.

The Fifth Republic was to crystallize situations of fact, to accentuate the Atlantic disengagement, and finally to implement the break. But despite the General's nationalist position taking, voices have never ceased to be raised in condemnation of a vision of France which appeared as an anachronism to those supporting a future Europe.

## FRENCE DEFENSE POLICY
## UNDER THE FIFTH REPUBLIC

### The Aims

To begin with, the aims appeared resolutely Atlantic and European. A co-signatory of the treaty of Dunkirk (March 1947), the treaty of the Western European Union signed in Brussels (March 1948), and the North Atlantic Treaty (ratified in July 1949 by 395 votes against 189 with 15 abstentions), France opted for collective defense in the face of threat from a monolithic Soviet bloc whose military power gave rise to the justified apprehensions of a divided Europe, drained of its life blood and weakened by the political vacuum resulting from the defeat of Germany. One of the initiators of the European defense community plan, it seemed to want to speed up the rate of building a political edifice which would cap the establishment of the European Coal and Steel Community and strengthen the Atlantic Alliance while taking precautions against an independent German rearmament through military integration within a European grouping.

But the achievement of these initial aims was to be subject to the influence and constraint of three major factors. They were the pursuit and the extension of overseas wars linked with the phenomenon of decolonization; the fear of a German hegemony linked with the rearmament of the Federal Republic; and the apprehensions aroused by the growing weight of the United States within the Alliance. These three factors were, moreover, interdependent. The colonial wars were to absorb all the real strength of the French Army, reducing its contribution to the Atlantic Alliance and no longer permitting it to provide a counter-balance to the forces progressively being established by Germany. This rearmament, which was violently struggled for by certain elements, was finally only allowed to take place within a purely Atlantic framework after the failure of the EDC and the coalition of oppositions.

The resolutely anticolonialist attitude of the United States and as a result its reticence about supporting the French effort (both in Indochina and in Algeria), and its unequivocal condemnation of the unfortunate Suez affair were to be the source of growing tension between the two countries. France was to be forced to wonder about its role and its relative importance, to listen to the sirens' songs of those hoping for a revival of independence in decision making and the restoration of unimpaired sovereignty and particularly to the possession of an independent nuclear weapon, the sole guarantee of security and the prerogative of great powers. In short, the defense policy of the Fourth Republic was to be distinguished by two main characteristics: ambiguity in the pursuit of declared objectives and a growing gulf between initial intensions and later evolution; and a disproportion between aims and resources in view of the manifest impossibility of waging exhausting colonial wars and maintaining an adequate military contribution on the continent at the same time.

During the era of the Fourth Republic which was marked by the chronic instability of power (from January 1946 to the nomination of Mendes-France, the Prime Minister changed eighteen times), we were to witness a confrontation between the past, i.e. the maintenance of the overseas empire at all costs—despite the most obvious signs of the process of decolonization and its irreversible nature—and the future, the time of the state-continents, of growing independence, of the development of the nuclear weapon forcing on the medium powered state-nations the choice between national withdrawal and association and even integration in a much wider grouping.

## Resources and Methods

The Paris Agreements laid down fourteen divisions as the ceiling for French contribution to NATO's conventional forces. In actual fact, this contribution was not to exceed six divisions during the Indochina war and it was to fall to two divisions during the Algerian War which was to break out in the Aurès in 1954.

In 1956, numbers reached 400,000 men as the result of sending national servicemen. The incompatibility between a colonial policy and an Atlantic and European policy was to come out into the open. "France's Atlantic policy is changed as the Fourth Republic weakens and Gaullist opposition makes progress."[1]

Despite its reduced contribution to the Alliance, France had a privileged position in it. It was represented on the standing group in Washington, the commander-in-chief of Central Europe was French, and it occupied many responsible posts in the inter-allied headquarters at Shape, Afcent and the central army group. It housed on its soil not only the permanent representatives of the Atlantic Council (in Paris) but also the supreme military command (at Rocquencourt), the central Europe Headquarters (at Fontainbleau), the NATO Defense College (in Paris), and many logistics and air bases. The entire logistic infrastructure of the central European theater lay in the French hinterland. All this meant that France was recognized as being of major importance within the organization. After the failure of the EDC, the European idea on the subject of defense weakened under the dual influence of external events and the absorption of the western European union into the Atlantic Alliance. At best it must be observed that at the beginning of January 1955, a proposal for a fresh start was introduced by Mr. Mendes-France and submitted to the seven members of WEU with a view to creating a European armament production agency. Its tasks were the distribution of arms stemming from American aid among the members of the European Union; the establishment of a program for European manufacturing; and the letting of orders and the distribution of armaments.

The plan quickly became bogged down and as General Stehlin said:[2] "The fundamental idea of convergence of efforts for a real collective security system speedily became absent from discussions." He continued with a statement by the British representative: "The system must be designed fully to take into account the special needs of the national economy of each country concerned."

The common production of armaments in Europe was to remain a dead letter and was to be limited to pious wishes or sterile recommendations. Furthermore, the Suez affair of 1956 illustrated the limits of independent strategy for a medium-sized power. The failure was fraught with consequences since it brought to light the first weakness in the Atlantic edifice and gave rise to criticisms from part of French public opinion against its American ally.

It was the Algerian war which was to monopolize all efforts during the years to come. None of the successive governments of the Fourth Republic was to be able to lift this fundamental burden.

"The fear of being accused of treason by the man who symbolised the resistance in the face of the invader paralysed the Government of the Fourth Republic which was to be tempted to cast off the cloth of colonialism."[3]

The time was ripe for May 13, 1968; from then on de Gaulle was to have the way clear for giving the defense of France a new outlook distinguished by the seal of his personality.

## FRANCE'S DEFENSE POLICY
## UNDER THE FIFTH REPUBLIC

Defense was essentially the policy of one man, General de Gaulle, who considered it a reserved area closely linked with his concepts of foreign policy, the grandeur of France, its worldwide role, the independence of its decisions, and a national concept which was to shift further and further away from the Atlantic option. (This policy was only possible because of the extent of power granted to the head of state by Art. 16 of the constitution.) His successors, Presidents Pompidou and Giscard d'Estaing, were to make no notable or fundamental change to their inheritance from the General. Was France thus forced into semi-isolationism and would it be absent from any grand design for Europe? It is premature to judge the answers to these questions, since France's defense policy is still up to its neck in Gaullist nationalism, and a hardly disguised hostility for anything relating to the military organization of the Alliance.

To understand the mechanism of this disengagement, the General's permanent objectives must be remembered. They were to withdraw France from a position he considered subordinate within the Atlantic Alliance; to give France's defense a purely French character; to promote Franco-German cooperation and, on the basis of this, to establish a European cooperation—and not an integration —based on the Europe of the States; and to join the "nuclear club" as soon as possible. There were many quotations and no lack of warnings to clearly indicate the policy to be followed from then on.

There is really no reason for surprise since, as long ago as November 1949 at a press conference, the General declared: "It would be inadmissible that French national defense and the direction of French military effort he controlled by somebody other than a Frenchmen." And in August 1954, in a statement relating to the EDC, he clearly stated his views: "To give the Atlantic Pact the character of a good alliance and not a bad protectorate, there lies the great undertaking offered to France by destiny."[4]

The achievement of General de Gaulle's objectives was to be carried out in successive stages, starting with the proposal to create the "Directorate of Three" (September 24, 1958) and ending with the withdrawal of France from NATO

(Aide-Mémoire of March 1966 and ending the assignment of the French forces in Germany to the Atlantic Command on July 1966) and, in between, with the creation of an independent deterrence force and progressive disengagement from the military alliance.

## The Stages of Disengagement
## and Withdrawal into the Hexagon

Using a unique and continuous authority and served by an economy which, thanks to the monetary reform of 1958, was to become steadily stronger, General de Gaulle was to achieve his objectives by applying the strategic principles of the economy of resources, freedom of action, and initiative in the choice of method and the point of application.

Considering *the economy of resources*, it is impossible to maintain considerable conventional forces, engage in wars overseas, and at the same time build up a credible nuclear armament. Before anything else, it was therefore necessary to lift the burden of the Algerian war—this was only to be achieved after the Evian Agreements of March 1962—and then drastically reduce troop numbers and the armed forces, and devote as much money as possible to the deterrent force. All this was to go on without compromising the security of France since, throughout this time, France was to be assured of American protection through the Atlantic Alliance. As Henry Kissinger has written: "de Gaulle saw little risk and the possibility of considerable gains in political independence."[5] It is striking to note that the stiffening of attitude was to be accentuated as France's deterrent force was established. The first experimental nuclear explosion took place at the Reggane firing range on February 13, 1960; the establishment of the Force de Frappe was to be practically completed with first generation weapons from 1964. It is not a mere coincidence that France's withdrawal from NATO was announced in 1966.

## Then, Freedom of Action

Freedom of action meant giving France a privileged place in the concert of powers which would be inconceivable without regained independence. France wanted to be able to assume the role of arbiter between East and West and, in this context, it was to play a preponderant role in Europe. But in the same way as de Gaulle rejected any Atlantic subordination as being incompatible with the grandeur of France, he refused the integration of Europe in which the image of France would disappear in a technocratic and stateless amalgam. Keeping his options open was to be his constant concern in political affairs.

This same concern was to be found in the strategic area. "France proposes to recover the exercise of its full sovereignty. It is intolerable for a great state that its destiny be left to the decisions and actions of another State" (press conference of April 11, 1961).

It was therefore necessary to provide France with an independent force which must necessarily be nuclear.

## Finally, the Initiative

Strong in the knowledge of France's world position, de Gaulle sent a secret memorandum to Eisenhower on September 24, 1958 with a view to "creating a tripartite organisation to take joint decisions on problems concerning the world."

The participation of France in NATO was subject to recognition of its world interests and its equal participation in a world strategy.[6]

After the failure of the attempt at a "Triple Directorate," de Gaulle stepped up the number of tangible signs of France's independence and her progressive disengagement. Each time he took the initiative, to disconcert his allies and his adversaries, to shuffle the cards, and to blow hot and cold; but he was never to lose sight of his main objectives. The Nassau Agreements were followed by the treaty on Franco-German cooperation signed in Paris in January 1963, and were the cornerstone of the Europe of the States that he foresaw.

Disengagement from NATO was taking place at the same time. On March 7, 1959, certain French naval units in the Mediterranean were withdrawn from the command of the Alliance; in June 1963, the French naval forces in the Atlantic were no longer assigned to NATO in wartime; in November 1965, the special nuclear committee met without France; and in March 1965, message was sent to President Johnson indicating France's intention to "alter the form of our Alliance without impairing its basis."

As we have seen, the establishment of the deterrent force was one of the main objectives of the defense policy of the Fifth Republic, and one of General de Gaulle's master cards for reaffirming national independence.

It therefore seems worth studying the origins, development, and composition of this force. It is still more important to wonder about the future of this deterrent force in the European context, and to try to see clearly the controversial problem of a European nuclear force.

## THE FRENCH DETERRENT FORCE
## AND THE STRATEGY FOR USING IT

### The Origins

The principle of a nuclear force was approved on December 26, 1954, in the council of ministers under the Mendes-France government.[7] We should remember that the French Atomic energy commission (CEA) had been set up in October 1945 under the direct authority of the prime minister. In 1955, everything was ready for an extension of its area of action to military application. Under Edgar Faure's government, Gaston Palewski, the atomic energy minister and a Gaullist from the beginning, doubled the credits of the CEA and ordered the construction of a nuclear-propelled submarine.

On April 11, 1958, a month before the fall of the Fourth Republic, Félix Gaillard's government had taken the final decision to extend the CEA program to the military field.[8] It is therefore wrong to attribute the paternity of the "Force de Frappe" to the Fifth Republic and General de Gaulle. The industrial and technical bases existed and the decision to go ahead had been taken. The merit of the General and his government was to free the necessary resources, to introduce major structural reforms, and to establish a close association between the civilians and military with a view to developing unity of action and indispensable coordination for the vast undertaking.

These reforms were to result in the creation of various institutions: the general scientific and technical research delegation (DGRST), the ministerial delegation for armaments (DMA) established in 1962, and the directorate of research and experimental resources (DRME). The framework for operations remained to be established and this was done through five-year programs covering the periods 1960 to 1965 and 1966 to 1970 and aimed at close cooperation between the activities of the atomic energy commission and the nuclear force plan.

Some figures may illustrate the stimulus given to the program. Between 1958 and 1966, the proportion of GNP devoted to research and development rose from 1.12 to 2.44 percent; the number of scientists rose from 18,000 to more than 47,000.[9]

More important, in 1972 the CEA's budget took half the funds allocated for military purposes. Out of a total of 4,444 million French francs, 2,116 were devoted to defense and 1,890 to industry and science.[10]

The second five-year program, which is more explicit than the first, laid down the initial composition of the future French deterrent force based on Mirage IV bombers (62 operational) and capable of carrying a fission bomb of 50 to 60 kilotons.

The French program developed entirely independently because, to begin with, no formal threat of abandoning the Alliance was uttered. On the contrary, the nuclear weapons were to increase France's value as a partner. In 1960, Michel Debré estimated that they would make France a "valid speaker for its allies."[11] This trend was regarded as inopportune by the Americans and the tensions between allies became more obvious. However, according to James Bellini,[12] de Gaulle's refusal to accept the offer of Polaris by President Kennedy after the Nassau Agreements was based on much more technical than political reasons. In 1962, French technology was not sufficiently advanced to adapt French weapon systems to the Polaris. Furthermore, an affirmative answer would have compromised the establishment of the first generation of the Force de Frappe centered round the Mirage IV aircraft.

Finally, it was inconceivable that the future French deterrent force should be included in a multilateral NATO nuclear force, as had been done with the British nuclear submarines.[13] As a result it was inevitable that France should adopt an independent line and that its foreign policy should change in the same way.

Another important consequence of acquiring a nuclear capability at all costs was the conflict of priorities in a certainly considerable but not unlimited defense budget. In 1960 to 1964, the nuclear forces took 27 percent of the total budget, against 72.4 percent for conventional forces. In 1965 to 1970, the proportion was 45.5 percent nuclear, and 54.5 percent conventional. In 1970 to 1975, the figures were, respectively, 36.9 percent and 63.1 percent.[14]

The land forces were the most affected; their share of the budget fell from 26.9 percent in 1960 to 1964 to 17.5 percent in 1965 to 1970 and then rose to 20.8 percent in 1970 to 1975.

It was not therefore surprising that a certain "malaise" arose in army circles as a result of the slowing down of the re-equipment programs and the feeling of being the "poor relation" of the French armed forces.

## The Establishment of the Deterrent Force and the French Strategic Concept

General Charles Ailleret's book retraces all the details of the arduous process, the reservations to be conquered, and the technical and psychological difficulties that had to be overcome before the "force de frappe" could be introduced.[15] The main details of the program to be carried out in five years were contained in plan K103 and included the establishment of the necessary organization; the creation and equipment of research centers; and the recruitment and training of specialized personnel.

This was a vast enterprise when one realizes that France had to go it alone with the exception of the sale of CF-135 refuelling aircraft by the United States, which enabled the radius of action of the Mirages IV A aircraft to be extended, and also the delivery of about 440 kilograms of Uranium 235.[16] The undertaking was a success, since only four years were to pass between the first experimental explosion at Reggane, on February 13, 1960, and the bringing into service of the first generation of the deterrent force based essentially on the Mirages IV A.

At that time and until the accidental death in 1968 of General Ailleret, the chief of defense staff, French strategy was to be one of all or nothing and was exposed in the doctrine called "Tous azimuts" ("all-round"). At the same time as the beginning of the independent force de frappe—whose small scale was recognized but whose importance was justified by the "functional deterrent"— the French line maintained that one could not be absolutely certain of United States intervention under all of the military circumstances which would be particularly concerning Europe. Here is how General Gallois expressed himself on this subject: "In France and for the defense of metropolitan France, there can be no question of flexible response. The very vitals of the nation are concerned and not merely advantages or marginal interests."[17]

Accordingly, there was no alternative to the immediate nuclear response, to massive reprisals on the rear areas and in depth in the enemy country, including its vital centers of high population density, without prior recourse to diversification of methods and the gradual use of the available arsenal.

As Pierre Messmer said in April 1963: "The only targets worthy of deterrence are demographic. Aiming at weapon sites would be absurd."[18] The explanation and theoretical justification for this strategic concept may be found in the article published by General Ailleret in the *Revue de Défense Nationale* in September 1964.[19] According to him, there are two possibilities for defending Europe, either solely with conventional forces or with the use of tactical nuclear weapons. Under the first assumption, in view of numerical inferiority on the order of three to one, the only solution would be to yield a major part of territory, practice the scorched-earth policy, and counter-attack the adversary when he had gone sufficiently far from his bases. "If the Russians can be stopped, we can be thankful if that happens on the Rhine. The Somme, the Aisne, theVosges, the Jura and the Alps seem more likely to me."

All that is hardly compatible with the forward defense strategy, and in view of the risks of reconquest, General Ailleret discarded this solution.

The second assumption was the use of tactical nuclear weapons from the beginning. This was feasible, but using the striking example of the octopus which suffers little harm if a tentacle is cut off but which must be hit in its vitals to have a real effect, the author considers that nuclear interdiction would extend 1,500 km. either side of the front, thus transforming Europe from the Atlantic to the Soviet frontier into a vast pile of ruins, "an assumption for which one must be prepared intellectually and materially, but which is one which cannot be recommended, but one can only be resigned to."

As a result only one way remains open. In the case of a real aggression, the enemy's strategic war capability must be reached after first checking his intentions by testing probes. In summary, as Raymond Aron says, "The French doctrine of the use of deterrent force inevitably reproduces the doctrine of massive reprisals ten years late on a Lilliputian scale."[20]

As technology developed and the second and third generation nuclear weapons were progressively installed, alterations were made to an initially and unduly rigid strategic concept, probably in adaption to the relative weakness of the weapons available. General Fourquet, the chief of defense staff, stated this on March 3, 1969, in an address to the Higher National Defense Studies Institute. The deterrent force of the 1970s is larger, more sophisticated than that which first appeared ten years earlier, and with it there is a rejection of the "all or nothing" concept.[21] Persuaded that the strategic weapon could not be brandished about at any moment and in any circumstances, he accepted the idea of a certain flexibility in the use of conventional and nuclear forces. The "frappe stratégique" was prepared to be preceded by graduated actions as a result of which enemy aggression could be assessed. There is no further question, moreover, of the "all-round" defense. "Against an enemy from the East, the battle corps will act normally in close cooperation with the forces of our allies."

It will easily be agreed that this infers foundations of a national defense policy, very different from that accepted since 1959, and indicating a new trend. This evolution of French strategic thinking is important since it marks an appreciable rapprochement with the "flexible response," recognized as the official strategy of the Alliance in 1967 (it has already been applied for several years but, in view of French opposition, it was only officially recognized after the withdrawal of France from the integrated military organization).

The introduction of tactical nuclear weapons in the form of "Plutons" completed the French panoply and enabled it gradually to fill the gap separating it from the orthodox procedures of the Alliance, with the exception, of course, of the independence of decisions and the strictly national assignments of the deterrent force. At this stage of our study, it is worth summing up the French nuclear program.

## Nuclear Resources of France

Between now and 1980, there will be four components of the nuclear arsenal:

- The Mirage IV squadrons, 36 aircraft (plus an operational reserve of 20 more) carrying a 70 kiloton bomb. The radius of action is 850 nautical miles without flight refuelling and 4,300 with 2 refuellings by CF 135.
- The intermediate range ballistic missiles of the Albion plateau consisting of three groups of 9 missiles in silos. The first two groups are capable of carrying a 150 kiloton warhead over a distance of 500 to 1,875 nautical miles. The third group, now being installed, will carry a warhead of about a megaton.

—The missile-launching nuclear submarine force of four vessels, the "Redoutable," the "Terrible," the "Foudroyant," and the "Indomptable." A fifth submarine, the "Tonnant," will be operational in 1979. The first two ships, equipped with 16 missiles carrying 450 kiloton warheads, have a range of 1,500 nautical miles. The third, equipped with the M-2 missile, has an increased range of up to 1,875 nautical miles; the fourth, with similar endurance, will be equipped with thermonuclear warheads of about a megaton.

—The tactical nuclear weapons, spread out in two sectors: four squadrons[22] equipped with the AN-52 tactical nuclear bomb of 10 to 15 kilotons, and the Pluton ground-to-ground missiles with a range of 120 km. with which 6 regiments will be equipped.

If we add that France seems to have mastered the technique of multiple nuclear warheads, we can get an idea of the vast effort accomplished in about fifteen years in the technological and financial fields.

Has this effort been worthwhile? This brings us to the strategic and political *value* of the French deterrent force. Its disparagers have denied it any credibility, saying that it did not meet the essential criteria of a real deterrent because of its vulnerability and its limited capability. Its devotees, using as arguments "the equalizing power of the atom," "the unacceptable destruction," or again the increased uncertainty in the use of nuclear weapons as a result of the large number of decision centers, recognize that it has a vital role in the defense of France and the overall strategy of the Alliance.

It would seem that the force de frappe deserves neither this excess of honor nor this indignity. It is certainly not on the same scale as the nuclear arsenals of the superpowers and the vulnerability of its missiles in silos, and of its first generation vehicles. It cannot be questioned if the enemy is resolved to use sufficiently powerful means in a first strike. However, it cannot be denied an intrinsic value, a sufficient reprisal capability to inflict considerable losses on the enemy which, generally speaking, makes a specific contribution to the deterrent power of the Alliance.

As Ambassador de Rose has said: "If the Russian leaders believe that in certain circumstances the United States would not intervene in a conflict in Europe, this might be an error of judgement. But it would be an error that no one in the West could prevent.... An effective force deployed in Europe and not subject to an American veto would increase the security of each one of us, including the United States, by diminishing the danger of a war by error of judgement."[23]

As regards the controversial notion of "effective force," he adds that the American reaction to the attempt to set up forty intermediate range missiles in Cuba has demonstrated that "the fact that a force is small, does not necessarily mean that it is ineffective."

In conclusion, let us say that the value of the French effort was officially recognized in the Ottawa Declaration of June 1974. Speaking of the British and French nuclear forces, the final comminiqué points out "that they are capable of playing a deterrent role of their own, contributing to the overall reinforcement of the deterrence of the Alliance."[24] France's long march toward unreserved admission to the nuclear club was therefore coming to an end. Thus we can agree with Raymond Aron that the French "force de frappe" constitutes "a beginning of insurance against the unforeseeability of the diplomatic future."[25]

We shall see later what it means in the context of European defense policy.


## FRANCE'S TRUMP CARDS

How does France's position look with regard to the future construction of Europe, or more particularly the field of defense? General Maurin, at the time chief of defense staff, gave an unambiguous answer: "It is certain, and many of my European colleagues agree with me, that if one day a European defense becomes a fact, France will, in view of the contribution it will make to it, have a privileged position."[26]

This opinion was shared by Mr. Pompidou, who expressed himself as follows in July 1962: "The day may be very close when political union will be established and it will certainly extend to defense. The contribution made by France's possession of atomic weaponry will certainly be an essential asset to this defense. Then the question might arise of a nuclear force in a European framework."

The fundamental elements of this contribution are, first of all, the deterrent force we have just been talking about; then the conventional land, air, and sea forces; and finally the industrial and technological foundations of an armaments market which is in third position in the world. (In 1974, world orders amounted to about 100 milliard French francs, including 41 milliard for the United States, 25 for the USSR, 19 for France, and about 10 milliard for the United Kingdom.)

*The deterrent force* could serve as the basis for a European nuclear force in the context of Franco-British cooperation. The problem is not new and comes to the surface periodically without, however, being converted into fact.

In December 1962, Harold Macmillan suggested to General de Gaulle the possibility of amalgamating the nuclear capabilities. In 1970 to 1971, renewed interest was shown in the question[27] and there were even those in favor within the Gaullist ranks, such as Mr. Michel Doscher, vice chairman of the foreign affairs commission of the National Assembly, and Mr. Jobert who, in November 1973, had advocated a Western Europe nuclear committee before the WEU Assembly as a preliminary and significant step towards future amalgamation of the Franco-British deterrent forces. From the technical point of view, the decision must be taken in good time if the modernization of the nuclear weapons is to be carried out jointly.

We shall have occasion to come back to this problem and to study its practical aspects and the chances of achieving it.

*The conventional forces*, in view of the manpower resources involved, put France in second place in Europe, after Germany but in front of the United Kingdom. The air-land battle corps consists of five mechanized divisions equipped with nuclear weapons and tactical air support also equipped with nuclear weapons. (The army, as we shall see later, is in the process of full reorganization.) The operational defense of the territory (DOT) is not limited to the protection of strategic bases, but extends to a form of warfare covering the whole territory and based on the will of every citizen to fight everywhere. Although the army is strong in numbers (332,000 men), its program of re-equipment must be speeded up, since this has only progressed at a slow rate as a result of competition from the deterrent force and the large share devoted to the latter in defense budgets. Furthermore, account will have to be taken of the morale element, which seems to be the weak link in a not very satisfactory army-nation context where recent events have demonstrated an explosive situation.

The navy component is undergoing complete modernization. From 1958 to 1963, the total tonnage had fallen from 400,000 to 169,000. In 1973, the navy already had 325,000 tons in service with 50,000 under construction.

We now come to *the industrial and technological foundations for an armaments market* which is without question the leader in Western Europe. This vital area cannot be considered without stating the role and importance of the *Ministerial Armaments Delegation* (DMA), created in 1961, with the basic principle that "A rational policy for armaments manufacture—particularly the manufacture of the most modern weapons—requires a concentration of authority and resources leading to better use of manpower, a higher output from the industrial infrastructure involved and a more efficient use of the funds" (Preparatory Report for the Budget).

Let it be said in passing that the transposition of this principle to a European scale would allow elimination of the duplication of efforts and would solve the always topical problem of the standardization of weapons and the interoperability of equipment. We use figures to show the importance of the DMA and the wide range of its missions which cover state, industrial, and commercial activities. It produces half the weapon equipment for the army and deals with almost the whole of naval construction, employing about 80,000 people including 4,400 engineers. Commercially, its sales reached 7 milliard French francs in 1971, 9.5 milliard in 1973, and 19.5 milliard in 1974. Thanks to the programs and industrial affairs directorate (DPAI), it controls the whole of the industrial armaments potential whether it be state, para-public, or private.

Two other bodies are subordinate to the DMA, the international affairs directorate (DAI) and the research and test facilities directorate (DRME), the first dealing with international cooperation in armaments and the export of military equipment, and the second with the development of weapons using the most advanced technologies. Two tables in the Appendix show the general organization of the DMA and its general position in France.

We have dealt at some length with this third aspect of the French contribution, since it will undoubtedly be required to play a primary role in the attempts at European cooperation which seemed to be developing in arms production matters. The results of the exploratory meeting in Rome, on February 2, 1976, were positive in this connection and it is significant that the French delegation was led by Mr. Jean-Laurens Delpech, the ministerial armaments delegate.

One thing is certain in any case. France intends that any cooperation of the kind should have a strictly European character. This is why she obstinately refused to participate in the Eurogroup and, until the recent past, has considered Western European union as the ideal forum for achieving progress in European cooperation in defense matters. Our comments on the French contribution would not be complete if we failed to mention *its geo-strategic weight* and the favorable prospects for its *economic development*.

Increased depth of the theater of operations, Atlantic and Mediterranean coastlines, logistic and air bases, normalization of the communications systems, and ensured operational cooperation and the decisive advantages that the geographical position of France would give the Alliance and, as a result, give Europe. From the economic point of view, taking into account the growth of the gross national product (which in 1970 was fifteen percent below that of the United Kingdom, twenty percent above it in 1970, and sixty percent above it in 1976), it may be seen that French apprehension in the 1950s about its relative weight in Europe is no longer justified. It remains to develop the political will, so that European aspirations in defense matters do not remain a dead letter.


## CONCLUSIONS


A long road separates the declared Atlanticism of the Fourth Republic and the national independence policy of the Fifth Republic. General de Gaulle succeeded in equipping France with a nuclear capability which, without putting it on the same level as the superpowers, gave it a privileged status on the world chessboard and, more particularly, in Europe. The price to be paid was considerable, since the withdrawal from the military organization of the Alliance was a severe blow to Atlantic cohesion and diminished its credibility and its homogeneity while accentuating the tensions between the United States and France.

Without, however, endorsing the extremely harsh measures taken at the time, we can only support the very principle of a policy based on a fundamental fact: "The states are unwilling to allow another state, even an ally, the exclusive responsibility for decisions controlling their life and death."[28] It is indeed here that the European dilemma lies. Regarding the construction of a political Europe, can we rely indefinitely on the American guarantee to ensure the security and defense of Europe, even when fundamental changes have altered the strategic environment and the force relationship at the nuclear level? If the answer to this question is in the negative, we must consider how a credible European defense can be built up, and its scope.

One thing is certain. Such a prospect is inconceivable without France and what it represents geo-strategically, as well as in terms of its positive contribution to conventional or nuclear defense, i.e. to the deterrent at a purely European level.

Matters seem to be evolving in a particular direction under the double pressures of economics and politics. Despite its technological breakthrough and its own resources, France cannot isolate itself from the European context. Interdependence is a fact, and President Giscard d'Estaing seems to be convinced of this.

The statements by General Mery, chief of defense staff, and by President Giscard d'Estaing appear to justify the assumption that a rapprochement is developing between France and its Atlantic Alliance partners as regards operational cooperation, both in peace and war.

As Ambassador de Rose appropriately says, "The political reasons for such efforts are numerous: the interdependence of our destiny and our interests with our European neighbours, the need not to repeat the mistake, which cost us so dear in the past, of a contradiction between the aims pursued by our foreign policy and the capabilities and missions of our armed forces, evidence that the defense of Europe is not, for a long time to come, conceivable without the assistance of the United States and that the Alliance is the irreplaceable framework for this American support." He adds: "Security is not the adequate condition for safeguarding and handing down to posterity the values of our civilization. It is however one of the necessary conditions, at the same time as it permits the progressive change in the order of things."[29] In this work of quite remarkable clarity, the essentials of present French defense policy are concisely set out.

Certainly, independence of decision remains a fundamental axiom on the basis of avoiding being drawn into a general conflict on behalf of interests which might be specifically neither French nor European. On the other hand, European solidarity is constantly reaffirmed and takes for granted the engagement of France alongside its allies in the case of open aggression. This is the stand reaffirmed by Mr. Chirac in the 1972 White Paper on National Defense: "As a component part of the European continent, France intends to participate to the best of its ability in the defense of Europe in the case of a localized crisis as well as a general threat."

However reassuring these statements may be, they are only translated into facts to a modest extent. France is still absent from the NATO Defense College in Rome and this empty-seat policy, in addition to not being compatible with its own interests, deprives the Alliance of a highly qualified French participation and leaves the way free to more and more obvious Anglo-Saxon and German domination. France only takes part in allied maneuvers to a limited extent; and more alarming, it has made its intention known of reducing French troops stationed beyond the Rhine by 10,000 men before the end of 1977.[30]

This decision, which seems to run counter to the principle of the indivisibility of joint defense and the forward strategy, has been attributed to a general reorganization of the army which provides for eight new armored divisions and six new infantry divisions. It is however a question of not deluding oneself with words and of remembering that these "divisions" have been very much reduced in comparison with the earlier models, and probably represent little more than extra powerful combat brigades with troop numbers considerably lower than those of conventional divisions.

> The operation will apparently enable a triple aim to be achieved:
> —to stiffen the "DOT" (Défence opérationnelle du territoire) with mobile and armored formations stationed in metropolitan France;
> —to refine the logistics system based in the Federal Republic;
> —to partially solve the thorny problem of the maintenance of permanent military infrastructure on German territory, a source of dispute between the government of the FRG and the French authorities.

A general withdrawal of the French units from Germany seems however out of the question, despite the intentions attributed to Mr. Bourges, the minister of defense. Such a measure would be a considerable blow to European and Atlantic solidarity and would question the "participation of France in the forward battle," claimed by the chief of defense staff.

The stamp of nationalism has had a profound effect on French public opinion over a period of many years. It would be difficult, if not impossible, to return to the old Atlantic cooperation, but it is perhaps conceivable that a new form of association in which France would enjoy a privileged position, should be organized on the basis of a European defense policy.

To assess its chances of success, and to understand the reasons for it, it has been necessary to follow the evolution of French defense policy and strategy which have, before the event, developed in much the same way as Europe will in the future.

# 6 The Defense Policy of the Federal Republic of Germany Atlantic Solidarity

The Federal Republic of Germany was admitted to the Atlantic Alliance on May 9, 1955 and effectively started its rearmament in November of the same year. At the present time, it constitutes one of the "strong links" of NATO in its participation with the largest conventional forces, and in equipment which is among the best of the Alliance.

Yet, it is legitimate to ask if there is a real German defense policy. The answer is certainly negative for reasons which are, at the same time, political, geostrategic, and economic, and which give the German defense policy a particular nature characterized by ambivalence and residual competence.

To begin with, there are *political* reasons remaining from the end of the Second World War (see Chapter 3). German rearmament had aroused serious suspicions, particularly from the French. Accordingly, once the fait accompli had been accepted by all, precautionary measures were introduced to contain this rearmament within preestablished limits and *to prevent Germany from independently manufacturing nuclear weapons on its own territory*. The agency for the control of armaments, a body within the WEU, is responsible for checking these commitments under the terms of Art. VII of Protocol No. IV signed during the Paris Agreements of October 1954.

In the second place, the *deployment of forces* in the Federal Republic of Germany is so interlinked that it prohibits any attempt at the reestablishment of an independent German general staff or any action carried out by German forces alone. It seems clear that in this there also lies some concern not to permit any reunification of the two Germanys through any forceful action on the part of West Germany alone.

Finally, there is *the presence of American forces* whose general disposition reveals marked dependence, on the part of Germany, on its powerful American ally from the dual views of reinforcement of conventional forces but particularly of protection and nuclear intervention which the FRG is unable to ensure by itself and which explains and justifies its almost unconditional allegiance to the Atlantic Alliance.

Further, *the need to cover and defend the whole of German territory* has led to the introduction of the "forward strategy" which is open to discussion from the strategic point of view—particularly in a defensive environment—but irrefutable from the point of view of German internal policy.

From the geo-strategic aspect, three essential factors have to be taken into consideration:

the narrowness of the theater of operations which, between the Thüring salient and the Rhine at Frankfurt, is a mere 150 km.; an area 100 km. wide to the West of the demarcation line contains 17.3 million inhabitants whereas, widened to 200 km., it includes 41.8 million and 59 percent of the FGR's industrial manpower;[1]

the advanced position of the Federal Republic of Germany as Central Europe's defense bastion, in direct contact along 800 km. of frontier with Soviet East Europe;

*the unsatisfactory deployment of the allied forces in peacetime* resulting from splitting the country up into occupation zones and of peacetime contingencies rather than a coherent idea with a view to ensuring distant coverage and the forward strategy.

Finally, from the *economic point of view*, the Federal Republic has had to agree to offset agreements aimed at assisting the balance of payments deficits of its main allies, the United Kingdom and the United States, by way of the costs of stationing the troops of these two countries on its territory.

To some extent, these handicaps deny it full freedom of choice in its range of weapons and equipment. Similarly, the restrictive clauses of the Paris Agreements have not permitted it to develop its armaments industries to the same extent as its French or British European partners. All this means that German defense policy has a dual character.

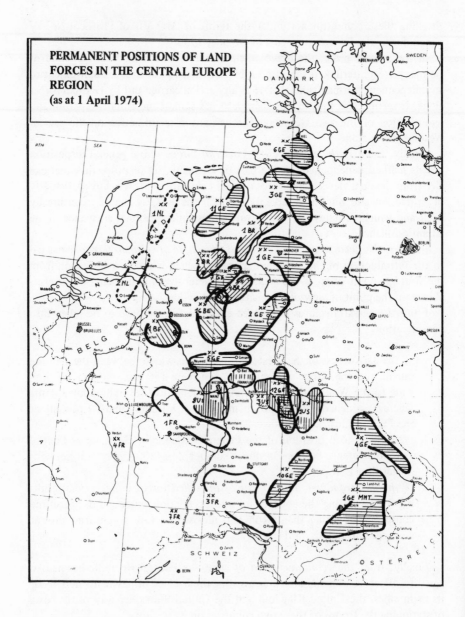

*Fig. 6.1.* Extract from Western European Union Assembly Document 663.

To begin with, it has a greater *dependence* on its allies, in particular the Americans, and, as a result, less independence of decision about the level of its conventional forces and the use of tactical or strategic nuclear forces.

Then, there exists *an ambivalence in trends and attitudes*. Split between its desire to encourage European integration in defense and its unconditional faithfulness to the Atlantic Alliance (the forced result of an American participation considered vital to its security) it tries to further these two aims simultaneously. The great obstacle to that pan-European design within the framework of the Alliance is France, with which it is linked through a bilateral treaty and which (without being restrictive to the extreme) imposes upon it a certain reserve or an attitude of reconciliation towards Paris.

From the external point of view and, paradoxically, the fear of a resurgence of a powerful united German state, possibly possessing the supreme weapon, the Federal Republic is envisaged with equal suspicion both by its European allies of the moment—even the most faithful—and by the Soviets who have openly declared that they would be unable to tolerate such a possibility. The permanent presence of foreign troops on its soil, previously felt as an unbearable burden, has been converted into a vital necessity with a view to ensuring the security and defense of the advanced posts of Western Europe in the name of European solidarity.

It remains for us to deal with a last point which is perhaps the most important one for the future trend of Germany in its search for security. I refer to the flexible response strategy and the certain use of tactical nuclear weapons on its own territory. When will it be necessary to trigger off the cataclysm and what will its results be for the mass of the German population whose density is one of the highest in Europe? What part will Germany play and what weight will it have in the decision about the use of tactical weapons? How will it be possible to coordinate the tactical use of nuclear weapons with the preservation of cities or East-West migratory movements of millions of refugees fleeing from the advanced zone of future combat?

Many conjectural questions involve delicate choices for the responsible German authorities who must take into account both the exigencies of internal politics and the imperatives of an assured security. From this stems Bonn's permanent concern not to reduce the level of its conventional forces, and its obvious irritation when its allies indulge in drastic reductions either in length of compulsory service, or in unilateral reductions in personnel or equipment.

Since the Federal Republic of Germany is by definition the geometric center of security of all the states of Central Europe, it seems appropriate to devote some thought to the organization, deployment, and strategy of allied forces in this particular theater.

Successive German White Papers have extensively dealt with this subject of common interest; a less known but no less remarkable document is General

Ulrich de Maizière's study made at the request of the WEU committee on defense questions and armaments, better known under its title "Rational Deployment of Forces on the Central Front."[2] We shall examine these problems in the first section, and in the second we shall review the present situation of the German armed forces, the political restraints, as well as the FRG armaments market. In the third and last part we shall propose solutions for improving the security of the Central European Theater within a strictly German and European framework.

## PRESENT DEPLOYMENT OF ALLIED FORCES IN THE CENTRAL EUROPEAN THEATER

Dealing with this problem makes us take a view which is no longer strictly German but which is also European and Atlantic since (by definition) defense is based on the double principle of *solidarity* and *effectiveness*.

The principle of solidarity is apparent when we consider the stationing of allied troops in the Federal Republic from north to south.[3] The central region extends from the Elbe in the north to the frontiers of Austria and Switzerland in the south. Six countries have forces stationed in it: Belgium, Canada, the Federal Republic of Germany, the Netherlands, the United Kingdom, and the United States of America. In addition, by virtue of a bilateral agreement, French troops (which are not included in the NATO integrated command) are stationed in the southwest Federal Republic of Germany. The central Europe region is divided into sectors:

> The northern army group (NORTHAG), in the area lying between the Elbe and the Harz mountains, consisting of four army corps. From north to south, the First Netherlands with two divisions, the First German Corps with four divisions, the First British Corps with three divisions, and the First Belgian Corps with two divisions (one of which has been stationed in Belgium since 1978, Headquarters Verviers—one brigade at Leopoldsburg, another at Marche).
>
> The central army group (CENTAG), to the south of NORTHAG, has, from north to south, the Third German Army Corps with two divisions, the Fifth U.S. Army Corps with two divisions, the Seventh U.S. Army Corps with two divisions, and the Second German Corps with four divisions.
>
> In addition, CENTAG includes the Fourth Canadian Brigade and the American dual-based (United States and FRG) First mechanized division and a regiment of armored cavalry.

The air forces are associated with the army groups: The second allied tactical air force (or 2 ATAF) with NORTHAG, the fourth allied tactical air force (or 4 ATAF) with CENTAG.

Allied solidarity also stems from participation in the double belt of surface-to-air defense missiles, either low altitude (the HAWK) or high altitude (the NIKE). (For more details see Western European Union Assembly 663, April 2, 1975, p. 12.)

The first chain is the most eastward, generally from Rendsburg to Munich, while the second, behind the first, extends from Wilhelmshaven to Ravensburg. In both cases the air defense units include Belgian, German, Dutch, and American units. Finally, mention must be made of the French Second Army Corps with two divisions in the area of Trier and Freiburg-im-Breisgau whose use, according to recent statements by General Mery, the chief of defense staff, is planned to support the forward defense, without however a particular and predetermined sector of the front line being allocated to it in peacetime. From the nuclear point of view, it appears that 5,000 nuclear warheads of varying powers are stored on German territory and therefore in the Central Europe region. These remain American property under strict American control but, *after authorization by the president of the United States*, are destined for supply to the launching facilities or vectors held by the various allied contingents.

At the end of this summary of the general deployment of Allied Forces in Central Europe, two comments are necessary. The alternation of allied and German army corps, in a general disposition which has been called the "layer cake," stresses the interdependence of the various national contingents and, in case of enemy attack, has the advantage of proving the *cohesion and solidarity* of the Alliance.

As a counterpart, it assumes that the various component parts of the disposition are of similar value and that there is no weak link to compromise the coherence of the whole. A marked weakening on the part of one or more allied army corps could, in case of conflict, result in a concentration of effort by the enemy (following the principle of attacking the weak point) leading to a break in the disposition and complete disorganization of the whole defense of Central Europe. In such a case of deep penetration followed by envelopment, the use of tactical nuclear weapons would become hazardous if not impossible.

The second comment relates to the obvious disadvantages of the present deployment. Born of the Second World War and of the division of the Reich into zones of occupation, it has been dependent on existing availabilities of barracks, airfields, and training areas but has not been designed to correspond closely with a preestablished strategic plan. This plan has, moreover, developed with time. Initially, the Rhine was the main defense line and only delaying actions were envisaged east of the river.

Progressively, as more (particularly German) divisions were established, the strategy was changed in order to organize defense as far east as possible and to cover almost the whole of German territory. The main line of defense was advanced to the Weser, the Fulda, the Main, and the Lech. Later defensive actions were planned to start directly at the frontiers with the German Democratic Republic and the Czechoslovak Socialist Republic.[4]

As a result, there is considerable difference between the peacetime garrisons and the planned positions for wartime, so that the divisions must cover varying, and sometimes considerable, distances to reach their area of operations.

This deployment does not only apply in the west-east direction, but sometimes also north-south or south-north with possible overlappings and crossings if the delicate arrangements of the movement plans get out of step.

The most unfavorable deployments are those of the Netherlands First Army Corps, almost completely sited in its home country; an appreciable part of the Belgian First Army Corps; units of the German First Army Corps and of the British First Army Corps; an American division, and a division of the German Second Army Corps.[5]

An examination, even a superficial one, of the distances to be covered gives sufficient proof that these movements would take time, varying from a few hours to several days in the most unfavorable case.[6]

A question arises immediately about the possibility of improving the present deployment by a new siting of units. The answer is unfortunately in the negative for two reasons, both political and economic. The sovereign countries are reticent about stationing the major part of their armed forces in the Federal Republic of Germany. (Until the recent past, Belgium was a remarkable exception to this rule. Our two divisions had been stationed in the FRG from the beginning. One of them has been redeployed to national territory.) In the case of the Netherlands Army Corps, a single brigade out of six is stationed on German territory.[7]

From the economic point of view, the costs involved would be enormous if it is realized that the re-siting of a single brigade (headquarters, four battalions, support units) in two newly constructed barracks would involve infrastructure costs of about 350 to 450 million DM.[8] Accordingly, we may wonder about the cost-effectiveness ratio of such an operation which would cause a parallel reduction in investment expenditures on equipment for the armed forces. This leads immediately to dealing with the respective *effectiveness* of the allied contingents taking part in the common defense of Europe in the Federal Republic of Germany (an obviously delicate matter). Some of them are made up entirely of professionals (United States, Canada, and United Kingdom), and others have adopted a mixed formula, part conscription and more or less advanced professionalism (Belgium, FRG, Netherlands). But here again there are differences according to length of *conscript service* and the qualitative level of the volunteers.

Finally, economic pressures or internal politics have led certain States to gradually, and sometimes in striking fashion, reduce the "availability" and the "instant combat readiness" of units. Periodic adaptations of the manning tables to the numbers actually existing, dismal cuts in active service personnel replaced by insufficiently trained national service reserve NCOs, and social arrangements argued to absurdity, have through their cumulative effect reduced the operational value of some units by fifty to sixty percent. (In the First Belgian Army Corps, the regular volunteer soldiers and NCOs who mount guard on the weekend have three rest days in compensation! They are therefore only required to be on duty again on Thursday morning.)

As regards matériel and equipment, these are noteworthy for their disparity, resulting in serious operational consequences from the interoperability point of view. We shall come back to this later.

An objective comparison must be made of the time for training; motivation; national public opinions; mobilization or recall times to bring personnel up to combat readiness; availability of training ammunition, etc. Although this would take us outside the framework of the present study, these questions deserve to be mentioned. At the end of this analysis of the "solidarity" and "effectiveness" factors of the allied forces in Central Europe, I think it worth quoting the conclusions reached by the Maizière report:

> If the presence of forces is reduced to such an extent and their deployment becomes so unfavorable that the time required for the deployment to wartime positions is no longer reasonable, quick military response—at least with regard to surprise attacks—is no longer ensured.
>
> Such a situation would be nothing short of inviting the potential aggressor to take possession of a pawn by surprise—*i.e. without a warning time and any early indications* (my emphasis)—and to establish a fait accompli.
>
> . . . Only the readily available forces are capable of effectively resisting surprise actions of the enemy. . . . The forces at present available are the minimum forces required for the implementing of the strategy of flexible response and forward defense in view of the present threat. The potential aggressor is well-informed about these available forces and will take into account their strength and type in his estimates, when preparing his own possible military actions. He will also register exactly any unilateral reduction of the military presence and will draw his conclusions.[9]

"Availability" and "operational immediacy" have therefore appeared to be vital requirements for the defense and security of Europe. In this respect, only the American Seventh Army and the Bundeswehr appear to offer the necessary guarantees.[10]

The following section of this chapter will examine in greater detail the organization and present situation of the German Armed Forces.

# ORGANIZATION, MISSION, AND FUTURE DEVELOPMENT
# OF THE GERMAN ARMED FORCES

The Bundeswehr is just over twenty-three years old and its development phase may be considered complete, at least in its present form. Its main role is a defensive one and stems moreover from Art. 87a of the "fundamental law." Any preparation for a possible aggression is excluded from both the legal and operational points of view. The same fundamental law prohibits any action of the kind in its Art. 26. Furthermore, the fact that there is no self-contained major German headquarters; the mixing of the German corps among the allied contingents; the absence of adequate logistics stocks; and the integration of the land, sea, and air forces in the Atlantic system make it clear that any such possibility can be excluded.

Interdependence and integration are, as we have seen above, at the root of the Federal Republic's Atlantic commitment and faithfulness. Isolation would be considered a disastrous end since Germany is well aware that, left to its own devices, it would be in no position to ensure the security of its territory. These are the reasons for the importance of the American presence on its soil and of permanent participation, not subject to change, on the part of its European partners.

The limitations imposed on it result from Protocols II and III of the Brussels Treaty (revised in 1954) which laid down the ceilings for its conventional forces—broadly, 12 divisions and 1,000 military aircraft—and which prohibit the manufacture of atomic, biological, or chemical weapons on its territory (as well as certain conventional weapons).

Protocol IV instituted an "Agency for the Control of Armaments" under the Western European Union responsible for keeping a check on the limitations. The Federal government has never questioned its commitments under the Paris Agreements and it has restated its position in the 1970 White Paper.[11]

The Federal Republic's contribution to the joint defense is the largest of NATO's conventional forces. In Central Europe, the army by itself represents fifty percent of allied forces. Participation in the deterrent strategy, forward defense, and preservation of its territory are the main mission of the armed forces. What is their relative importance and what are their main characteristics?

## The Army

This consists of three Army Corps with a total of twelve divisions. The key unit is the brigade of which there are 36, an increase of three compared with the previous organization. These thirty-six brigades consist of seventeen mechanized and "Jäger" brigades, sixteen armored brigades, and three airborne brigades. Their internal structure is being developed in accordance with the "Brigade 80" model. In brief, the trend is an increase in combat units—companies and battalions—as well as increased operational readiness and combat effectiveness, without recourse to prior mobilization or replacements.

Stress will be laid on an improved antitank defense capability.[12] There are 3,026 per armored brigade and 3,730 per mechanized brigade. This new structure will give the Army more tanks, artillery, and antitank missiles than is the case in the present organization. In addition to the army (entirely under NATO command) the internal defense forces or territorial army must also be mentioned. These are authorized by the 1954 Paris Agreements which permit the existence of national forces "earmarked to NATO for the defensive battle in Northern and Central Europe and for the internal defense of the territory" (excluding any other national forces, in the form for example of strategic reserve or overseas intervention forces). Their size is subject to prior agreement by WEU. At the present time, German territorial forces number about 70,000 men (as compared to about 250,000 in the battle corps), and are split up into six territorial commands and a certain number of "Jäger" regiments equipped with tanks and artillery. Their mission is to ensure freedom of action of the battle corps by protecting vital points and ensuring the security of the rear areas against any possible airborne actions by the adversary. It appears that both their size and role will increase in the future because of the large number of trained and available reservists, which now number nearly two million. More than 100,000 are recalled each year for exercises or maneuvers of varying duration.

The area of action of the Battle Corps lies mainly in the Central European theater. There is however one division in the Northern European theater.

## The Air Force

The air force has more than 100,000 men, mainly regulars. With 24 combat squadrons, totaling about 500 aircraft, it takes part in reconnaissance and conventional combat missions. Some of its forces have an atomic capability and are available for nuclear engagement as part of the deterrence strategy (under the double key system, the nuclear missiles supplied by the United States and for use after approval by the President). Its role is solely tactical and not strategic and its operational air space extends from the Baltic Straits in the north to the Alps. As well as the combat aircraft, air defense also includes twenty-four surface-to-air "Nike Hercules" missile batteries and thirty-four "Hawk" batteries. The aircraft types used in the air force are "Phantoms" (RF-4E reconnaissance, F-4F as fighter and fighter bomber aircraft), the FIAT G-91 (ground support), and the F-104 G "Starfighter." In the near future, the "Alpha" jet (a Franco-German aircraft) and the MRCA "Tornado" (produced jointly by Germany, the United Kingdom, and Italy) will respectively replace the FIAT G-91 and the F-104 G. German air force participation in Central Europe represents one third of the allied air forces in the theater.

## The Navy

The navy's peacetime manpower amounts to 38,000 men. Three squadrons of destroyers, one of escorts, four of fast patrol boats, two of submarines, six of minesweepers and one of landing craft make up its operational forces operating in the Baltic and the North Sea. To these must be added four squadrons (fifty-two aircraft) of F-104 G fighter-bombers and reconnaissance aircraft and one squadron of Breguet Atlantic aircraft.

## Characteristics of the Armed Forces

The 1975-1976 White Paper considers the essential attribute of the armed forces to be an almost instantaneous reaction capability and a permanent state of operational readiness. It may be added that the quality of the equipment, high level of the training, high proportion of regulars or medium-long-term volunteers make the German armed forces the backbone of European defense.

It is appropriate to dwell a moment on the ability to react immediately and almost without warning against any hostile enterprise on the part of the adversary. We should remember that the vulnerability of the Federal Republic and the narrowness of its territory demand a maximum degree of preparation of its armed forces, particularly the army, for its very survival. This stems from the strategic assumptions made by the Federal Government and from the massive superiority of Soviet conventional forces. Interesting assumptions are to be found in the 1975-1976 White Paper (pp. 16-18) which deserve quotation in full.

*On the strategic principles* applied by the Soviets, in para. 30 and 31:

> The salient feature of military strategic thought in the Soviet Command is the conviction that, in any military conflict with NATO, strategic offensive must be the basis of Soviet operations.
>
> The striking power is being boosted so that strong operationally ready forces can exploit the element of surprise, and, by means of an operational breakthrough, can quickly create situations in which the initial use of nuclear weapons by the defender would occur at too late a stage.

And further on:

> Initiative and surprise occupy a place of paramount importance in the military strategic thinking of the Warsaw Pact. According to the Soviet military doctrine, a surprise outbreak of hostilities is the most dangerous form of beginning a war since the attacker holds the initiative.

*On strategic possibilities*, the following may be read in par. 32:

> A surprise attack could be launched by the Warsaw Pact with practical-
> ly no preparation and without any build-up—from manoeuvre situations,
> for instance. It could, in such an operation, exploit the advantages of the
> attacker and determine the time of the attack as well as its points and key
> effort.

And, finally, in the following paragraph:

> The Warsaw Pact can exploit internal political weaknesses in Western
> democracies through the medium of subversive actions conducive to
> achieving its goals. Moreover, it can use this resource independently of
> armed conflicts. Subversive actions can pave the way for a military conflict
> and be used as flanking measures.

It seems that the 1975-1976 White Paper has lucidly analyzed the most
dangerous assumptions for the security of the West and, therefore, the most
favorable to a potential adversary.

Since prefaces to this document were written both by Chancellor Helmut
Schmidt and by the Minister of Defense Georg Leber, it is difficult to understand the profound reasons leading to such public protest in certain political
circles in the Federal Republic when a study based on these same assumptions,
and initially printed in "The Times,"[13] drew the logical conclusions. The author
considered that, under specific conditions, the forces of the Warsaw Pact had the
feasibility to reach the Rhine in forty-eight hours, preventing the use of tactical
nuclear weapons and the implementation of the flexible response strategy by
means of the rapidity of their advance.

Naturally, we shall return in detail to this scenario and compare the im-
peccable logic of facts and the harshness of realistic deductions against
unchecked or unduly convenient assumptions (see chapters 9 and 10 of this
study).

Now we must examine a last characteristic of the strategic considerations
affecting German defense policy—the ambivalence of the FRG's attitude about
the use of tactical nuclear weapons.

On the one hand, it is recognized that the existence of these weapons is an
essential factor in deterrence and therefore in the prevention of a conflict. On
the other, the German government, extremely sensitive to the fact that its
territory would in any case be the inevitable battlefield of an East-West confrontation, has always been the advocate of a selective and last resort use of the
tactical nuclear weapon. It has never ceased to defend to the last the point of
view that, by themselves, powerful conventional forces would permit the
avoidance of premature recourse to massively destructive weapons and, what is
more, would strengthen the credibility of their use.

When we remember that a team of scientists, led by Professor Carl Friedrich von Weizsäcker, has undertaken a long study concluding that 22 megaton bombs would lead to the death of 10 million Germans and that 200 bombs would destroy 50 million,[14] we can easily understand the reticences and perplexity of the Federal Government as well as its interest in participating in the decision to use nuclear weapons through the "nuclear planning group."

What must be concluded from all this? The special position of Federal Germany, its vulnerability, dual dependence on the United States of America and its European allies obliges it to do everything possible to guarantee its security which is identical with that of Europe, a fact which is not always recognized by its partners in the Alliance.

Accordingly, the dilemma is as follows, *either Germany must be freed from the restrictive and limitative clauses of the Paris Agreements* and be given its own full initiative, authorizing it to raise and maintain adequate conventional forces to ensure its own security and survival; or else, the allies, aware of the interdependence of their interests in matters of security and defense, must abide by the *rules of participation and uniform, equitable, and intangible contributions* and not undertake to subject their forces to periodical fluctuations resulting from the economic circumstances of the moment or pressures—mainly electoral—of their internal politics. This assumes a minimum of European solidarity.

It remains for us to see, in the next section of this chapter, what the attitude of the Federal Republic is regarding European cooperation and defense from the triple points of view of politics, economics, and operational efficiency.

## POSITION OF THE FEDERAL REPUBLIC
## WITH RELATION TO A EUROPEAN DEFENSE POLICY

"The pursuit of a policy aiming at European unification is the cornerstone of German foreign policy. At the end of this road, we must have developed a European foreign policy which included a European security policy." So much for the principles, as clearly expressed in the 1975-1976 White Paper (European Security Policy, paragraph 105, p. 54).

However, the Federal government has hardly any illusions about the slowness of the process and it recognizes that full cooperation in defense will only be realized on the basis of political cooperation.

A major concern dominates all German efforts towards the achievement of a European solution—not to cut itself off at any price from the United States whose strategic nuclear guarantee remains essential, even for a united Western Europe. Accordingly, recognizing the absolute necessity for increased European cooperation between East and West, the Federal Republic is obliged to set any European solution within the framework of the Atlantic Alliance. So far, it has never altered its attitude.

It is here, too, that it disagrees with the French positions, despite bilateral agreements which link the two countries in a privileged fashion. The priority for the construction of a united Europe is certainly recognized, but a reasonable balance must be maintained within the Atlantic Alliance between the European Community and the United States.

Federal Germany has always favored international economic coproduction, particularly European, for obvious reasons of operational efficiency, rationalization, and standardization.

It is true that the structure of its armaments industry—nonexistent in 1955—has characteristics which are fundamentally different from similar industries in France and the United Kingdom. It is only lately that Germany has seriously started on arms construction programs. There are psychological inhibitions perhaps, political restrictions certainly, due to the limiting protocols of the Paris Agreements.

However, since the 1960s, it has forged for itself a prime position in the field of conventional weapons, particularly in the construction of fast patrol boats and conventional submarines, armored matériel (of which the "Leopard" and the "Marder" are the best-known examples), in the electronics field (radars, missiles, etc.), and finally in a rebirth of the aircraft industry in the form of international cooperation with the Alpha jet and particularly the MRCA. The whole armaments industry employs 200,000 people.

Despite the spectacular successes, *exports* represented only 0.2 percent of the total against 12 percent for France and 18 percent for the United States. In 1974, these exports represented a value of 800 million French francs against 12 billion for France. There are two reasons for this phenomenon. On the one hand, there is very severe legislation by the Federal government concerning exports outside the NATO area; and on the other, a fairly considerable internal market results from the reequipment of the Bundeswehr which covers seventy percent of requirements for national protection alone.

Another difference is that the armaments industry is almost wholly in the hands of private industry whereas, in France and particularly in England, it is largely in the hands of state shipyards and factories or nationalized industries. Finally, considered as a function of total industrial production, the German armaments industry barely represents 2 percent of the total (as opposed to 6.5 percent for the French armaments industry).

Accordingly, Germany has been able, more easily than its partners, to encourage international solutions. Here are some of the more striking examples: in the antitank missile field, the Milan and Hot systems, in cooperation with France, the Roland 2 antiaircraft missile and the ground support and training Alpha jet aircraft, also Franco-German. We have already mentioned the MRCA project completed jointly by B.A.C., Messerschmidt-Bolkow, and FIAT. Growing costs of equipment and fixed or reducing financial resources impose a cooperating solution regarding equipment. Germany is one of the strongest partisans of initiatives in this direction, to such a point that its minister of defense, Georg Leber, has stated that "even if the national military requirements were only met to 80 or 85% by a solution leading to better standardisation, this would still have to be given preference because of the advantages it has within the Alliance."

From the operational standpoint, the 1975-1976 White Paper lists these advantages rapidly. Standardization facilitates uniformity of command, logistics support, and training. Furthermore, in the final analysis, it leads to a much more rational use of military material from the cost-effectiveness point of view. Finally, by the very fact that different allied contingents are required to participate in combined operations in Central Europe, the combination of European technological resources in joint development projects can only strengthen the common defense capability.

It is moreover only on this European scale that transatlantic cooperation can be conceived between partners of equal sizes, the United States and Europe. As we have seen, Germany has made itself the champion of more advanced European cooperation in the production of military equipment, the first step towards increased harmonization preparing the way for a common defense policy. First through the Eurogroup, but also the CNAD (Conference of National Armaments Directors), and the European Programming Group in which France is represented, it constantly pursues its efforts towards Europeanization with a view to the progressive elimination of "one of the most serious weaknesses of the defense effort, the lack of interoperability and compatibility."[15]

Alongside the operational advantages achieved by standardization of equipment, we must also mention those which stem from common instruction and training. Much remains to be done in this field, although present achievements are by no means negligible. Since the formation of the Alliance, contacts at staff or unit level have become more and more frequent and have engendered a climate of confidence and friendship between allied military personnel.

The territory of the Federal Republic has been the favored area for numerous interallied maneuvers in which integration has been pushed particularly far. German units of various sizes are regularly put under the orders of allied formations or vice versa (as was the case in the "Reforger 76" maneuvers under the direction of the Supreme Allied Commander Europe, General Haig).

The resulting solidarity, the comparison of methods, the elimination of possible disparities, and, more simply, cooperation in the fulfillment of a common task, can all be counted as positive aspects of the Alliance and of meeting the Bundeswehr's concern to develop the feeling of solidarity and interdependence to the maximum.

# CONCLUSIONS

There is no question that, in defense matters, the Federal Republic is aware that it finds itself at the crossroads and that rationalization measures, even new trends, must reestablish a balance of forces which is becoming more and more precarious. The cumulative effect of the quantitative erosion of the forces of the Alliance and of the progressive growth in Soviet conventional capability calls for urgent solutions. Nuclear parity at strategic level and the qualitative improvement of Soviet equipment make conventional forces of vital importance. Germany is aware that implementation of the forward strategy—imperative from the political point of view but hazardous from the strictly defensive aspect—cannot be conceived without considerable reinforcement of the conventional forces.

How can this be achieved in a climate of latent economic crisis, of restriction, and of "détente"? It would probably be necessary to plan, alongside mobile, modern, and extremely costly major units, the possibility of almost instantaneously calling up territorial units which would be less sophisticated, locally mobilized, and equipped with modern high-performance antitank weapons with a view to stiffening the defense sector, to making a network over the entire country, to act against the flanks and rearguard of the adversary, to relieve the conventional divisions of security problems, and to guard vital points or to carry out the almost insoluble task of preventing infiltration by night.

The territorial units of the Bundeswehr may perhaps be developed along these lines. But they would not have to be the only ones to carry out this task, the allied units of similar structure would have to be added to them, if only to demonstrate interallied solidarity in all aspects of joint defense. (We shall return to this possible solution in greater detail in chapter 11.)

It is on this note that I should like to conclude that the defense of the Federal Republic—the advanced bastion of Central Europe—*goes hand in hand with the defense of Europe*, i.e. with that of all the member countries of the Alliance. Ignoring this vital truth stems from either stupifying ignorance or from a narrow and outdated nationalism. *Any unilateral diminution in contribution to the common effort reduces the credibility of the deterrent and increases the risks of a war we want to prevent at all costs.*

# 7 The Other European Members of the Alliance: Juxtaposition of National Defense Forces

We started the previous chapter with an extensive review of Central Europe before discussing the importance of the Bundeswehr in greater detail in the common defense organization. It is now appropriate to examine the contributions and defense efforts of the Benelux countries since, apart from Luxembourg whose participation is limited to a single battalion, Belgium and the Netherlands each furnish an army corps to the Northern Army Group of the Central Europe theater.

But the defense of the European continent is united and indivisible. The importance of the northern and southern flanks is crucial to the survival of the whole, which is closely dependent on its sea communications, either through the Atlantic and the North Sea or through the Mediterranean basin. Accordingly, we shall deal successively and succinctly with the northern flank of the Alliance—Norway and Denmark; and then the southern flank—Italy, Greece, and Turkey.

This chapter will therefore consist of three sections, Central, Northern, and Southern Europe, and will end with a review and an analysis of the defense policies of the European members of the Alliance, from the failure of the EDC to the present time.

## THE BENELUX CONTRIBUTION TO THE DEFENSE OF
## CENTRAL EUROPE AND THE DETERRENCE STRATEGY

### General Factors

The defense policy of Belgium and the Netherlands has not escaped the triple influence of geography and history, internal political climate, and the objectives of foreign policy.

*The geographical factor* is a permanent one. The Benelux countries are a crossroad among the Latin, German, and Anglo-Saxon worlds, with a truly strategic position commanding the Channel and the North Sea, and is situated on the natural routes of the great invasions.

*Internally*, there is a certain reticence about providing an independent military effort which is considered derisory in comparison with the military power of the blocs, and this is a trend whose roots have a long history.[1] There is no real symbiosis between the nation and its armed forces, and so in Belgium as well as in the Netherlands, domestic problems often take precedence over defense policy.

The political parties, more concerned with internal affairs than with external problems, are sensitive to the pressures of a public opinion which is not always aware of the need for the financial sacrifices demanded by the defense effort, because it is either ill-informed or not informed at all about the necessary conditions for its security. Accordingly, these same parties most often give way to a demagogy of immediate relationship and turn defense into an electoral stake, rather than retaining its character as an apolitical instrument in the service of the nation on a permanent basis. The result is a *discontinuity of effort* which fluctuates according to the men and regimes in office.

We must now examine the third factor, *the influence of foreign policy*. At the end of the Second World War, faced with the threat of an expansionist Soviet bloc and understanding finally the bitter lesson of previous years, the Benelux countries definitely opted for a defense policy within an Alliance. In a world whose solidarity and interdependence were growing, it was no longer possible for countries within the heart of the European continent and at the crossroads of the great economic and commercial currents to go it alone and to retreat within isolation in the name of a national defense they no longer had the means to provide independently.

Furthermore, there is no comparison between the role played by these same countries in the concert of Europe in the nineteenth century and at the beginning of the twentieth, and that which they can claim and intend to assume in the Europe of the present day and of tomorrow. Formerly, it was out of the question that Belgium, the Netherlands, and Luxembourg could make themselves heard in the big international conclaves. In contrast, although demographically and territorially their relative importance has remained unchanged, the full members of the community of the nine are participating in the development of a common policy (certainly still very limited) which affects more than 250 million Europeans and goes far beyond the traditional framework of national and exiguous frontiers.

It therefore seems absolutely correct, having full rights in Europe (most of whose institutions are situated in our territories), that they should assume rightful share of the common burdens in defense matters. Is this really the case? This is what we shall have to examine in the analysis of the contributions of each country. But first let us remember the importance of other factors affecting the development of the defense of all the members of the Alliance which are linked with the transformation of the contemporary world.

*Technological progress* has led to full mechanization, to the considerable increase in fire power, to specialization, to the expansion of logistic, administrative, and infrastructure support, to a *reduction in fighting troops* as well as to an *exponential growth* in costs. The *sociological factor* associates the personnel of the regular forces with the planning of the public sector, with legal arrangements controlling the number of working hours and days of leave and *makes the continuing increase in personnel costs inevitable.*

These two decisive factors, complexity and cost of equipment and constantly growing personnel costs, have led to a continuing reduction in the armed forces and in the correlative reduction in international commitments. Successive reductions in national service time, apparently compensated for by greater recruitment of volunteers, has led to a considerable reduction in the troop numbers available. This process, which could be called "the history of shrinkage" and which will be examined in greater detail later, has led to an erosion and we may rightly wonder whether the units on the spot are still able successfully to ensure the defense of a sector which, by definition, has remained unchanged. As an example, a 1979 model Belgian division now has only half the personnel numbers it had twenty years ago and only one third of the battle tanks of the 1956 divisions.[2]

Despite qualitative improvements, there are limits to the continued pruning of troop numbers. The imperative law of numbers is just as true today as it was yesterday. Faced with the choice between ultramodern and therefore extremely costly equipment and an increase in numbers, the responsible authorities do not always appear to have applied the correct priorities. We make war particularly with men, and not solely with sophisticated robots. It would, moreover, be disastrous from the psychological point of view if the NCOs and men whose morale and enthusiasm still remain intact were to have the agonizing feeling of being condemned to carry out a hopeless mission for lack of adequate and appropriate equipment.

## Present Situation and Future Trends

We have just reviewed the common characteristics of the three countries under consideration. Regarding achievements, there are differences which stand out relating to the budgetary field, equipment, the relative importance of the air-land-sea components of the armed forces, peacetime deployment, or fitness for war missions.

Finally, *psychological factors and motivation* play an appreciable role in the overall evaluation of the respective contributions.

### Belgium

The Belgian armed forces are made up of three components: land, air, and sea. During the initial rearmament period (1949-1953), corresponding internationally to the awakening of conscience about the Communist threat, the Korean War (1950), and the implementation of the containment policy, Belgium undertook (from July 1952) to raise an army of three active divisions and two reserve divisions. By December 1952, it was to establish an air force with at least 400 aircraft and a naval force of about 15 ships. In addition to the units assigned to NATO, Belgium organized *"internal forces"* responsible for ensuring the security of the lines of communications and nerve centers.

The air defense of the territory was ensured by the territorial antiaircraft guard which, in addition to the warning services, consisted of about 40 antiaircraft artillery battalions. In addition, two metropolitan bases—Kamina and Kitona—were set up in the colonies. These measures resulted in a considerable increase in military expenditures, which went from 5 billion francs in 1948 to more than 14 billion in 1951 and reached 21 billion in 1952. In 1953 to 1954, troop numbers were nearly 150,000 men (about double the figures for 1948); national service was twenty-four months; and about six percent of gross national product was devoted to defense expenditures.

The death of Stalin, the start of the so-called détente period, and the progressive development of nuclear weapons were to lead to three successive reductions in national service time, resulting in major reorganization of the army.[3]

In 1956 one active division became a reserve division; later, within the framework of the MC-70 plan, commitments included the raising of two M-day active divisions, two reserve divisions, and surface-to-surface and surface-to-air missile units. The air force was reduced in the same proportions and the naval force was to consist of oceangoing and coastal minesweepers plus four support ships.

From 1960 on, because of the reduction of national service time to twelve months, the army reorganized the intervention forces into Landcent divisions of three brigades each; the territorial antiaircraft force was disbanded; and surface-to-air missile units for low- and medium-altitude defense were created (Hawk and Nike units).

The air force was equipped with high performance interceptor aircraft with air-to-air missiles, and, as a result of the work of the 1966 joint service commission, the army corps was reduced to two divisions each of two brigades, and the reserve consisted only of two reserve brigades (one mechanized and the other motorized). For their part, the internal defense forces underwent successive reductions but could count on the firm nucleus of the para-commando regiment which developed as time went by to incorporate artillery and light armored vehicles in its organization.

That in general is the present situation which is the final result of a reduction in overall numbers to a total of 87,000 men.

At the same time, a policy of "professionalization" of the army has been going on through the recruitment of volunteers, together with new reductions in conscript service time, which is now nine months in Germany and should be lowered to six months if the volunteer contribution proves adequate.

Another trend, whose development is about to be completed, relates to the deployment of our two-division army corps. In the end, one division, the sixteenth, will be wholly stationed east of the Rhine with its two component brigades, whereas the other is now spread out in Belgium with one brigade at Leopoldsburg and the other at Marche. It is probably no longer possible, for psychological reasons relating to distance from the home country, to maintain almost the entire fighting land force in the Federal Republic of Germany. Even so, from the operational point of view, the cumulative results of the trends in defense matters are considerable increases in the times required for emergency deployment in case of crisis and a lowered availability of fighting troops.

The "professionalization" should certainly lead to a raising of the qualitative threshold and reduce the periodical training cycle; however, these real advantages must not be counterbalanced by a reduction in the troop numbers of the intervention units which are already approaching the limit of acceptability.

The *air force* (20,000 men), after undergoing reconversion and having adapted its aims and its resources, has been relatively stable during the last few years. It has succeeded in renewing its major combat equipment despite a considerable growth in costs. It now has 147 combat aircraft, F-104 G and Mirage B, and 40 transport aircraft including C-130 Hercules S and 10 HSS 1 helicopters. The multilateral contract committing Belgium, the Netherlands, Norway, and Denmark has enabled Belgium to plan the future replacement of its F-104 G Starfighters with the modern American F-16 aircraft. In addition, it participates in the antiaircraft protection ring with three groups of Nike-Hercules surface-to-air missiles.

The *naval force* (4,000 men) is divided into three groups (operational, instruction, and training [logistics]). Its main mission is "mine warfare" but has recently been extended to include submarine search and destruction and convoy safety. As a result, work is being started on its escort program. Its area of action is restricted to the channel and the southern part of the North Sea.

Financially, Belgium's defense effort amounts to 3.1% of its gross national product which puts it in tenth position amongst its allies, after the Netherlands (3.8 percent), and before Italy, Denmark, Canada, and Luxembourg.

EQUIPMENT POLICY FOR THE ARMED FORCES

Until recently, it was fair to wonder whether an equipment policy, in the real sense of the word, had ever existed in Belgium. This situation was probably attributable to a whole series of factors, the main ones being:

—*dependence*, in the immediate postwar and subsequent periods, *on external aid*, British to begin with and then mainly American under the MDAP;[4]

—the *absence of integration* from the European and Atlantic points of view (logistics remained strictly national by political decision);

—the *minor role played by national industries* in national production and lack of governmental support for these industries;

—the *absence of concrete and long-term directives* aimed at encouraging the appearance of a *European armaments market* in which Belgium could play an appropriate role; and

—the almost automatic and probably traditional application of the *"lowest price" criterion*, an understandable concern in an environment of extremely limited funds but remarkably restrictive in a wider framework aiming at promoting cooperation agreements, stimulating research, and encouraging standardization.

It is only over the last few years that bilateral or multilateral agreements have been made and that a favorable trend towards standardization, if not "Europeanization," is appearing. Largely dependent on external markets, Belgium has every interest in encouraging co-production agreements or, better still, in participation of the founding of an association starting at the research and development stage. Purely national production, without the assurance of extensive outlets in a European context and with only a limited production run must be rejected, precisely because of its prohibitive unit costs. (A relevant case is the national and independent production of about seventy armored vehicles for the gendarmerie.)

The Netherlands

Like Belgium, the Netherlands maintains land, air, and sea components of its armed forces. Because of its geographical situation, and long tradition, the navy plays a more important role in the armed forces than in Belgium. In the Netherlands, more than elsewhere, the trend is toward a reduction in the forces as was expressed in the 1974-1983 White Paper on "Reform of the Armed Forces." Basing great hopes on reductions from the MBFR conversations, the

Netherlands has reduced the active and permanent portion of its available troops by putting greater accent on recourse to mobilization, despite the bitter criticisms made among its Atlantic Alliance partners. (The MBFR, mutual balanced force reductions, have been discussed in Vienna for many years without appreciable results so far because of differences of view between East and West.)

Certainly, the Netherlands government does not question its adherence to the treaty but it is reduced to tightrope exercises in the face of the socialist and radical component of its coalition. But it is in the Netherlands that the "nuclear obsession" reaches its peak. Nonproliferation, reduction of the role of nuclear weapons, and absolute opposition to a European force de frappe, are the themes which are endlessly discussed in the political arena or by a public opinion little inclined to sacrifice the "welfare state" to the imperatives of security. In the meantime, the minister of defense's pet subject is based on standardization together with specialization. Although The Hague believes that an integrated European defense presupposes a common foreign policy, it nevertheless supports all initiatives which might advance European cooperation in arms production, provided, naturally, that it remains within the Atlantic Alliance context.

Should the reforms recommended in the White Paper be implemented, they would represent a hard blow to the solidarity of the Alliance and to the integration of air defense systems. However, the Netherlands has never been in the forefront of the defense effort. We have to remember that its First Army Corps of two divisions (i.e. a total of six brigades) has always been stationed on national territory (with the exception of a single brigade deployed in the FRG in peacetime) whereas its wartime mission makes it responsible for the extreme northern section of the northern army group line. Of all the allied formations, its deployment is the most unfavorable since it must cover considerable distances to reach its operational positions. Its armored formations can only be transported after the Bundesbahn has sent special heavy equipment wagons, a slow and complex operation which obviously does not facilitate the implementation of the "forward strategy" but which does not seem to be in the forefront of the Netherlands' concerns. The cumulative effect of "ill-deployment" and recourse to mobilization to complete the troop numbers of its intervention forces runs counter to the urgent measures which need to be taken to improve the security and reestablish the balance of the forces in Central Europe.[5]

Are the northern neighbors therefore not aware of solidarity in the defense effort and of the increase in danger? It appears that, for many years, the motivation of the youth of the country has been falling considerably. Weakening of discipline, a distinct laxity of manner and behavior, and growing militant trade union activities within the armed forces have not contributed to a strengthening of the image of our Dutch ally among its Atlantic partners. Belgium's ambassador to NATO stressed this moreover in an historical moral tale which is worth repeating.

When the Persian danger which had given rise to the League of Delos created by Athens—the America of those times—became rather less obvious, the little island of Sphacteria progressively and unilaterally reduced its contribution in triremes and money.

The defaulting island was no longer summoned to the meetings of the Council of the League and was upset as a result, claiming the Treaty as its right to attend. Pericles invoked its failures to pay its contributions to the Federation, thus showing that one is consulted and listened to to the extent to which one contributes to the common effort. (Quoted in the 1974 "Annual Political Report" dated January 20, 1976, p. 24.)

### Luxembourg

The participation of Luxembourg—whose population and area are minimal in comparison with its partners—is a striking example of the disparity between political participation in Europe as a whole and contribution to the common defense effort. The abolition of conscription reopened the question of its earlier participation in the form of a brigade-group, now reduced to a single battalion. Certainly, it cannot be expected that the Luxembourg contribution will have a determinative influence on the balance of forces facing each other. Even so, it cannot easily be accepted that the "smalls" of the Alliance should leave the care of their defense to their medium-sized partners or to the United States. The principle of national sovereignty is devoid of meaning if a country is incapable of assuming a reasonable share of the collective defense effort in proportion to its resources.

## THE NORTHERN FLANK:
## ITS IMPORTANCE AND THE CHARACTERISTICS OF
## NORWEGIAN AND DANISH PARTICIPATION

From a geo-strategic point of view, the northern flank is of twofold importance. On the one hand, Denmark controls the outlets from the Baltic through the Little and Great Belts; on the other, Norway, as a result of its enormous sea coastline extending over nearly 2,000 km., plays a paramount role both in SACLANT's (Supreme Allied Commander Atlantic) maritime strategy and in the continental strategy of the northern flank of Europe.

The discovery of oil deposits under the North Sea has added a new and important economic dimension to the whole problem. Participation in the Atlantic Alliance by the two Nordic countries is matched by *restrictive* conditions. *No foreign troops* may be stationed permanently on their territory; and no nuclear weapons may be stored there in peacetime.

These reservations increase the complexity of the defense problems of the northern flank, since the defense of that enormous area of 400,000 square km.

cannot be satisfactorily achieved without bringing reinforcements from abroad and without the possible use of tactical nuclear weapons.

To get an idea of the extreme length of the northern theater which extends from the North Cape to the Elbe, we have only to remember that if it were folded down southward, it would cover the distance between the Baltic Straits and Naples. The applicable defense budget contributions are 3.8 percent of the gross national product for Norway and 2.6 percent for Denmark.

### Norway

This immense territory has only a population of 4 million. Together with Turkey, it is the only country of the Alliance having a common frontier with the Soviet Union, in the extreme northern Finmark region, along a length of 196 km. Its defense is essentially based on mobilization, the organization of which is indeed a model of its kind. Preestablished depots; local mobilization; modern equipment; the high level of endurance, fighting qualities, and training of the Norwegian soldier; and close relations between the army and the country, are the main characteristics of the Norwegian defense effort.

The geographical configuration of the continental land offers some advantages. There is only one road in (the E6) which is often obstructed by snow; and the enormous distances to be covered would probably allow the necessary time to complete the mobilization operations. There remains the possibility of sea landings. The length of the coastline and the large number of fjords make the entire maritime front line extremely vulnerable and impossible to defend.

This leads us to a few words about the maritime threat in this theater of operations which has considerably increased over the years as a result of the construction of the enormous shipyard on the Kola Peninsula with Murmansk as the focal point, the biggest naval base in the world. There are 110,000 men—civilians and military—in the Kola area which provides shelter for 200 warships and nearly 200 submarines, half of which are nuclear-propelled. Three quarters of the "nuclear second strike" capability (including the strategic submarines with intercontinental missiles), 200 naval aircraft, 300 fighter bombers, 2 army divisions (24,000 men), and 2 intermediate-range rocket complexes are all located in the Kola Peninsula, whose civilian population has risen from 360,000 in 1940 to one million in 1976.

What can Norway line up against these impressive forces? From the naval point of view, two frigates, six fast gunboats equipped with sea-to-sea missiles, fifteen submarines, and two minesweepers exist; the air support consists of forty aircraft based at Bodo. Six thousand men in the Finmark region who can be increased to 22,000 by mobilization (including a fast reaction force from southern Norway whose depots are permanently preestablished in the north), make up the army contribution.

The disproportion of forces is overwhelming, but it must be remembered that the considerable forces maintained in the Kola Peninsula are not solely directed against Norway but are also used to control the sea lines of communication in the North Atlantic. It is not therefore surprising that the proximity of this formidable neighbor should make Norway a faithful partner in the Atlantic Alliance upon which, in the final analysis, its security and survival depends.

## Denmark

From the geographical point of view, Denmark consists of the Jutland Peninsula—an extension of the European continent—and about 500 islands, of which the two biggest are Zealand and Fünen. We should also mention Bornholm, the isolated rocky island in the Baltic whose importance to the radar coverage of the Nadge system is paramount. The three straits controlling the outlets from the Baltic are respectively the Little Belt between Jutland and Fünen (.5 mile wide), the Great Belt between Fünen and Zealand (9 miles), and the sound between Denmark and Sweden (2.5 miles).

A special interallied command has been set up in this region. Its strategic importance is obvious. It is called COMBALTAP (Commander Allied Forces Baltic Approaches) and the commander is always a Dane. Like Norway, Denmark relies on extensive mobilization to bring its armed forces up to adequate level. Since the 1973 agreement on defense, which appreciably reduced peacetime numbers, an effort has been made to increase the number of volunteers that now amounts to 13,000 in contrast to 9,000 conscripts.

The *army* in peacetime consists of a "training force" of 7,750 men; schools, headquarters, and administrative units totaling 7,250 men; a "standing force" of 8,500 men; and a "United Nations contingent" of 500 men (source: "Handout on Danish Armed Forces," chief of defense, Denmark, unclassified, September 1975). In wartime, army numbers increase to 78,000 men, 41,000 for the field army and 24,000 for the local defense forces. The standing force of 8,500 men is the active nucleus of the army and is split up into twelve mechanized battalions, support units, and an infantry battalion on the island of Bornholm.

Conscript military service time is nine months but the combat units of five brigades (three in Jutland and two in Zealand), are theoretically fully manned. An interesting characteristic of the "army home guard," with 48,500 men and 7,000 women, is that its personnel keep their weapons, ammunition, and equipment at home in order to speed up the mobilization operations in case of crisis.

The equipment of the Danish army is rather out of date but is in course of renewal; 120 of the 200 Centurion medium-sized tanks will be replaced by German Leopards and this will improve the standardization of major equipment in the Northern Europe sector, and particularly in Schleswig-Holstein.

The *navy* has a total of 5,700 men including about 1,900 conscripts. With 52 ships, of which 5 are frigates or corvettes, 18 fast patrol boats, 6 submarines, and about 15 minelayers or minesweepers, it ensures surveillance and control of the Straits and the Baltic in a particularly important maritime area. Modernization of the Danish fleet is in progress.

The *air force* has 7,000 men, of whom 1,370 are conscripts. There are squadrons (2 air defense, 3 fighter bomber, and 1 reconnaissance) with a total of 116 aircraft. To these must be added 1 transport squadron (13 aircraft) and 1 squadron of 8 helicopters. The surface-to-air missile group consists of one Nike unit and one Hawk unit; the combat aircraft are F-100s (40 Super Sabres), F-104s (40 Starfighters) and F-35 fighter bombers (20 Swedish Drakens). Regarding modernization, a joint contract with Belgium, the Netherlands, and Norway provides for forty-eight American F-16s (with an option on ten additional aircraft) to replace obsolete aircraft.

Overall, after complete mobilization, the Danish armed forces should total about 200,000 men. Although it is accepted that the home guard (land, sea, and air) can mobilize in an extremely short time, it is doubtful whether their light weapons will enable them to take part in extended operations. Its role is important however in the protection of vital points—guarding airfields, coast surveillance, and so forth. In any case, the Danish system under which personnel keep their weapons, ammunition, and sometimes explosives at home is worth retaining since it results in a considerable reduction of the time required to bring reserve units of this type to readiness.

To complete the picture, we must stress the handicap of the absence of preestablished nuclear weapons depots on Danish soil. It is difficult to see how this state of affairs could be remedied in the case of a surprise attack (bearing in mind the relative weakness of Danish conventional forces) if the flexible response strategy is desired in this Northern Europe area.[6]

## THE SOUTHERN FLANK:
## STRATEGIC IMPORTANCE AND
## INCREASING "BALKANIZATION"

The southern flank of the Atlantic Alliance has two essential geo-strategic characteristics—*extreme length* from the Straits of Gibraltar in the West to the borders of the Black Sea and the Caucasus in the East;[7] and *geographical separation* between its Mediterranean countries, Italy, Greece, and Turkey. (Like France, Greece still belongs to the Atlantic Alliance but has withdrawn from the integrated military organization.)

The link between these politically and economically dissimilar entities is the Mediterranean Sea, whose strategic importance is obvious to all because of the trade routes which cross it, the immediate proximity of North Africa and the Near and Middle East, and the naval bases it can offer. This exceptional situation has not escaped the Soviets whose indirect strategy, supported by a growing maritime power, has for several years chosen the Mediterranean Basin as its favorite area.

The land strategy of the southern region is more the sum of almost independent national efforts than the result of a general grouping. Transfers of forces from one sector to another are geographically and politically almost unthinkable. Only the presence of the NATO mobile force, consisting of multinational detachments, is capable of demonstrating the solidarity of the Alliance if serious tension arises at a vulnerable point of this vast theater. At sea, the situation is otherwise; the presence of the American Sixth Fleet is the decisive guarantee of the maintenance of the equilibrium in this vital region, although the problem of its bases has been considerably complicated by the Greek withdrawal and the cooling of American/Turkish relations.

It is the political aspect of the southern flank situation which seems to be the most alarming. We have already mentioned the attitude of Greece, which has preferred to go it alone following its serious dispute with Turkey over Cyprus. The American embargo, following the decision by Congress to suspend deliveries of weapons to Turkey, has provoked retaliatory measures on the part of the latter which have affected, among others, the American bases in Turkey. The psychological climate has certainly not been improved as a result of this. Greco/Turkish relations are still in a state of tension which could become acute if a solution is not found to the problem of the oil deposits under the Aegean.

Italy has been the subject of passionate discussions and controversies about its remaining in the Alliance and the validity of its contribution, should Mr. Berlinguer's Communist party share power or accede to it. Could there be compatibility between membership in NATO and a governmental formula that includes Communist representatives? The debate has been cut short following the results of the June 20, 1976 elections, but the problem remains in view of the growing influence of the Italian Communist party (PCI) in Italian political life.

We must mention the impact of the *economic situation* of the countries under consideration on the maintenance of an adequate equilibrium in the Southern Europe Region.

The position of Italy is alarming and the fall of the lira, together with galloping inflation, does not arouse great hopes about the substantial improvement of its armed forces. Greece and Turkey are barely about (without external aid) to maintain their present efforts or to improve them. The question remains whether a European solution could solve all or part of the present difficulties.

Of the three countries under consideration, Turkey is the only one in direct contact with the Soviet Union through their common Caucasus frontier. Greece only touches the Eastern Bloc through Bulgaria. Italy is separated by a ring of neutral or nonaligned states, Switzerland, Austria, and Yugoslavia. A swing by this latter country to the enemy camp would cause a marked change in the strategic balance of the southern flank. This is why there is much speculation about the political evolution of Yugoslavia after the death of Tito. Maintenance of the status quo would be an ideal solution, but it seems doubtful that the USSR would not do all it could to increase its influence in this country and to obtain its tacit or open adherence to the Warsaw Pact.

Strategically, a surprise attack is less to be feared than on the Central Front, because of the difficulty of the terrain and because of the depth of the theaters of operation and their isolation. The most sensitive areas seem to be Thessalonica, vulnerable to a thrust from Bulgaria in order to gain access to the sea, and European Turkey, in the case of operations against the Straits.

After this rapid review of the general problems of the southern flank, we shall go on to a brief examination of the particular situation and of the contributions of its constituent parts.

### Turkey

There is no question about Turkey's strategic importance, not only because of the considerable contribution it makes to the conventional forces of NATO (453,000 men including 261,000 conscripts), but above all through the permanent control it exercises over the Straits by virtue of the Montreux Convention.

The withdrawal of Greece from the integrated military organization of the Alliance has accentuated, even more than in the past, the geo-strategic position of Turkey which is also a member of CENTO, together with Iran, Pakistan, the United Kingdom, and the United States. Its land forces consist of three armies, with a total of nineteen divisions positioned in European Turkey, on the Caucasus front and on its southern frontier.[8] Until recently, its air forces were well equipped—thanks to American support—and well trained.[9] Its navy plays an important role in the Black Sea in controlling the Straits leading to the Aegean.

Overall, Turkey devotes more than four percent of its gross national product to defense which, for a country whose economy is clearly less advanced than its central European partners, represents a considerable if not excessive effort. The armed forces have been and remain the cornerstone of the reforms which have led Turkey from an almost feudal state to that of a country trying to reach the level of the modern democracies.

This has a twofold consequence. On the one hand, the defense budget is almost completely absorbed by personnel and infrastructure expenditures. Without external aid, it is unable to meet the considerable investment needed for the modernization of equipment and the procurement of sophisticated equipment. However, the discipline of the Turkish soldier, his fighting qualities, endurance, and his combat effectiveness are among the best in the Alliance, and proof was given during the Korean War. We can rely on the fighting qualities of the Turkish people, on their pride, and their extreme nationalism.

It is all the more deplorable that the Cyprus crisis has created an unbearable tension between former allies, has widened the split between Greece and Turkey, has rearoused a secular antagonism, has intensified national feelings about territorial and other claims, and, as a result, has appreciably harmed American/ Turkish relations. It appears that these difficulties are on the way to settlement following an agreement reached in June 1976 (valid for four years) providing for American military aid to Turkey amounting to $1 billion.

The embargo decreed by Congress a short while ago had serious consequences, material and psychological, for this proud and sensitive people. Like all countries, their dependence on others hurts pride and nationalist feelings, and can easily turn towards xenophobia camouflaging internal problems.

There are two dangers to be feared which must be removed at all costs. The first is open conflict between Greece and Turkey, whose result would either way benefit the Soviet Union. (A new Aegean command has been set up at Izmir which obviously has Greece's sea areas in mind.) The second is a reorientation of Turkish policy, either by withdrawal from the organization, or by neutrality or nonalignment, which would further weaken the southern flank of the Alliance.

Such an eventuality would have disastrous consequences for Europe, which depends on others for ninety percent of its energy supplies. Twenty-one percent of its imports of crude oil pass through the Mediterranean where the Soviet presence is growing stronger every year.

An indirect strategy, weighing heavily on essential supplies to Europe, a direct or hidden threat, could hardly help being felt severely by the industrialized nations of Central Europe. Accordingly, we must know how to pay the price for interdependence and recognize the southern flank for the vital importance that it has. More active solidarity would be desirable and, in this connection, it is not impossible that a European solution to joint defense could gain the support of Turkish public opinion and contribute to the solution of the main difficulties. Under present circumstances, we can hardly do without Turkey's considerable contribution in conventional forces, which immobilize on its frontiers a corresponding number of Soviet divisions. And we cannot be satisfied with a solution which would leave the door open to Soviet naval squadrons by delivering the outlets to the Mediterranean to them.

### Greece

Like Turkey, Greece furnished the Alliance with a substantial contribution in conventional forces. Its armed forces number 160,000 men, 112,00 of whom are conscripts. The army, with four active service divisions, eight reserve divisions, five independent brigades, and eight reserve brigades, absorbs 120,000 men.

The air force consists of 15 squadrons with 250 combat aircraft and a total of more than 22,000 men (including 16,000 conscripts). The navy—17,500 men and 85 ships (including 5 submarines and 15 destroyers)—plays an important role in the surveillance of the Mediterranean Basin.

The characteristics of the Turkish armed forces (the fighting quality and endurance of the soldier, patriotism, and the inability to modernize equipment without external aid) also apply to a large extent to Greece.

Strategically, Greece occupies a crucial position in the Alliance as the link between Italy and Turkey and in regard to control of the central Mediterranean. The NADGE radar chain is essential for the surveillance and detection of air movements in the East, and the naval bases and training installations are important. Their loss would have a serious effect on the general cohesion. In this connection, the withdrawal of Greece from the integrated military organization may be a serious blow not only to the Alliance but also to the country itself.

The bases and firing ranges on Greek territory are part of a common infrastructure program which has benefitted Greece to a considerable extent.[10] So far, the missile firing range in Crete and the American Polaris base at Canea have not been affected by the Greek withdrawal.

Negotiations are continuing and the United States will retain its four bases in Greece for four years for $700 million worth of credits for military purposes,[11] but it is certain that the Karamanlis government's decision has profoundly shaken a theater whose split into separate units and instability were already weaknesses on the southern flank of the Alliance. In view of the preferential relations which have been established between Greece and France, it appears that a European solution with France taking part may rally public opinion and help Greece become the tenth member of the European Community and thus improve European security. Despite its external balance of payments deficit, largely due to the increased cost of oil, Greece's economic situation is less alarming than that of its neighbors. It is doubtful, however, whether it can continue its present military effort without substantial aid, either from the United States or from the EEC.

One of the important consequences of the Greco-Turkish dispute, as is stressed in WEU Document 671,[12] has been the almost complete break in communications, particularly air, between the two countries, thus at the same time isolating Turkey from NATO. A break in the continuity of the NADGE network would also have considerable repercussions on the Alliance's air detection capability. Moreover, the Cyprus crisis has led to the withdrawal of the Greek officers serving at the headquarters of Allied Land Forces South Eastern Europe. The position of Greece is vital to the functioning of the whole defense structure because European security demands a stable military situation on the two flanks of Allied Command Europe.

It is therefore essential that Greece should, in the immediate future, reintegrate its forces into the Alliance and once again play its part in cooperation with its European allies.

### Italy

The Italian armed forces have, for a very long time, remained at a constant level of about 420,000 men, with the army alone taking more than 300,000 and the navy and air force having 44,000 and 70,000 men, respectively. As a percentage of government expenditure, the defense budget has been steadily falling—from 11.3 percent in 1972 to 8.6 percent in 1975. The same trend is to be found in percentage of gross national product, 3.1 percent in 1972 and 2.8 percent in 1974.[13] This constant reduction in financial resources has not failed to have an adverse effect on the condition of the armed forces, mainly in terms of chronic underequipment and increased aging of matériel.

Nevertheless, the Italian contribution in conventional forces was proportionally among the highest in the Alliance, particularly regarding the army with seven divisions (two armored), four infantry brigades, five alpine brigades, one parachute brigade, and an amphibious regiment. The navy, with more than 50 ships—including 3 cruisers, 9 destroyers, and 10 submarines—and the air force, with its 372 combat aircraft, made a strong contribution to the defense of the southern flank and the balance of forces in the Mediterranean.

The economic crisis and the devaluation of the lira has severely cut the financial resources available and, in a climate of chronic inflation, has led to a fundamental "restructurization." This has resulted in a drastic contraction of units by the deletion of many battalions,[14] a reduction in conscript service time (from fifteen to twelve months), and personnel cuts in the auxiliary services, all aimed at allowing modernization of the equipment of the three forces.

It is certainly time to act, since the air force is "living off its own fat" and, unless its aircraft are replaced, will have to disband one squadron every year. It is true that Italy is a participant in the MRCA (Tornado) project, but it cannot hope for the appearance of this ultramodern aircraft in squadron service before the end of the decade.

Conversion of the underequipment of the Italian air force into budgetary figures is striking. Whereas, in percentage terms it is normal to devote thirty percent of budgetary resources to reequipment investment, this figure has fallen to ten percent for the Italian air force.[14]

The navy, on the other hand, in view of its primary role in the security of the Mediterranean, has managed to secure parliamentary approval for the necessary financial resources for its reequipment over a ten-year period.

With an external debt of $16 billion,[16] it is doubtful whether appreciable progress can be hoped for in the organization and reequipment of the Italian armed forces. If drastic measures have to be taken to improve the economy, it is certain that the defense budget will have to contribute to their costs.

Here again, a willingness on the part of Europe to cooperate in the joint defense might, even if it does not solve all the problems, appreciably approve the situation which (if we are not careful) will inevitable lead to an upset, if not collapse, of the southern flank.

It is *politically* that the Italian situation has given rise to the most serious concern. The striking progress achieved by Mr. Berlinguer's party among the Italian electorate; the growing favor in public opinion for the "historical compromise" solution between Communists and Christian Democrats; and the dynamism, discipline, and verbal moderation of the PCI have made it seem likely that the Communists will participate effectively in the future Italian government.

As a result, all sorts of speculations have come to the surface about the attitude the Alliance would adopt should defense and foreign affairs be entrusted to Communist ministers; about protection of the secrets of the nuclear planning group—of which Italy may be a nonpermanent member—or of the highly confidential deliberations of the NATO ministerial meetings. There is also speculation about what would happen to the American or allied bases on Italian soil; or to the southern theater command with its headquarters at Naples. These extreme and (in my opinion) to some extent unrealistic ideas have led to no less extreme solutions and attitudes. The unveiled warnings by Presidents Ford and Carter, Henry Kissinger, the former American ambassador to the Quirinale, Volpe, General Haig, and many others, left absolutely no doubt about America's determination to proceed with a "major revision" of its participation in the security of the southern flank should the Communists come to power.

Incompatibility with the declared aims of the Alliance; uncertainty about Berlinguer's real intentions with regard to NATO and fears of a future setting up of Communist cells; memories of the "Prague Coup" and of preferential links with Moscow; and the important situation of Italy in the case of an "after Tito" era alive with possible incidents—all explain the rigid attitude of the Americans, the thinly disguised threats, and the extreme assumption of a new Atlantic bloc generally including Central Europe, with the Federal Republic as the hard economic and military nucleus.

It was not necessary to implement these extreme measures, and the results of the June 1976 elections without however clarifying the situation have enabled any threat of an Italian secession to be dismissed, a secession which nobody really wants (Berlinguer no more than his opponents). But it still remains that one-third of the Italian electorate votes for the Communist party and this proportion is inevitably repeated in the armed forces. Although the regular officers and noncommissioned officers, who are traditionally conservative, do not seem to be affected by the Communist advance, the high proportion of conscripts—nearly 300,000—means that one Italian soldier in three is, if not an active member, at any rate in favor of the PCI.

A major program of setting up Communist cells is not impossible and this moreover seems to have started, if the demonstrations among the NCOs or the conscripts are anything to go by. The operation is carried out in steps, subtly with formidable efficiency, and according to proven practice.

The PCI has established preferential links at different levels in the Italian armed forces in exchange for its parliamentary support for the vote on the budget. Berlinguer has openly declared that, should the Communists accede to power, he would not denounce the Atlantic Pact and the party would not claim either the defense or the foreign affairs portfolios, in accordance with this Euro-Communism line which is less subject to directives from Moscow than in the past and which has been reaffirmed at the recent Congress of European Communist Parties. Is this a break with the past or the use of tactics designed to gain confidence and then to proceed to a realignment more in conformity with the dynamism of Marxism? All these assumptions are valid and only the future will tell who was right.

Could the situation develop more favorably if Europe took responsibility, both politically and economically, for its own security? It is certain that in a huge European parliament, the Communist voice would be much diluted and its influence more limited. The magnetic attraction of a politically united Europe might counterbalance the traditional influence of Moscow and accentuate the split between Eastern and Western Communists, thus encouraging the electoral pluralism and the human-face socialism which Dubcek was claiming at the time of the "Prague Spring."

Is this unrealistic speculation about the future, or an irreversible trend in keeping with the spirit of the century? It is barely possible, at the present time, to give a positive answer to this crucial problem for the security of the West and the political stability of the southern region. The future is never as black or as rosy as supporters of one or the other camp like to believe.

The phenomenon of Communist expansion in the peninsula is an undoubted fact, probably resulting much more from the economic causes and a far from perfect sharing of national income, than of purely ideological considerations. A policy of austerity with basic reforms, supported by increased discipline and conditional European aid, would probably permit the situation to be reestablished and at the same time strengthen the stability of a theater of operations on which the security of all of Europe depends.

### The United Kingdom, France, Spain, and the United States

An examination of the situation on the southern flank would not be complete without mention of these four countries. The first because its Mediterranean interests have always had a considerable bearing on its foreign policy and the deployment of its naval forces; the two others because they are states with Mediterranean coastlines and either play or are destined to play a considerable role in the stabilization of the Mediterranean theater; and, finally, the last of these countries because it alone, by virtue of the presence of the Sixth Fleet, ensures the balance of forces in this vital sector and represents the only real nuclear deterrence instrument.

As regards the United Kingdom, we have already shown in chapter 4 how the influence of a difficult economic situation has made its mark on defense and forced a general withdrawal from "east of Suez."

Initially, the Mediterranean bases had suffered little from this abandonment of England's world role. They have not however been able to stand up to the latest Labour government reforms due to the aggravation of the economic crisis.

The withdrawal of the fleet marks the end of an era and of a continuous presence in the Mediterranean for more than two centuries. As a result, destabilization was growing and France announced its intention of transferring part of its Atlantic forces to the Mediterranean to reestablish a balance compromised by the British withdrawal. This did take place and the increase in French naval influence in this area will certainly have beneficial effects on cooperation between France and its Atlantic allies in the southern European theater.

Spain's strategic importance has once again been stressed before the American Congress.[17] The new Hispano-American Treaty recognizes the "contribution of Spain to the security of the West" and "requires the two signatories of the Treaty to promote the development of appropriate coordination with NATO." (The treaty was ratified on June 21, 1976 by the American senate. Concluded for a period of seven years, it provides for credits amounting to $12 billion to Spain, in return for the provision of three air bases and the ROTA strategic submarine base.)

Among other things, Mr. Bergold stresses the importance of the treaty to the prospects of integrating Spain into the European defense system. Indeed, Spain controls the approaches to the western Mediterranean through which more than 130 ships pass every day. In addition, the Canary Islands lie in a position favorable to control the oil tanker traffic from the Persian Gulf to Europe. Sufficiently distant from the iron curtain countries, the Iberian Peninsula offers first-class logistics facilities for European reinforcement and resupply. The crucial importance of Spain to the United States is demonstrated by Torrejon, a logistics air base; Saragossa, where more than seventy percent of the air-to-air missile training of the American forces stationed in Europe is carried out; Spanish bases for the strategic submarines and SAC (strategic air command); logistical support for the Sixth Fleet; and a protected communications system. It appears that this interest is contagious and that Mr. Leber, the German ex-minister of defense, is planning closer bilateral cooperation with Spain. This initiative could be the precursor of a general rallying, developing as the regime progresses towards democracy.

It seems certain to me that, within a few years, Spain will be able to become a full member of the Atlantic Alliance. If it were to join the European Community at the same time as it was admitted to the Alliance, we might see interesting developments from the point of view of European security. Should France once again agree to accept logistical bases and reestablish the continuity between the advanced operation zones in Germany and the rear logistics zone provided by Spain, immense progress would be achieved. Depth would be restored to the European theater, and there would be reestablishment of direct contacts between the central and the southern theaters, and stabilization and reinforcement of the latter. It remains to be seen whether the Soviet Union, to counterbalance this, might be tempted to gamble all in Yugoslavia and demand its closer support for the Warsaw Pact.

The importance of the role of the United States has been stressed throughout this study. This is because its Mediterranean presence serves its interests in both the near and middle east and in the defense of Europe. This superimposition of a world and regional political role results in the Commander of the Sixth Fleet having dual functions. On the one hand, he is responsible to CINCSOUTH (the commander of the southern theater) and on the other, he is directly subordinate to Washington for tasks which are not directly concerned with the Alliance but which affect the national interests of the United States.

For this reason, I feel that it is unlikely that the American naval presence in this vital area will be reduced to any serious extent. Too many economic and political interests are involved and they can only be properly attended to and guaranteed through the strategic weight of a sixth fleet whose destructive power is matched by the sophistication of its ships and the quality of its matériel and personnel.

It is the permanent illustration of an obvious truth. In the present state of Europe—and even if the latter were to achieve political union—it would take decades to develop an overall self-sufficient European defense with no dependence on the United States. This extreme solution is, moreover, not desirable because it would be harmful both to Atlantic and European interests. This in no way prejudges a joint effort on the part of the Europeans themselves to strengthen both their position, their security, and that of the southern European flank.

## CONCLUSIONS

After this inventory of the three main theaters of operation, Northern, Central, and Southern European, and of the contributions made by the member states, what can we conclude?

A common characteristic is the progressive *erosion of the conventional forces* to various extents, sufficient enough to fear that there will be a destabilization of the forces facing each other if this trend were allowed to continue.

The *reduction in conscript service time* or the suppression of conscription altogether has affected a large number of the member countries: Denmark, the Netherlands, Belgium, Italy, the United States, and Luxembourg. The first of these measures has resulted in an appreciable fall in the quality of training and combat readiness (we should remember that, while the conscript service time is nine to fifteen months in the West [with the exception of Greece, Portugal, and Turkey], it is two to three years for the Soviet Union and the members of the Warsaw Pact). Modernization of equipment has been achieved either at the cost of reducing fighting troops or has been left pending for lack of external aid.

The *increasing vulnerability of the northern and southern flanks of the Alliance* compromises the security of the center which relies on sea lines of communications being kept open for its very survival. This interdependence has not been translated into fact by increased solidarity and cooperation.

The "balkanization" of the southern flank has been accentuated following the Greco-Turkish dispute, as a result of the chronically adverse economic situation and endemic political instability, particularly in Italy where the pressure of the Communist Party in internal affairs will certainly raise problems for the future.

The *American contribution, mainly naval, is essential and indispensable for an indeterminate period.*

This section could be brought to an end with a prediction of the forthcoming breakup of the southern flank or the general weakening of the Alliance, leading to even worse catastrophes. We do not believe that such a pessimistic viewpoint can be accepted.

Better developed European cooperation, leading to an integrated European security organization in the future—without however rejecting the Atlantic aspect—would be capable of appreciably improving a poor situation.

The *accession of Spain to the European Community and to the Alliance* seems to be an established fact in the eyes of the other countries of the Alliance, in view of its progressive evolution toward a democratic regime. There is no question of its strategic importance. Its presence would facilitate cooperation between the center and the south in terms of logistics bases and cooperative training. The sealing off of the two theaters from each other would be eliminated at the same time if France were to adopt a positive attitude to such a new situation.

Therfore, there are grounds for hope but before we consider the concrete measures which might lead to an overall European solution to the problem, we must review the specific problems which have been facing the members of the Alliance for decades and for which no satisfactory solution has so far been found due to lack of political will and spirit of cooperation.

# 8 Specific Problems of European Defense

In the atmosphere of détente which has marked East-West relations for several years, the problems of European defense closely depend on economic, social, and psychological factors whose combined effects tend to push into the background the maintenance of a minimum security which is a guarantee of the values held by the Western world as well as of its economic development and its social gains.

The basic data are simple and even obvious. On the one hand, the budgets devoted to defense do not increase in proportion with the gross national product; at best, they reach a constant value ceiling or else they imperceptibly lose their purchasing power. On the other hand, the cost of personnel and equipment is constantly increasing as a result of the improvement in standard of living and special costs and also of the growing complexity and technicality of the equipment. There is no convincing indication in an environment of latent economic crisis and continuing social claims that points to a reversal of trends in the future.

The results can only be a constant reduction in the forces available to ensure security and to permit the application of the "flexible response" strategy and the deterrence of any threat of aggression.

Faced with this apparently irreversible situation, what can the Alliance as a whole and Europe in particular do to guarantee a minimum level of security? The answer is quite clear. It is a question of achieving a better return from the resources available through closer cooperation or integration at European and Atlantic levels.

In the following pages, we shall try to demonstrate the truth of the premises and define constructive proposals for maintaining the credibility of the defense of Western Europe with the means available to it. Without a speedy solution, the entire defense system would find itself compromised. The present strategy is based on three components: strategic nuclear forces (of which the United States has the monopoly), tactical nuclear weapons, and conventional forces.

The reduction of the last of these below an unacceptable level brings with it two inevitable consequences, the lowering of the "nuclear threshold" and mandatory recourse to atomic weapons in a very short time (either the return to massive reprisals and its apocalyptic consequences or speedy capitulation) and the lack of credibility of the European effort for ensuring its own defense, i.e. either a more and more pronounced dependence on the United States or a disengagement of the latter and a return to partial isolationism.

In both cases, Europe would have shown its incapability of organizing itself politically as a result of failing adequately to participate in the defense of its territory. The "Grand Design" would be stillborn since it is impossible to conceive a sovereign Europe indifferent to its security or giving to others the responsibility for defending it.


## THE EXPONENTIAL INCREASE IN DEFENSE COSTS

At a time when most of the European States are trying to reduce or at least contain their defense budgets, the cost of development and production of the most modern weapons is constantly increasing. In particular, anything involving the most advanced technology (aerospace, computers, electronics, nuclear energy) requires considerable investment exceeding the individual capability of the nation-states of average power.

Furthermore, Europe faces a potential enemy, the USSR, which is competing with the United States and is on the same defense technology level. This leads to a reduction in the useful life of the most complex weapons which become superseded by a new generation of more modern and, generally, more costly systems.

The increase in costs (in thousands of dollars) may be illustrated by the following examples. In 1940 to 1950, the cost of F-51 and F-47 aircraft were respectively $50 and $90; in 1950 to 1960, the F-84 and the F-100 were $500 to $800 and $700 to $800; in 1960 to 1970, the F-104 and the F-111 were $800 to $1,800 and $7,000 is $15,000. As for tanks, the Churchill (1940 to

1950) was $50, the Centurion (1950 to 1960) was $100, and the Chieftain (1960 to 1970) was $300.[1]

In short, the F-111 cost 300 times more than the F-51, its predecessor during the last war. This increase in costs, which cannot be compared to the increases resulting from inflation and the increase in salaries, results from the growing complexity of the weapon systems which tend to include highly advanced technology in their development. This assumes a parallel increase in a highly skilled, specialized labor force which must be maintained during the intermediate periods separating the completion of one development project from the next.

While one of the first military aircraft (the Handley Page) produced in 1915 required 300 weeks of research (or 6 research workers for 50 weeks), it now requires 200,000 or, for the same period of 50 weeks, the number of specialists would rise from 6 in 1915 to 4,000 in 1970. Conversely, accepting a constant number of 6 technical experts, the research time would go from 50 weeks in 1915 to 28 years in 1938 and 100 years in 1970.[2]

The same escalatory trend in costs is found in the considerable differences between the initial funding estimate for a weapon system and the actual total which may reach two to six times the initial figure. The increase in costs goes hand in hand with the size of funding involved. The investment for the research and development cycle for aerospace engines is 300 times greater than the unit cost. Most of the aerospace industries moreover depend to a large extent on government support, the level of their borrowing being 40 and even 60 percent of the capital involved. In 20 years, from 1954 to 1974, the average cost of research and development for thirteen American weapon systems replacement projects increased by 540 percent and the average unit cost by 420 percent.

The enormous cost of financing the most complex projects is no longer within the power of the medium-sized powers. It must be admitted that the facts of the problem of security are profoundly altered by the evolution of the technicality of the weapons. When artillery first appeared, the feudal lords were unable to collect the necessary funds for equipping themselves with this new weapon. They had to unite or join the great European monarchies. The present-day nation-states are in a situation similar to that of the feudal lords of earlier times. They can no longer afford the modern weapons which are the prerogatives of the Empires.

## THE RIGIDITY OF DEFENSE BUDGETS

An analysis of defense budgets indicates two almost constant trends: a regular reduction in the percentage of defense expenditures compared with the gross national product; and an appreciable increase in personnel costs resulting from social claims and salary charges. These result in a corresponding reduction in

Table 8.1. Indices of NATO Defense Expenditure, Current and *Constant* Prices[a]
(in local currency, 1970 = 100)

| Country | 1960 | 1966 | 1967 | 1968 | 1969 | 1970 | 1971 | 1972 | 1973 | 1974 | 1975 | 1976[b] | % Growth[c] 1960-1970 | 1971-1976 |
|---|---|---|---|---|---|---|---|---|---|---|---|---|---|---|
| Belgium | 53.9 | 75.1 | 81.1 | 87.1 | 90.4 | 100.0 | 105.8 | 117.7 | 130.5 | 153.0 | 186.5 | 212.0 | 6.4 | 14.9 |
| | *72.5* | *85.6* | *89.8* | *93.9* | *94.0* | *100.0* | *101.3* | *107.0* | *110.9* | *115.4* | *124.7* | *129.8* | *3.3* | *5.0* |
| Britain | 67.7 | 88.1 | 93.1 | 95.4 | 94.2 | 100.0 | 115.2 | 133.3 | 143.4 | 172.1 | 211.3 | 253.1 | 4.0 | 17.0 |
| | *100.6* | *106.0* | *109.3* | *106.9* | *100.2* | *100.0* | *105.2* | *113.7* | *112.0* | *115.9* | *114.6* | *117.8* | *0* | *1.4* |
| Canada | 80.3 | 85.7 | 95.3 | 93.5 | 92.1 | 100.0 | 103.4 | 108.6 | 116.7 | 138.9 | 151.7 | 174.4 | 2.2 | 10.9 |
| | *105.3* | *99.8* | *107.2* | *101.1* | *95.2* | *100.0* | *100.6* | *100.8* | *100.6* | *108.0* | *106.6* | *114.0* | *-.05* | *2.5* |
| Denmark | 40.4 | 75.4 | 81.6 | 94.0 | 95.8 | 100.0 | 115.9 | 122.8 | 127.6 | 161.0 | 191.3 | 206.0 | 9.5 | 12.2 |
| | *71.4* | *97.0* | *97.3* | *103.7* | *102.0* | *100.0* | *109.4* | *108.9* | *103.6* | *113.2* | *122.9* | *121.3* | *3.4* | *2.1* |
| France | 57.7 | 80.5 | 87.1 | 91.0 | 95.5 | 100.0 | 105.4 | 110.8 | 121.2 | 147.4 | 171.3 | 196.2 | 5.6 | 13.2 |
| | *85.7* | *97.1* | *102.3* | *102.3* | *101.1* | *100.0* | *99.8* | *99.2* | *101.1* | *108.1* | *112.5* | *116.5* | *1.6* | *3.0* |
| Germany | 53.7 | 89.7 | 94.8 | 85.5 | 95.6 | 100.0 | 112.7 | 127.2 | 141.4 | 157.9 | 166.5 | 172.0 | 6.4 | 8.9 |
| | *70.2* | *98.7* | *102.6* | *91.1* | *99.2* | *100.0* | *107.2* | *114.6* | *119.0* | *124.2* | *123.6* | *122.2* | *3.6* | *2.7* |
| Greece | 36.0 | 50.5 | 66.1 | 77.4 | 89.8 | 100.0 | 109.0 | 121.1 | 139.8 | 169.8 | 309.1 | 401.8 | 10.8 | 24.3 |
| | *44.2* | *54.3* | *70.0* | *81.7* | *92.6* | *100.0* | *105.8* | *112.6* | *112.9* | *108.1* | *172.6* | *198.4* | *8.5* | *11.0* |

| | | | | | | | | | | | | | | |
|---|---|---|---|---|---|---|---|---|---|---|---|---|---|---|
| Italy | 45.5 | 85.9 | 87.0 | 89.8 | 90.4 | 100.0 | 118.6 | 138.4 | 153.1 | 182.6 | 198.7 | 227.9 | 8.2 | 13.9 |
| | *67.0* | *97.1* | *95.0* | *96.8* | *94.8* | *100.0* | *113.1* | *125.0* | *124.7* | *124.8* | *116.7* | *113.0* | *4.1* | *0* |
| Luxembourg | 63.2 | 119.5 | 99.3 | 89.9 | 94.0 | 100.0 | 106.3 | 124.3 | 144.5 | 170.7 | 201.0 | 236.3 | 4.7 | 17.3 |
| | *81.5* | *134.1* | *109.1* | *96.3* | *98.3* | *100.0* | *101.6* | *112.9* | *124.1* | *133.5* | *141.8* | *151.9* | *2.1* | *8.6* |
| The Netherlands | 43.5 | 70.3 | 80.6 | 82.7 | 92.8 | 100.0 | 112.6 | 125.4 | 137.7 | 161.9 | 182.6 | 194.4 | 8.7 | 11.6 |
| | *65.6* | *84.0* | *93.1* | *92.0* | *96.1* | *100.0* | *104.7* | *108.2* | *110.0* | *117.9* | *120.7* | *118.1* | *4.3* | *2.5* |
| Norway | 38.1 | 70.2 | 75.6 | 82.9 | 90.2 | 100.0 | 108.9 | 116.8 | 126.4 | 142.0 | 171.0 | 188.2 | 10.1 | 11.6 |
| | *59.2* | *86.5* | *89.3* | *94.5* | *99.8* | *100.0* | *102.5* | *102.6* | *103.3* | *106.0* | *115.0* | *115.3* | *5.4* | *2.5* |
| Portugal | 24.1 | 59.0 | 76.4 | 85.3 | 86.0 | 100.0 | 117.2 | 128.0 | 133.5 | 200.3 | 158.0 | 147.6 | 15.3 | 4.6 |
| | *37.3* | *76.4* | *93.7* | *98.7* | *91.0* | *100.0* | *104.7* | *103.3* | *95.4* | *114.4* | *78.6* | *60.5* | *10.4* | *-11.6* |
| Turkey | 38.6 | 64.1 | 73.7 | 82.7 | 86.5 | 100.0 | 136.1 | 159.7 | 195.5 | 253.8 | 532.6 | 699.2 | 10.0 | 31.0 |
| | *68.4* | *87.0* | *87.7* | *93.0* | *92.6* | *100.0* | *114.3* | *123.6* | *131.1* | *147.0* | *259.8* | *253.2* | *3.9* | *13.3* |
| United States | 58.3 | 81.7 | 96.9 | 103.7 | 104.6 | 100.0 | 96.2 | 99.7 | 100.8 | 110.3 | 116.8 | 127.3 | 5.5 | 5.7 |
| | *76.5* | *97.6* | *112.7* | *115.7* | *110.8* | *100.0* | *92.3* | *92.6* | *88.1* | *86.9* | *84.3* | *86.8* | *2.7* | *-1.2* |

*Source:* The Military Balance 1977-1978, International Institute for Strategic Studies, p. 86.

*Notes:*

[a]To produce constant price series (in italics) defense expenditures are deflated by consumer price indices. These reflect general rates of inflation, not rates in the defense sector.

[b]1976 figures are provisional, those for Greece and Turkey being estimates; hence 1971-76 growth rates are approximate.

[c]Average annual compound growth rates over periods shown.

investment expenses (equipment and matériel) which, together with the increasing cost of weapons, inevitably brings about a reduction in the armed forces, or in structural reorganizations aimed at reducing expenditures in sectors considered secondary.

A detailed examination of Table 8.1 (defense budgets in percent of GNP) from 1965 to 1974, indicates for all countries—with the exception of Portugal—a fall in the percentage of GNP devoted to defense.[3]

This is particularly noteworthy for certain countries: the United Kingdom (6.3 percent to 5.2 percent), France (5.6 percent to 3.4 percent), Germany (4.4 percent to 3.6 percent), the Netherlands (4.3 percent to 3.4 percent), and the United States (8 percent to 6 percent). For others it is less pronounced: Belgium (2.9 percent to 2.8 percent) and Norway (3.9 percent to 3.2 percent). But the decreasing trend is general.

During the same period—1960 to 1974—the budgets have obviously undergone spectacular increases in absolute value because of the regular increase in GNP and inflationary trends.

This is why it is preferable to refer to the evolution of the budgets at *constant prices* if it is desired to establish objective comparisons. Examination of the 1975 to 1976 indices show that the average growth rate at constant prices varies between 0 (Canada), 0.8 (United States), 0.9 (United Kingdom and France) and 6.6 (Greece), 6.9 (Portugal) if the extreme variations are considered. The middle values lies between 3.2 (Denmark), 3.4 (Belgium), 4.1 (Italy), 4.2 (Germany), 4.3 (Netherlands), and 4.5 (Norway). At *current prices* we go from 4.5 (United States) to 14.4 (Turkey) for the extreme values, while the other countries remain within the 7 to 10 percent area (Belgium: 7.7; United Kingdom: 6.8; France: 6.1; Germany: 8.1; and so forth.[4]

This trend was stressed by former president Ford in a speech delivered in Boston on November 7, 1975:

> Under the most optimistic circumstances, there could be a reduction in our defense budget of more than 7,000 million dollars. . . . It is not just this year's cuts that worry me. Let's look at the trend: ten years ago, expenditures for defense represented 41 percent of the total federal budget; five years later, it was 36 percent. For the fiscal 1976 budget, defense represents approximately 27 percent.

> If this trend continues to the year 2000, according to mathematical projections, the United States will be reduced to one soldier carrying one rifle—just like the statue at Concord Bridge![5]

A similar phenomenon may be observed in other countries of the Alliance. In Germany, the increase in defense expenditure from 1957 to 1975 is far less than the growth rate of the Federal budget shown in Fig. 8.1. For the year 1974 for

Federal budget and defense budget
(in billions of DM).

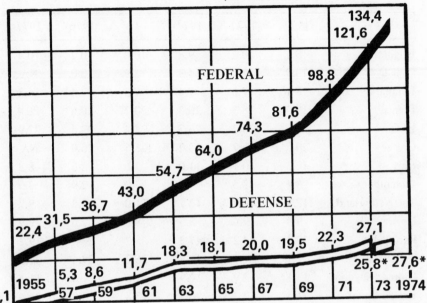

Evolution of defense budget portion
of the federal budget from 1962 to 1974.

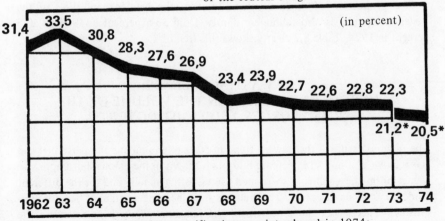

*A new budget specification was introduced in 1974;
1973 budget is converted to the new specifications.

Fig. 8.1.

*Table 8.2.* Percentage of state expenditures devoted to defense.

|                   | 1972 | 1973 | 1974 | 1975 | 1976 | 1977 |
|-------------------|------|------|------|------|------|------|
| Belgium           | 10.1 | 10.2 | 9.8  | 10.0 | 10.2 | 10.4 |
| Canada            | 13.9 | 12.0 | 14.3 | 11.9 | 10.0 | NA   |
| Denmark           | 8.1  | 7.6  | 7.4  | 7.3  | 7.4  | 6.8  |
| France            | 19.0 | 18.3 | 20.3 | 20.2 | 20.6 | 20.4 |
| FRG               | 25.9 | 26.2 | 26.7 | 24.4 | 23.5 | 22.9 |
| Greece            | 20.8 | 21.7 | 25.2 | 25.5 | 26.0 | NA   |
| Italy             | 11.3 | 10.1 | 11.0 | 9.6  | 8.6  | 8.3  |
| Luxembourg        | 3.1  | 3.5  | 3.5  | 3.0  | 2.9  | 2.9  |
| The Netherlands   | 12.9 | 11.9 | 12.2 | 11.0 | 9.8  | 9.7  |
| Norway            | 9.9  | 9.4  | 8.5  | 8.2  | 7.6  | 9.9  |
| Portugal          | 39.3 | 34.2 | 47.3 | 35.2 | NA   | 19.2 |
| Turkey            | 21.1 | 21.1 | 19.2 | 26.2 | 29.4 | 21.1 |
| United Kingdom    | 13.1 | 12.9 | 12.9 | 11.6 | 11.0 | 11.4 |
| United States     | 31.5 | 29.2 | 26.5 | 23.8 | 26.0 | 24.4 |

*Source:* International Institute for Strategic Studies, The Military Balance 1977-1978.

example, the increase is 6.7 percent for defense against 10.5 percent for the Federal budget.

The proportion of defense expenditures in the total expenditures of the Federal Republic is also falling constantly, from 33.5 percent in 1963 to 20.5 percent in 1974. Table 8.2 clearly shows this trend.[6]

# THE WASTING DISEASE:
## CONSTANT REDUCTION IN THE VOLUME OF THE ARMED FORCES AND FIGHTING UNITS

The obvious result of the upward trend in costs of equipment and personnel and the relative diminution in defense budgets is shown in the gradual but impressive reduction in the volume of the armed forces both generally and for the different land, air, and naval forces. The budgets have become veritable "beds of Procrustes." Faced with the problems of the inordinate growth in costs and the competition from other areas (social charges, education, scientific research), those responsible for the defense have tried to maintain the investments at an acceptable level but as a result they have found themselves forced to cut personnel numbers radically.

Table 8.3 shows the extent of these reductions, in total and for each force separately, in the countries of the Alliance.[7] The examples of Belgium, Canada, Denmark, the United States, the Netherlands, and the United Kingdom are particularly significant. From 1960 to 1976, the reductions *in personnel* are respectively 33,000 (BE), 43,000 (CA), 9.600 (DK), 359,000 (US), 22,500 (NL) and 109,230 (UK).

In percentage of initial numbers, these figures represent reductions of 27.5 percent for Belgium, 35.83 percent for Canada, 21.7 percent for Denmark, 14.42 percent for the United States, 16.66 percent for the Netherlands, and 24 percent for the United Kingdom. The levels are relatively constant for Greece and Turkey which until recently benefited from a substantial United States equipment aid program.

Italy, faced with the need for equipment modernization, has announced considerable reductions in the number of fighting units.

The trend towards reduction in numbers is still continuing for the United Kingdom as Fig. 8.2 shows. In April 1979, total numbers will fall to 321,000, i.e. a further reduction of more than 24,000 men (or 7 percent) compared with the 1975 numbers which will bring the reduction in troops, from 1961 to 1979, to nearly 30 percent. (Most of the reductions have related to forces overseas following the government decision to concentrate defense efforts in Europe and to proceed with the withdrawal East of Suez.)

It may be argued that the modernization of equipment, the increase in fire power, and the additional mobility compensate for the reduction in numbers. This is only partially true since there is a limit to the defensive capability of the units in a predetermined geographical context. "Quantity cutbacks cannot go on indefinitely. Having cut aircraft quantities from 1,800 to 500 over roughly the past decade, we have substantially run out the string."[8]

The continuing decrease in conventional forces, and as a result their lowered capacity for resistance and fighting, involves premature recourse to tactical nuclear weapons and thus reduces the elasticity of the flexible response strategy. We shall return to this essential point later because we must now talk about the disparity of equipment and the consequences of the lack of standardization on the efficiency of the defense and security system.

Table 8.3. Armed forces of NATO countries.

| | | 1960 | 1961/62 | 1966/67 | 1968/69 | 1971/72 | 1975/76 | 1977/78 |
|---|---|---|---|---|---|---|---|---|
| Belgium | Total | 120,000 | 110,000 | 107,000 | 99,000 | 96,500 | 87,000 | 85,700 |
| | Land | 95,000 | 85,000 | 83,500 | 75,000 | 71,500 | 62,700 | 62,100 |
| | Sea | 5,000 | 5,000 | 4,500 | 4,000 | 5,000 | 4,200 | 4,200 |
| | Air | 2,000 | 20,000 | 19,000 | 20,000 | 20,000 | 20,100 | 19,400 |
| Canada | Total | 120,000 | 119,300 | 107,000 | 101,600 | 85,000 | 77,000 | 80,000[a] |
| | Land | 48,000 | 47,800 | 44,000 | 41,500 | 33,000 | 28,000 | 23,500 |
| | Sea | 20,500 | 20,000 | 18,100 | 16,600 | 15,000 | 14,000 | 13,400 |
| | Air | 51,500 | 51,500 | 45,000 | 43,500 | 37,000 | 35,000 | 36,600 |
| Denmark | Total | 44,000 | 43,000 | 50,000 | 45,500 | 40,500 | 34,400 | 34,700 |
| | Land | 29,000 | 29,000 | 30,000 | 28,000 | 24,000 | 21,500 | 21,800 |
| | Sea | 7,500 | 7,000 | 7,200 | 7,200 | 6,500 | 5,800 | 5,800 |
| | Air | 7,500 | 7,000 | 12,600 | 10,300 | 10,000 | 7,100 | 7,100 |
| United States | Total | 2,489,000 | 2,606,000 | 3,093,960 | 3,500,000 | 2,699,000 | 2,130,000 | 2,088,000 |
| | Land | 870,000 | 967,000 | 1,200,000 | 1,535,000 | 1,107,000 | 785,000 | 789,000 |
| | Marine Corps | | | 261,600 | 302,000 | 212,000 | 197,000 | |
| | Sea | 619,000 | 635,787 | 745,000 | 763,000 | 623,000 | 536,000 | 728,000 |
| | Air | 825,000 | 824,900 | 887,300 | 900,000 | 757,000 | 612,000 | 571,000 |
| France | Total | 1,026,000[b] | 1,008,791 | 522,500 | 505,000 | 501,500 | 502,500 | 502,700 |
| | Land | 812,000 | 804,000 | 338,000 | 328,000 | 329,000 | 331,500 | 330,000 |
| | Sea | 68,000 | 67,791 | 84,000 | 69,000 | 68,500 | 69,000 | 68,500 |
| | Air | 146,000 | 137,000 | 113,000 | 108,000 | 104,000 | 102,000 | 103,600 |
| Greece | Total | 157,900 | 159,000 | 159,000 | 161,000 | 159,000 | 161,200 | 200,000 |
| | Land | 120,000 | 120,000 | 118,000 | 118,000 | 118,000 | 121,000 | 160,000 |
| | Sea | 16,400 | 17,000 | 18,000 | 20,000 | 18,000 | 17,500 | 17,500 |
| | Air | 21,500 | 22,000 | 23,000 | 23,000 | 23,000 | 22,700 | 22,500 |
| Italy | Total | 400,000 | 466,392 | 376,000 | 365,000 | 414,000 | 421,000 | 330,000 |

| | | | | | | | | |
|---|---|---|---|---|---|---|---|---|
| | Land | 310,000 | 369,000 | 270,000 | 265,000 | 295,000 | 306,500 | 218,000 |
| | Sea | 40,000 | 40,814 | 40,000 | 40,000 | 45,000 | 44,500 | 42,000 |
| | Air | 50,000 | 55,978 | 66,000 | 60,000 | 74,000 | 70,000 | 70,000 |
| Luxembourg | Total[c] | 3,200 | 5,500 | 1,545 | 560 | 550 | 550 | 600 |
| Norway | Total | 40,000 | 37,000 | 34,000 | 35,000 | 35,900 | 35,000 | 39,000 |
| | Land | 21,000 | 20,000 | 17,000 | 19,000 | 18,000 | 18,000 | 20,000 |
| | Sea | 8,000 | 7,000 | 6,000 | 7,000 | 8,500 | 8,000 | 9,000 |
| | Air | 22,000 | 10,000 | 9,000 | 9,000 | 9,400 | 9,000 | 10,000 |
| The Netherlands | Total | 135,000 | 142,000 | 129,250 | 128,500 | 116,500 | 112,500 | 109,700 |
| | Land | | 98,000 | 85,000 | 83,500 | 76,000 | 75,000 | 75,000 |
| | Sea | | 23,000 | 21,250 | 21,500 | 19,000 | 18,500 | 17,000 |
| | Air | | 21,000 | 23,000 | 23,500 | 21,500 | 19,000 | 17,700 |
| Portugal | Total | 79,000 | 80,000[d] | 148,000 | 182,500 | 218,000 | 217,000 | 58,800 |
| | Land | 58,000 | 58,000 | 120,000 | 150,000 | 179,000 | 179,000 | 36,000 |
| | Sea | 8,500 | 9,000 | 14,500 | 15,000 | 18,000 | 19,500 | 12,800 |
| | Air | 12,500 | 12,500 | 13,500 | 17,500 | 21,000 | 18,500 | 10,000 |
| FRG | Total | 260,000[e] | 330,000 | 440,000 | 456,000 | 467,000 | 495,000 | 489,000 |
| | Land | 172,000 | 224,000 | 307,000 | 326,000 | 327,000 | 345,000 | 341,000 |
| | Sea | 24,000 | 26,000 | 33,000 | 32,000 | 36,000 | 39,000 | 38,000 |
| | Air | 64,000 | 80,000 | 100,000 | 98,000 | 104,000 | 111,000 | 110,000 |
| United Kingdom | Total | 593,000[f] | 454,330 | 437,600 | 427,000 | 380,900 | 345,100 | 339,200 |
| | Land | 317,000 | 200,000 | 218,200 | 210,000 | 185,300 | 174,900 | 175,300 |
| | Sea | 102,000 | 96,330 | 97,200 | 96,000 | 84,600 | 76,100 | 76,700 |
| | Air | 174,000 | 158,000 | 122,000 | 121,000 | 111,000 | 94,100 | 87,200 |
| Turkey | Total | 500,000 | 500,000 | 450,000 | 514,000 | 508,500 | 453,000 | 465,000 |
| | Land | | | 360,000 | 425,000 | 420,000 | 365,000 | 375,000 |
| | Sea | | | 37,000 | 39,000 | 38,500 | 40,000 | 43,000 |
| | Air | | | 53,000 | 50,000 | 50,000 | 48,000 | 47,000 |

*Source:* For 1977/78, The Military Balance 1977-1978, International Institute for Strategic Studies.

*Notes:* [a]The Canadian Armed Forces were unified in 1968; the strengths shown here for army, naval and air forces are only approximate. [b]Algerian War. [c]Land forces only. [d]30,000 in Angola. [e]7 divisions in existence out of 12 authorized. [f]Conscription abolished in 1962.

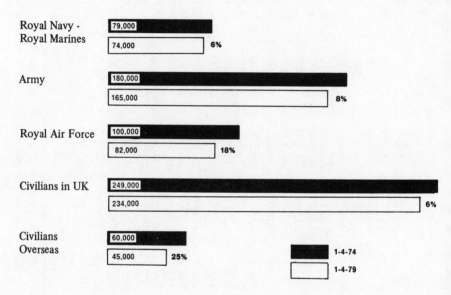

*Fig. 8.2.* Reductions in Personnel, 1974-1979.

## THE SPECIFICITY OF EUROPEAN EQUIPMENT
## AND ITS IMPACT ON OPERATIONAL EFFICIENCY

The European Defense Community proposed to achieve considerable progress in weapon standardization. Through the commissariat which was to place its orders in a vast market and which had its own budget, Europe was to be able to lower the cost of production and increase the efficiency of its conventional arms. Nothing came of it since, as Raymond Aron wrote, "Europe temporarily preferred security in lack of power to the agonies and dangers in regained independence."[9]

Since then, nationalist tendencies have been reaffirmed particularly in the armaments industry field. Despite worthy attempts at cooperation, both bilaterally and multilaterally, the specificity of equipment continues while research and development are coordinated only regarding the basic criteria for the acquisition of a particular weapon system. (See Chapter 11—The Defense of Europe; Means Available, Achievements, and Political and Strategic Prospects.)

The final results are distressing as demonstrated in the assessment made by the secretary general of NATO, Mr. Luns, in a lecture delivered at The Hague on October 8, 1975.[10] The main points of his argument follow.

All our strategy depends closely on the aptitude of our national forces to carry out joint operations and to be able to resupply each other. Despite past achievements in joint projects (the G-91 tactical reconnaissance aircraft, the F-104 Starfighter, the Hawk, Sidewinder, and Bullpup missiles, the Jaguar and MRCA aircraft, the Puma, Lynx, and Gazelle helicopters), these represent at best multinational cooperation but not NATO standardization.

What are the consequences? Let us consider the particular case of NATO's mobile force ("ACE mobile force") composed of contingents from seven nations. These units have seven different types of aircraft, six types of recoilless guns, and at least three varieties of guided antitank weapons, mortars, and machine guns. This mobile force, which must be capable of intervening in the shortest possible time in five or six areas in the theater of operations is forced to transport with its logistical supplies which are as diversified as its types of equipment. As a result, instead of being able to intervene in five days, it needs two weeks to reach the spot, and it uses double the air transport capability that it would need if its equipment were standardized.

On a wider scale, it will be noted that there are twenty different types of aircraft in the Alliance, a hundred different warships (destroyers or larger), and forty 30 mm. or larger caliber guns. The duplication and proliferation of types of equipment have led to the parallel multiplication of maintenance, supply, training, logistical systems, costs, and personnel.

It seems hardly conceivable that the military "experts" of the European countries of the Alliance can seldom agree on the characteristics of the equipment used. This indifference to cooperation is surprising and runs counter to common sense. Indeed, four European countries of the Alliance, Belgium, the United Kingdom, the Netherlands, and the Federal Republic of Germany (five if France is added) have troops stationed in Germany, and their war missions are carried out under identical circumstances. Why then is it so difficult to make a common choice? Why is the equipment considered appropriate by Germany but not by Belgium or the Netherlands? Why choose an item of equipment used by a country which is not a member of the organization and why, after a common choice, are parts of equipment modified nationally thus reducing interoperability or the standardization of spare parts?

Even accepting that the choice of a country should relate to a better weapons system than that of its neighbors, is it thought that the advantage thus achieved is not totally destroyed by the absence of standardization and therefore of any possibility of operational cooperation?

It is probably that no general evaluation finds its place in the choice procedure. But there are tactical and strategic consequences. The Warsaw Pact's equipment is completely standardized which gives it unimpaired flexibility of action and interoperability. In the West, as a result of the disparity of equipment, each national contingent is confined to a preestablished sector. In practice this means giving up any idea of readjustment of forces, any flexibility of maneuver, and any alteration in the defensive or offensive effort.

The British division equipped with Chieftain tanks and called upon to intervene in the Belgian or German sector must be followed by its own logistical support without being able to operate from the basis of neighboring divisions because of lack of standardization of spare parts and, particularly, ammunition.

We thus find waste of effort, increased ponderousness of movement, and as a result a rigidity in the operational concept which goes hand in hand with preestablished national efforts.

The possibility arises of going into reverse, changing the industrial factors to achieve real standardization in European and Atlantic equipment, without falling wholly under the technological domination of the United States. Can a valid compromise be found to coordinate and harmonize European efforts with those of the United States?

There are concrete measures which might be taken. The Callaghan Report, in response, tried to find answers and make suggestions, and some have already been discussed at higher levels. Let us examine the contents of this report, recently revised.[11]

Dr. Callaghan begins by noting that the maintenance of peace for nearly thirty years has been NATOs greatest success. But this success masks NATOs most persistent failure—unnecessarily weak conventional forces.

When NATO began, the economic means of achieving military ends was always seen as one and the same problem. It was believed that economic necessity required all duplication of effort eliminated. But duplication has never been eliminated. The past thirty years have witnessed an incalculable waste of tens of billions of dollars of American and European defense resources—manpower, money, energy, materials, and structures. NATO has not provided the maximum defense possible for the resources available, or the resources expended.

Callaghan states that this is because the common Soviet threat—channeled into a common European/North American economic, technological, and industrial effort. The defense budget burdens we bear are therefore much larger than they ought to be, for the quantity, quality, and diversity of tactical forces they provide. Put another way, the military effectiveness of NATOs conventional forces—the so-called conventional deterrent—is far below the standard that the American and European allies should expect from the more than $130.0 billion per year that we spend together on general purpose forces.

Since 1961, Allied leaders have warned repeatedly of the danger of the North Atlantic Alliance having but two strategic options: surrender or nuclear war. These warnings have never been heeded. NATOs conventional forces are now *collectively so weak* that the day could come when the only difference between NATO and The Alamo is that NATO would have the option of bringing about nuclear holocaust before being overrun.

Dr. Callaghan maintains that too much attention is being paid to what the massive conventional force buildup of the Warsaw Pact is doing to NATO. *Not enough attention is being paid to what the nations of the Alliance are doing to each other.* The Russians are not ten feet tall. They just seem that way because NATO nations have cut themselves off at their knees.

Every Allied nation determines what it will buy, when, in what quantity, and for what military purpose. Unnecessary duplication (indeed multiplication) of Allied defense effort abounds. Logistical support for what General Johannes Steinhoff called "a museum of weapon systems" is provided by fourteen national defense ministries for thirty-nine armed services. No wonder that NATO Secretary General Joseph Luns spoke of "a logistics nightmare that may well prove impossible to support."

The provisioning of forces and the provisioning of war reserve stocks is a national responsibility. Defense departments (American and European) buy weapons without adequate ammunition, aircraft without adequate repair parts, missile launchers without adequate numbers of missiles. In addition, fuel and ammunition shortages limit training and reduce allied readiness. The short-war/long-war argument is effectively foreclosed by the long lead times and gaps between war reserve replenishment orders and first production deliveries. As a consequence, NATO produces a destandardized *collection of forces*, qualitatively uneven, quantitatively inferior to those of the Warsaw Pact, unable to fight for the same period of time at the same munitions expenditure rates, and with only a limited ability to rearm, refuel, repair, support, supply, or even communicate with each other. The Warsaw Pact, on the other hand, produces a massive, standardized, *collective force*, capable of operating together effectively.

The tragedy, meanwhile, is that Europe and North America, the two richest, most technologically advanced industrial economies in the world, have combined gross national product (GNP) *289 percent greater* than that of the Warsaw Pact. Together, they are *spending more money* on the development, production, training, maintenance, operation, and support of general purpose forces than the Warsaw Pact!

But NATO's failures are not primarily military. NATO's forces are large enough to maintain the conventional force balance in Europe. Nor is the failure primarily economic—there is *no economic reason* for NATO to be inferior to the Warsaw Pact. The failure, Dr. Callaghan argues, is political—a conceptual failure on the one hand, and a structural failure on the other. The concept, as Callaghan puts it, that fourteen sovereign nations could forge an effective military Alliance *without a collective military-industrial effort* has failed miserably.

The primary causes of this alarming and absurd situation must be investigated when it is remembered that the Alliance loudly proclaims its desire to maintain common security at the highest possible level, and that in any case the Allied armed forces will have to fight side by side in the same theater of operations.

When the Atlantic Alliance was first formed, the armed forces of NATO had weapons systems and equipment which were relatively homogeneous thanks to off-shore supplies from the United States of America. As Europe regained new political and economic vitality, the national armaments industries underwent a parallel rebirth to ensure the priority equipment of their national forces and to extract themselves from the American monopoly. It was, however, clear that standardization of equipment, the reduction in the number of types of equipment, specialization of manufacturing, the determination of the optimum dimension of production units and common research and development had to be encouraged at all costs to contribute to the lowering of production costs and to smooth out transitions between national markets and a common armaments market.

The European reply to this need for standardization was twofold. There was strict adherence to national production, or else there was an attempt to reach cooperative agreements.

At a meeting of NATO parliamentarians, General Norstad was asked the reasons preventing closer standardization of weapons and unity of opinion on strategic concepts. His reply was short and to the point: "There are three reasons or obstacles. The first is called the United States, the second is called England and the third is called France!"

This explains why NATO, which could have appeared as an ideal forum for the development of a common policy, has never succeeded in overcoming national interests and particular interests (despite the agreement of the Atlantic Council in 1949) to establish the necessary procedures for formulating and promulgating NATO Basic Military Requirements (NBMRs). (The term is defined as follows in document C-M(59)82 approved by the Council on November 4, 1959: "An indication in general terms of the kind and type of equipment required, and also of the quantities needed and the date when it is desirable that the equipment should be in service.")

Without going deeply into this problem, it should be remembered that, out of 49 NBMRs promulgated by the end of 1966, nineteen were a total failure, twenty-three were "under study," and only seven were the subject of bi- or multilateral concrete achievements.

The reasons for this indifference were the preponderant position of the United States and their wholly understandable aversion to a voluntary limitation of their share of the European armaments market; the lack of realism in the formulation of some of the NBMRs by the military authorities and the differences in the basic criteria; the withdrawal of France from the military organization of NATO; and finally (and above all) the absence of any budget financed from common funds and any authority with powers of compulsion over the member governments.

In short, NATO was unable to provide the economic means equal to its ambitions.

## American Penetration into European Markets

The strategic hegemony of the United States in NATO has resulted in a parallel domination of the armaments market. Whether it is the result of the means used and the immensity of the domestic market and the unity of purpose, rather than any real inferiority in European technology, there can be no question that it exists. But the dominating position of the United States results in scientifically skilled labor and financial resources which duplicate those that non-Communist Europe devotes to research and development. Furthermore, the characteristics of production cover a complete range of weapon systems (from the tactical to the strategic), a shorter development period, better organization and productivity, and a continental market which results in a lower finished product cost than that of its European equivalent.

As a result, the European dilemma may be stated as follows. Considerable research and development investments are committed only to find out in the end that an equivalent American project has been developed in a shorter time and that its unit cost is lower. This encourages the European partners which have not committed the initial investments to turn to the American market. There then follows a reduction in outlets and a waste of resources (the case of the "contract of the century" is significant in this connection). A project is abandoned after a delay, the teams of scientists are made redundant with the resulting risk that they are attracted by the United States and its enormous financial means, while the investments allocated are lost without compensation. The case of the British TSR-2 and the French A.C.F. (Avion de Combat Futur) are the best illustrations of this side of the dilemma.

The imbalance in American-European exchanges in the military equipment field is illustrated by the Table in Appendix C which demonstrates, according to a recent Western European report[12] that the present ratio is 1 to 15 in favor of the United States.

According to the Callaghan Report[13] during the 1960s the United States:

- Sold $8.0 billion of the most sophisticated aircraft, weapon, and electronic systems to Europe;
- Bought only $700.0 million of subsystems, components, and much less sophisticated equipment in return; and
- Eventually captured 20 percent of the European defense procurement budgets.

In order to understand Europe's reaction, Dr. Callaghan states that Americans need only reflect upon what the political situation would be in the United States if Europe were producing twenty percent of the most sophisticated weapons systems procured by the Pentagon, and buying little in return; if European firms were at the same time acquiring America's most promising growth industries; and if European industry was producing ninety-five percent of our integrated circuits, eighty-three percent of our commercial aircraft, eighty percent of our computers, and all of our communications satellites.

## Recent Developments and the
## Present "Two-Way Street"

It would be wrong to say that the alarming situation regarding equipment for the forces and the growing "destandardization" has escaped informed opinion. Both the Alliance's military authorities and certain political circles have not failed to stress the loss of substance represented by the lack of standardization and have applied pressure on the responsible authorities to take the necessary steps to remedy the situation.

Generally speaking, the results have been disappointing both because of existing obstacles (which we shall bring up again later) and because of the conservative approach of certain military circles and the absence of firm and unanimous political directives. The Assembly of the Western European Union has been concerned for a long time about the problem of better cooperation in the military equipment field but it is only very recently that the governments have become aware of the importance and seriousness of the problem and have decided to plan joint measures. A special meeting of the ministers of defense of the member countries of Eurogroup was held at The Hague on November 5, 1975 to achieve a twofold objective, intensification of intra-European cooperation and the start of a real current of exchanges with the United States.

In this latter context, it seems that our transatlantic partners are favorable to the idea, commonly called the "two-way street," regarding armaments. It appears that the initiative started in the United Kingdom and that it was defended in the Eurogroup by the United Kingdom minister of defense, Mr. Mason.

Dr. Schlesinger, at the time American secretary of state for defense, took this idea up again at the last ministerial meeting of the Atlantic Council. With the aim of strengthening NATO's conventional capability in Europe, the United States would plan to define with their Allies the basis for a long-term common policy for the acquisition and production of armaments. The criterion of competition between the American and European programs would be strictly applied and this would put an end to the "captive markets" and protectionist practices. There is no question that the new United States attitude represents a considerable step in the right direction. In 1975 and 1976, Senator Sam Nunn (Dem., Georgia) was joined by Senator John C. Culver (Dem., Iowa) in sponsoring legislation which now bears their names, and which declares it to be the "policy of the United States" that weapons procured for American forces in Europe shall be standardized, or at least interoperable, with those of the European Allies.

In 1977, Chairman Jack Brooks (Dem., Texas) of the House government operations committee began the first of a series of oversight hearings to determine the progress being made in implementing this declared, statutory policy of the United States. The Committee's first interim report noted that:

> The enactment of this policy reflects the realization that the continued decline of NATO's conventional strength poses an unacceptable security risk, and that real cooperation and burden-sharing among the NATO Allies is a prerequisite to reversing this conventional force imbalance.

In May 1977, at the fourth NATO summit in London, President Carter laid the groundwork for the Long-Term Defense Program (LTDP). He also expanded upon the theme of the Culver-Nunn legislation, saying:

> We must make a major effort—to eliminate waste and duplication between national programs; to provide each of our countries an opportunity to develop, produce and sell competitive defense equipment; and to maintain technological excellence in all Allied combat forces. To reach these goals our countries will need to do three things.

First, the United States must be willing to promote a genuinely two-way trans-Atlantic trade in defense equipment. . . .

Second . . . a common European defense production effort would help to achieve economies of scale beyond the reach of national programs. A strengthened defense production base in Europe would enlarge the opportunities for two-way transatlantic traffic in defense equipment, while adding to the overall capabilities of the Alliance.

Third, . . . together, we should look for ways to standardize our equipment and make sure it can be used by all allied forces. We should see if ways can be found to introduce into our discussions a voice that would speak for the common interests of the Alliance in offering advice about cooperation in defense equipment.

Though some progress has been made at both the London and Washington NATO summits of 1977 and 1978, the North Atlantic Alliance is still a long way from the promises, the hope, and the challenges that President Carter laid before the Allied heads of government at the London NATO summit. Unfortunately, today and for the past thirty years (in Dr. Callaghan's words), the heads of Allied governments, Allied foreign and defense ministers, national parliaments, and Allied military leaders are still concentrating on *cooperative projects* rather than *cooperative structures.*

Not one of them, Dr. Callaghan states, would seriously argue that a domestic procurement program could be managed on an ad hoc, unstructured, project-by-project basis. But Allied political leaders expect an Allied procurement effort to be coordinated by fourteen sovereign nations, *without* structure, *without* rules, *without* predictability—and *without* public and political comprehension and support.

### The Specific Proposals of
### The Callaghan Report

Dr. Callaghan's proposals emphasize the need for new structures within the North Atlantic Alliance, within Europe, and between Europe and North America.

Allied economic cooperation in weapons development, production, trade and support is no small nor easy task. It involves the combined Allied expenditure of *more than $40.0 billion per year* on weapons development and procurement— and an even larger sum on support. The North Atlantic Alliance has committed sufficient resources to *maintain* the conventional force balance, *once it is redressed.* How then, asks Callaghan, do we overcome the political inertia that keeps the Alliance from employing the necessary resources? He answers that the law of inertia was explained to him in high school in terms of a freight car—forty men were required to get that freight car moving, but once moving, one man could keep it moving. That is the task we face in the Alliance—to get a *collective* defense-industrial effort *moving*.

He notes that in April 1941, Canadian Prime Minister Mackenzie King met President Franklin D. Roosevelt at Hyde Park to discuss a similar problem: how to mobilize the resources of the North American continent. They decided that each country would produce and provide the other with the defense equipment it was best able to make. The weapons and equipment which Canada produced, and sold *to* the United States in turn provided Canada with the dollars it needed to buy weapons and equipment *from* the United States. To show they meant business, President Roosevelt and Prime Minister King established dollar purchase goals to be met by each country. Each country, would (in the twelve months following the Hyde Park Agreement) place orders with the other for between $200 million and $300 million of military equipment. The purchase targets may seem small until we translate them into 1977 dollars—between $800 million and $1.2 billion in orders from each other in twelve months!

In the thirty-seven years since the Hyde Park agreement, there has been a North American defense market between Canada and the United States. In the past eighteen years that statistics have been kept, there has been over $8.5 billion in military trade between the two countries. No attempt has been made to balance trade on either an annual or project basis. The peak American trade deficit (1971) was $544.3 million; the peak Canadian deficit (1977) stands at approximately $400 million. In other words, eighteen years have seen nearly $4.1 billion purchased by the United States *from Canada* and $4.5 billion bought by Canada *from the United States*. No similar trading structure exists within the North Atlantic Alliance.

Establishing a North Atlantic defense market would be the largest peacetime politico-economic cooperative effort ever undertaken by free people in their own defense. It would test whether the nations of the North Atlantic Alliance have the political will, political wisdom, and institutional flexibility to match the military-industrial discipline of the Soviet-dominated Warsaw Pact.

Building a cooperative structure (a two-way street) will require a public and political consensus generated first by a congressional resolution, and then by a treaty binding all Alliance countries. Enabling legislation will also be needed. The first step would be a Vendenberg-style resolution, passed this time by both the Senate and House, stating it to be the sense of Congress that the president of the United States should begin negotiations with our Canadian and European allies leading to a North Atlantic treaty of technological trade and economic cooperation. The president of the United States, with the declared bipartisan support of the United States Congress, would then propose a transatlantic bargain to Europe, to be embodied in the treaty. The United States would offer to match every defense dollar Europe spent in the United States with a dollar spent in Europe, and would, offer to match the cost of every system developed in Europe for NATO use by an American defense development, also for joint use, and commit itself not to duplicate such systems.

Thus the more Europe contributed to NATO's general purpose forces, the more the United States would contribute. In return, Europe would agree to fully offset America's balance of payments deficit on military accounts; to establish an institution within the North Atlantic Alliance (presumably the Independent European Program Group) which would permit Europe to plan, finance, and manage intercontinental, nonduplicative, multiannual, multiproject defense research, development, production, and support programs with the United States and Canada; and to increase Europe's collective defense expenditures by at least 3 percent per year in real terms for as long as there is a substantial imbalance in American and European defense budgets, or until lower levels are mutually agreed upon.

But there would be more to the bargain than that. The treaty would reaffirm the American pledge to defend Europe by every means at its disposal, including its theater and strategic nuclear forces, *providing* Europe agreed to join with Canada and the United States in building a collective, conventional capability sufficient to defend Europe against conventional attack, *without early recourse to nuclear weapons*.

The treaty would also lay down the following general principles to govern allied armaments cooperation:

- cooperation must provide balanced collective forces for the defense of Europe;
- all unnecessary duplication of effort must be eliminated;
- benefits and burdens must be equitably shared;
- cooperation must provide maximum standardization, at reasonable cost;
- cooperation must achieve maximum joint follow-on configuration control and logistical support; and
- no allied country will deny weapons production to another ally, except in accordance with multilateral allied agreements governing arms transfers within and outside the alliance.

With the bargain struck, Europe and North America would follow the lead taken by President Roosevelt and Prime Minister King, and they would establish goals.

The Soviet Union's fifteen-year head start in the buildup of Warsaw Pact conventional forces would not permit the alliance to focus on new development projects only. Short-term results must also be sought. We must achieve the optimum interoperability of current inventories; we must bring our war reserve "days of supply" to agreed uniform levels. The standardization agreements (STANAGs) must be implemented and there must be procurements from one another, and a start made on common logistical support.

Employment and other political benefits must begin to appear within the terms of incumbent congressmen and parliamentarians. But long-term goals must also be established, so that the alliance never again finds itself fielding forces that cannot refuel, rearm, repair, support, supply or even communicate with one another.

The president of the United States, working with Congress, would propose the following mid-, short-, and long-term goals.

### Short-Term Goals (by congressional resolution, and then treaty)

Current Inventories and Days of Supply: Europe and North America would each pledge to spend $1.0 billion per year, for the next five years, over and above current defense budgets in order to achieve optimum interoperability of current weapons, equipment and communications, and to reach agreed uniform "days of supply" throughout the Alliance.

### Equipment Standardization Agreements (STANAGs)

Europe and North America would together implement each year at least 20 percent of the material STANAGs already agreed upon, and would implement each new material STANAG within a year. Within three years of implementation, each STANAG item would be procured by open, competitive bidding by both Europe and America.

*Procurement*

A three-year goal of $3.0 billion of defense procurement occurs from one another. In case there was a short-fall in Europe's ability to produce $3.0 billion of competitive systems of their own, Europe would co-produce American systems for its own forces, and for possible sale to the United States and Canada.

### Mid-Term and Long-Term Goals (by resolution and treaty)
*Research*

A three-year goal for harmonizing all basic defense research, with agreement on a fixed minimum percentage of defense procurement funds to be devoted each year to research.

*Development*

An initial three-year goal of $4.0 billion of complementary development projects underway on each side of the Atlantic, with agreements on a fixed minimum percentage of defense procurement funds to be devoted each year to "technological building blocks."

*Logistics*

A four-year goal for common logistical support of all common weapons and equipment now in Allied inventories.

### North Atlantic Defense Markets

By successive development, procurement, and logistical support goals, Europe and North America would (by the twelfth year) achieve complete military-industrial interdependence within a fully structured North Atlantic defense market.

Some say these goals are ambitious. They are, but they are not *too* ambitious. Assume for a moment that the transatlantic bargain is agreed upon by all Alliance nations; that the treaty has been negotiated and ratified; that the new cooperative structures are in place, and fully manned; and that the governments have ordered full speed ahead on January 1, 1979. Then reflect upon the fact that:

> Decision, development, production, deployment and training lead times are such that *we would be into the 21st century* before the North Atlantic Alliance could field the same *collective* conventional force capability that the Warsaw Pact has today!

Do we dare proceed any slower?

Fortunately, the short-term goals will correct our most glaring conventional force deficiencies. Interoperable equipment modifications could begin in the second year. Significant increases in war reserve stocks would also begin in the second year. By the mid-eighties, NATO forces could operate together. The short-term goals would also generate many tens of thousands of additional defense industry jobs on each side of the Atlantic—and within the terms of incumbent congressmen and parliamentarians.

The political and economic benefits would be widely distributed, thereby minimizing (if not completely eliminating) transitional economic and employment dislocations. And the political cohesion, the public confidence, and the real and measurable military results obtained in the early years would guarantee the political commitment to see the job through. All efforts need not come to a halt pending negotiation and ratification of the treaty. When Congress has passed the Vandenberg-style resolution, the hand of the Secretary of Defense would be greatly strengthened in his dealings with the twelve armed nations of Europe. He could halt all bilateral dealings with the individual countries and Europe and he could offer the Independent European Program Group (IEPG) the right of "first refusal" on off-set agreements, and complementary or cooperative development, or procurement projects. Thus, progress could be made toward structuring an intercontinental defense-industrial base, even while the treaty was being negotiated and ratified.

The goals Dr. Callaghan has outlined would get things moving. They would provide more jobs, more business, and more challenges for American and European industry. Most important, Kremlin leaders would see that Europe and

North America, the two richest, most technologically advanced industrial economies in the world, had finally pooled their enormous resources for their common
defense. The ability of the North Atlantic Alliance nations to cooperate in
peacetime would unequivocally signal a will to cooperate, if necessary, in the
event of a Warsaw Pact attack. Dr. Callaghan concludes that in the post-Brezhnev
period sometime in the eighties, this could be the most effective deterrent to
Soviet military temptations.

These are the essential points of the Callaghan Report which has had the merit
of contributing to the alerting of the Atlantic Allies and of making public
opinion aware of the major problems of the standardization of weapons and of
prospects for cooperation between the United States and Europe. Although his
proposals may appear unduly ambitious, they have the merit of being formu-
lated and could serve as the basis for possible politico-economic agreements.

The stake involved is vital—the maintenance of European security by means
of a more rational use of the available defense budgets. But the obstacles to be
overcome are considerable although they are not absolutely insurmountable. The
entire validity of the proposals made lies in one essential but not yet achieved
condition—the political willingness to meet the American challenge *on a European basis*, the only practical possibility of achieving a realistic cooperation
agreement between partners of equivalent size and resources.

This brings us to the consideration of the existing situation and the ways of
altering it.

## THE OBSTACLES TO COOPERATION:
## THE FRAGMENTATION OF EUROPE'S NATIONAL
## DEFENSE MARKETS

The obstacles to cooperation are to be found at two levels, one political and the
other economic.

*From the political point* of view, since the army is not an end in itself but the
instrument of foreign policy, matters of defense have always been reserved to
the nation-state. In the absence of any supranational political power transcend-
ing national patriotisms—this is the weakness of the Western European Union—
and after the failure of the European Defense Community, no worthwhile
attempt has been made to coordinate or integrate defense policies or therefore
the European armaments market. The fundamental observation is that, in this
connection, Europe may be seen as an aggregate of rigidly protected national
markets determined to defend at all costs their positions and their external
outlets. It is clear that considerations of the internal politics, the protection of
traditional national industries, problems of employment and local manpower,
participation in technological progress, and the development of key industries all

play their part in the absence of any real initiative in the field of European cooperation.

But it seems clear that all this is a shortsighted policy which will be damaging in the future since it could lead either to the disappearance of the European defense industries because of their inability to keep up as a result of their limited size and resources, or to take their relegation to the role of subcontractors in American undertakings capable of dealing with future programs.

Furthermore, the fear of being cut off from the United States by setting up a self-sufficient and protectionist market or at the very least of catalyzing an American disengagement from Europe, has for a long time been the origin of the timidity of certain attempts. Wrongly or rightly, it was considered that the purchase of equipment was linked with the presence of their forces in Europe, and it was feared that the flow of technological information from the United States might dry up at the moment that a self-sufficient and competitive market was established.

Another important factor is the deficit in the balance of payments between the United States and Germany on the one hand, and the United Kingdom and Germany, which has a strong influence on the armaments market through compensation agreements and limits the possibility of cooperation at the European level.

Finally, mention must be made of French reticence about becoming involved in an undertaking in which American influence would be unduly apparent. Jealous of its independence in matters of defense policy and concerned with facing criticism from those condemning any Atlantic rapprochement, France intends to preserve its achievements and its external markets and shows itself extremely reserved about any non-European cooperation. Its obstinate refusal to participate in Eurogroup is a proof of this and it is only very recently that France has agreed possibly to join an ad hoc organization open to all the European countries of the Alliance aiming to promote cooperation in the procurement of defense equipment.

*From the economic point of view*, the essential problem is the fragmentation of the European defense industries which are directed toward the national markets which are too small for the enormous investment required for present programs. As a result, any cooperation agreement between the United States and a European country is, at the present stage, an impossibility if it is desired to respect the principles of cooperation and interdependence. These principles assume partners of equivalent size with equivalent resources. No European state on its own meets these conditions.

The crushing weight of the United States would from the very beginning distort the conditions of the agreement whether it referred to the sharing of the financing of research and development, sharing technology, or production on an Atlantic scale.

This statement may be illustrated by two convincing examples. The aviation side of the United States Marines has taken more British Harrier V-STOL aircraft than the whole of the RAF. The total number of F-4 Phantom aircraft delivered to the Federal Republic of Germany is less than one-tenth of the total production for the United States Navy, Air Force, and Marines. Furthermore, cooperative projects on an Atlantic scale can only be achieved progressively as current projects are completed. Being well aware of the considerable time intervals between the initial concept of a weapon system and its delivery to the armed forces, it is reasonable to estimate the time needed for achieving full cooperation at more than a decade from when the principle is accepted by the governments concerned.

Finally, the importance of the sale of weapons abroad must not be underestimated since this widens the unduly narrow base of rational markets and also contributes to the balance of payments (or the reduction of its deficit). Delicate negotiations will have to be undertaken in order to respect previously acquired positions. Steps to be taken in this area also raise complex political problems. Furthermore, technological transfers to third party countries which are not members of the Atlantic Alliance are liable to create risks from the military security point of view for the preservation of manufacturing secrets.

This brief enumeration of the political and economic obstacles would not be complete if the psychological factor were omitted. Public opinion has a definite influence on political decisions. It would be vain to disregard the resurgence of nationalistic spirit, of a certain demobilization of minds, and of the little impact of defense problems on the European masses. Certainly a rather tardy awakening may occur as a result of enlightened and realistic information. But in the present state of affairs, it must be accepted that public opinion is more sensitive to the economic crisis and to threats to the standard of living than to distant ill-defined prospects of a common Atlantic defense market, even if there is a well-understood interest in promoting its achievement.

For several years now, the European states have been making steady progress towards transitional formulas lying between strictly national positions and integration in the wider sense. Attempts at cooperation, either ab initio at the stage of research and development or on the basis of an existing project have been worked out with more or less fortunate results.

The continued erosion of the defense capability, the waste of resources resulting from duplication of effort, and the fragmentation of the European defense industries require constructive and bold initiatives implying a European cooperation, appropriate institutions, and an autonomous budget.

It is only in paying this price that a dialogue between the United States and Europe is conceivable.

What are the means that need to be brought into operation? What institutional organization must be chosen, and what are the stages to be gone through before substituting a real Europe for what Mr. P.H. Teitsen has called the "Europe of Conversations"? The following chapter will try to find answers taking the progress achieved and the existing institutions into account.

But before going on to the positive measures to be taken at short notice, we must clarify the threat facing Europe and the possible scenarios of a direct confrontation between two opposing worlds.

# 9 European Security in Danger

In the midst of détente, in the apparently optimistic atmosphere reigning in Western Europe at a time when tensions seem to be relaxing and when more than thirty years of peace seem to justify the idea that war is unthinkable, it appears difficult to imagine that war with the East could ever break out.

Nuclear parity of the two superpowers seems to be the best guarantee of peace since the Soviet Union and the United States are both aware of the impossible price of a confrontation. The expenses on costly armaments also seem useless since, from the outset, any war appears to be impossible.

We would like to believe that this is the situation, that there is perfect harmony between the peaceful intentions manifested by the Kremlin and the armed forces it maintains on its own territory and at the very frontiers of the West. As President Nixon said: "Is not this formidable fighting tool only meant for stabilizing peace by force?"

We would like (and hope) this to be true if Europe could claim for itself a satisfactory balance of forces. But the pressure of a public opinion little inclined to accept a defense and security effort which they consider excessive; the foreseeable troop reduction in (if not the long-term withdrawal of American troops) Europe; moral demobilization; the lack of cohesion of still poorly united European groupings are all warning signs of a dangerous weakness which could one day be brutally exploited and present the world with a fait accompli fraught with consequences for the balance of power in the world.

Of course, such a possibility does not seem likely to arise in the immediate or the short-term future. Since no one can predict the mutations of history, the changes of men in power, or the unforeseeable reverses in economic and social conditions, perhaps it is crazy to live in a sense of complete euphoria with no regard whatever for the most dangerous, but also the most probable assumption —that of a war in Central Europe along the 800 km. of common frontier between two concepts of the world which so far have shown themselves to be completely contradictory.[1]

The question is vital since the very existence of our Western countries depends on their resistance capability and particularly on the maintenance of peace. The latter relies entirely on the so-called flexible response strategy, i.e. the combined use of tactical nuclear weapons closely associated with adequate conventional forces. This is because men and combat units are first of all needed to make the adversary reflect on the futility of an armed conflict which would speedily degenerate into a nuclear holocaust and then to force it to establish a worthwhile goal—in space and time—to justify the use of nuclear weapons.

But in the face of the increasing tenuousness of our forces along the iron curtain, wouldn't the East be tempted to make a surprise attack without prior mobilization, with a view to conquering from the outset a major part of West Germany without permitting nuclear reprisals? We would like to answer this vital question since we wonder whether the enormous power that the USSR never ceases to develop may not one day incite it to take a calculated risk to gain mastery of the European continent and break up the geo-strategic balance of power in its favor.

In this chapter we shall deal with the concept and preparation of a plan of operations for an offensive directed against Western Europe and aimed at taking possession of a sufficiently important stake to ensure future domination of the Eurasian continent.

Chapter 10 of this work will describe the broad outlines of the surprise attack and the political and strategic consequences which would stem from it. Let there be no expostulation or cries of "science fiction" or talk of the delirious illusions of overexcited imaginations. All the assumptions made are based on concrete facts which can be seen in daily realities and are difficult to refute.

It is perhaps cruel to load public opinion with truths which are difficult to accept; it is certainly not very courageous to modestly conceal the real situation at the risk of compromising European security and, at the price of much blood and tears, to heavily mortgage the future of generations to come.

Above all, the defense of Europe means the ability to meet threats against its security with adequate means. It also means the maximum return from the billions voted by the European peoples to guarantee the values they claim to be proud of.

## THE POLITICAL ASPECTS OF
## A SOVIET AGGRESSION
## AGAINST WESTERN EUROPE

### From Confrontation to "Détente":
### Reawakening of Apprehension in the West

Despite permanent ideological opposition, the cold war has apparently been stowed away on the shelf of cumbersome spare parts. It has given way to a relaxation of tension (known as détente) whose resulting diplomatic contacts, increased economic cooperation, and the desire to establish a European collective security system bear witness to it.

Is this concern for détente manifested by the Soviets credible? Without condemning it directly, it must be recognized that it is an integral part of the declared aims of Soviet foreign policy which include the "de jure" recognition of the status quo in Europe; the dissolution of military alliances; with withdrawal or, at the very least, the weakening of the American forces stationed in Europe; and the creation of a denuclearized zone in Central Europe.

Although these aims may appear reasonable in some people's eyes, they could only be achieved if the Soviets were to reduce their military apparel to the same extent. We are far from this and the progressive erosion of the armed forces of the West is creating a strategic imbalance which is accentuated by the continued growth of the gigantic Soviet potential (see Fig. 9.1).

Two examples will suffice to illustrate these contradictory trends. Troop numbers in the NATO divisions have not ceased to decrease and some are now below 10,000 men whereas they originally exceeded 15,000. On the other hand, the Soviet divisions, formerly considered appreciably lower in numbers, have raised their troop numbers from 11,000 to 14,000 for their mechanized divisions and from 9,000 to 11,000 for their tank divisions. (The diagrams on p. 34 of the *German White Paper of Defense 1975-76* are particularly eloquent in this connection.) The percentages of gross national product devoted to defense vary between 3 and 6 percent for the NATO countries; they are assessed at more than 11 percent for the Soviet Union.

This growing imbalance, even though the Soviet Union has a standard of living which is appreciably inferior to that of the West, leads the Europeans to ask questions.

Why this accumulation of mainly offensive means? Why maintain a force relationship of 2 or 3 to 1 if they want to adopt a defensive strategy? Why deploy eighty percent of their forces against Central Europe and only twenty

**Combat power of Soviet divisions**

**Boost in number of Warsaw Pact battle tanks in Central Europe**

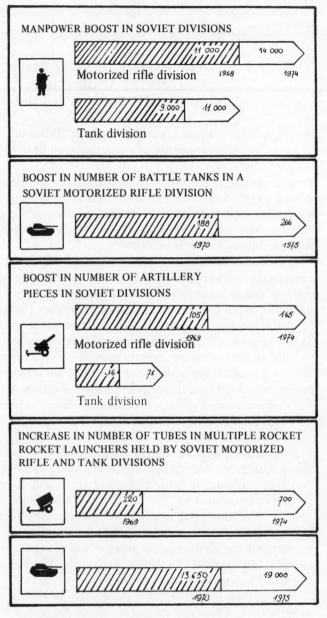

*Fig. 9.1.* Extract from
White Paper 1975-1976
of the Federal Republic of Germany

percent against China? Why, in a period of agricultural crisis, increase still further the level of expenditures on armaments?

In a recent article immediately taken up and commented upon in all the world's press,[2] this paradoxical and extremely alarming situation has been set in clear and explicit terms by General Haig, the supreme allied commander in Europe. In it he denounces the three to five percent annual increase in real terms of the defense expenditures of the Soviet Union which, in the space of seven years, have enabled it to increase its forces facing NATO in Europe by 100,000 men, to increase the number of its tanks by 40 percent, to make a considerable increase in its fire power on the battlefield, and to make fundamental changes in the characteristics of the air force.

From now on, the West can no longer claim the advantage of qualitative superiority. The third and fourth generation weapons systems, the supreme commander makes clear, are comparable or sometimes superior to the equipment available to the West. This considerable technological and qualitative progress has also been demonstrated by two German officers in a strict analysis based on uncontestable facts and accurate statistics.[3]

Stressing the overall character of the Soviet expansion, General Haig warns:

> During the period 1971-1975 the USSR outsold the U.S. in tanks and self-propelled guns by five to three; in artillery pieces by three to one; and in aircraft by 2.5 to one. Within the last year, they have supplied Ethiopia with more weapons than did the U.S. in its entire post World War II military relationship with that country. Supported by 4,000 military advisers and over 36,000 Cuban soldiers, responsive military assistance has become the cutting edge of expanding Soviet influence in over twenty African states.[4]

On this basis, it is logical to wonder about the motives which might incite the Soviet Union to undertake armed aggression against the West. Certainly, in the immediate future, such a possibility seems unlikely as long as a serious disagreement does not arise.

But history teaches us that it is dangerous and illusory to consider the circumstances of the moment as permanent and immutable. Reversals of the political situation are unforeseeable; the eclipse of the present leaders is inevitable in the long term. The death of Stalin led to a change for the better in East-West relations; the reverse phenomenon is perfectly plausible when Brezhnev disappears.

The de Gaulle era made its mark on the building of Europe. What will be the trends under Giscard d'Estaing and what might they have been under Mitterand? What will transatlantic relations be after the end of President Carter's term of office? These few examples suffice to indicate the importance of the human factor in the evolution of international relations and the margin of uncertainty remaining when we try to probe the future.

Invaded on several occasions and threatened to its vitals, the Soviet Union may fear the resurgence of a German hegemony.

A limited and preemptive attack would eliminate the obsession about Western aggression for a long time and at the same time would create a politico-strategic vacuum favorable to future expansion.

Another reason might be the suppression of a Western society whose prosperity and freedom of expression are in flagrant contradiction to the Communist ideology. The latter might, through contagion from the East, gradually become eroded, leading to the eventual collapse of the system.

Armed action against a common enemy would have the effect of turning the attention of the masses away from the internal problems of the Communist bloc; would avert the failure of the regime; and would strengthen the Soviet hold on the satellite countries of Eastern Eugope. We should add that the chronic indebtedness of the East and West—which has now reached the considerable figure of $50 billion—would automatically be cancelled.[5] From a geo-political point of view, and according to Lenin's strategy, the total or partial conquest and occupation (even temporary) of Western Europe would give the Soviet Union a considerable if not decisive strategic advantage and an undeniable economic gain capable of solving its chronic weaknesses. The seizure of a demographic and industrial potential without equal and technological resources as great as those of the United States would make the Soviet Union a first-class world power through the absorption of the "little Eurasion cape," the natural prolongation of the Soviet continental land mass. Whoever possesses the "heartland" is master of the world; access to Africa and the open seas would be acquired. Everyone must be aware of the determinative and vital importance of the stake.

The impact of a successful military aggression would mean the end of the Atlantic Alliance, a mortal blow to attempts at the political union of Europe, and would put a decisive end to United States influence in Europe.

"From the Urals to the Atlantic," the old dream cherished through the centuries, would become a reality, no doubt catalyzed by the predominantly Communist regimes in certain European countries. A general conflagration can arise from a local source of tension or protective or security measures may cause a preventive reaction. No one is in a position to predict the course of a future crisis. One thing is nevertheless certain and herein lies the decisive argument. If no confrontation between the two opposing blocs were to be feared, it would be futile, superfluous, and horribly costly to maintain such armed forces. There is apparently no one who unilaterally accepts this resolutely optimistic assumption. In view of the immense advantages of such an operation, the risks of the undertaking cannot be deliberately ignored.

First and foremost, despite what General Beaufre called the "paralysis of the thermo-nuclear systems" which allows us to envisage once again purely conventional wars, there remains a certain feeling of insecurity about the American decision to escalate speedily to atomic reprisals. The existence of the French nuclear deterrence system, and to a lesser extent the British, increases the uncertainty because of the larger number of decision centers.

A deliberate offensive by the Soviets would certainly provoke unanimous censure on the part of world opinion which might give rise to strategic and economic repercussions.

China might try to exploit the situation, in the case of a set back on the European front. In any case, the total or partial conquest of Western Europe would cause a definite rapprochement and even a treaty of alliance between the United States and China. In the future, the combination of the vast technological and industrial resources of the former together with the demographic reservoir of the latter could prove infinitely dangerous to the Soviet Union.

On the geo-strategic scale, it will therefore be necessary to weigh the immediate advantages of total mastery of Europe against the future consequences of a Sino-American collusion and the means for preventing it.

I shall now discuss the factors which might encourage the process or, in other words, incite the Soviets to go into action if they were to estimate that the risks incurred were small in comparison with the stake involved. One factor is *the reopening of the question of the credibility of the American nuclear deterrent.* This could result from the following causes, whose cumulative effect would obviously lead to an increased risk:

- disinterest and growing indifference on the part of American opinion about Europe and its defense based on the incapability of the Europeans to take on the responsibility for it;
- a more and more marked perception of the fact that nuclear intervention could only be unleashed if the vital interests of the United States were threatened, if their very existence was at stake;[6]
- the partial or total withdrawal of American forces stationed in Europe;
- the inability to apply the graduated response strategy through the increasing erosion of the conventional forces of the Alliance.

Then, there might be a *split among the European partners of NATO*, compromising the homogeneity and security of the whole. this might stem from inequality of cost sharing, unilateral production on the part of one member regarding troop numbers, national service time, or investment. Other causes might be political disputes in one or another theater of operations; the opposition of economic interests and the return to national egotisms; and a state of decay in the process of European unification.

*Much more important is the political will to ensure security and the state of public opinion about defense problems* which will play a decisive role in the Soviet appreciation of the situation. The psychological climate is an essential factor; if the will to defend does not exist either at the level of the populations or at that of the governments, the offensive could be carried out and a rapid and decisive success would be certain.[7]

Thus, any evolutionary factor tending to accentuate the imbalance of the forces facing each other, whether it be material or psychological, will provoke a destabilization and therefore an increased risk of the unleashing of a conflict we hope to prevent at all costs. Present trends on the Western side are however developing more and more towards a situation of imbalance, pregnant with potential risks as we shall see later. It remains to be examined whether the Soviet Union possesses the means for carrying out such an undertaking, and if it does, how it plans to go about it.

## The Strategic Aspect

In the first chapter of this study, we showed that technological progress has had the effect of considerably increasing mobility and fire power. This continued progress has led to an increase in the cost of more and more sophisticated equipment and a corresponding reduction in the forces whose size, generally speaking, is little more than one tenth of what was available at the beginning of the Second World War. This results in excessive stretching of the forces on the front, the absence of reserves, the tenuousness of defense units, the abandonment of the continuous static front in favor of mobile combat forces, the vulnerability of the rear areas and even of the airborne or partisan actions.

Accordingly, there is no question that the strategic advantage lies with the attacker who, free to choose the time and the place, can locally achieve a superiority of ten to one, and develop a ruthless thrust and exploit it in depth, before the defender has been able to mount coherent defensive action. The considerable development of attack or transport helicopters gives operations a new dimension and—under favorable conditions—enables the rear areas to be paralyzed, movements to be harassed, and, a priori, targets in depth to be neutralized.

However, the Soviet strategy is resolutely offensive and the trends observed in recent years confirm the growing adaptation of air and land resources to this fundamental concept. Massive use of airborne or helicopter-borne troops; large-scale strategic movements employing all the resources of the air transport capability of Aeroflot; complete mechanization; importance given to battle tanks and their continued improvement; integration of tactical nuclear weapons in operations; improved ability to cross rivers and obstacles; and logistical independence of forward divisions, all are undoubted signs of the establishment of an offensive capability which, in the form of the thirty-one Soviet divisions stationed in Central Europe, is immediately available, fully operational, and only a short distance away from its immediate targets.[8]

We should also remember that, although in 1963 Soviet strategic thought as expressed in the works of Marshal Sokolovsky, put the accent on the massive use of the thermonuclear weapon from the beginning of a conflict, the 1967 edition accepted the use of superiority in conventional forces without the a priori use of nuclear weapons. This indicated a basic change in the Soviet strategic concept. It has become still more developed during recent years and has been brought out in the lucid and fascinating report by Philip A. Karber which appeared in March 1977 and which was based on the most authoritative and highest level of soviet forces.[9]

This remarkable study shows us that the Soviet emphasis upon offense and maneuver has led them to put great stress on tanks and also on mechanized infantry vehicles (BMPs). Immediately after the Middle East war, senior military officers, up to and including the late Defense Minister Marshal Grechko, warned that antitank weapons (whose development had just begun) might come to dominate tanks.

Apparently the Russians are especially concerned that their BMPs will be particularly vulnerable to antitank weapons—a BMP is not as well armored as a tank—and that BMP vulnerability will preclude conventional offense which depends upon the survivability and mobility of mechanized infantry.

According to Karber, the Russians in 1975 saw two methods of keeping the offensive viable—nuclear weapons to suppress the defense or an increased emphasis on preemptive maneuver. They decided upon the latter and began to emphasize "daring thrusts." They observed that the fixed prepared defenses of former years were less likely and that NATO mechanized defense forces would provide instead a fluid environment in which meeting engagements (combat between two forces which are on the move) could be common.

In such a context, maneuver could be the key to success. They might prefer to rely upon *unreinforced attacks* (that catch the defense by surprise before it can get its antitank defenses ready) rather than to wait for Soviet reinforcements. These daring thrusts would be made possible by the Soviet consciousness of the absence, in NATO, of prepared linear defenses in depth of antitank weapons.

Karber urges a threefold increase in antitank guided missiles to a level of at least 10,000; greater combat readiness; more attention to conventional fighting capability rather than reliance on tactical nuclear deterrence; the construction of tactical defensive positions near the border which could be quickly manned; and the reexamination of NATO tactical nuclear weapon doctrine.

Based on Soviet sources, this study backs up still further the assumption of a surprise attack, getting NATO on the wrong foot in the middle of moving up its forces before any coordinated defense can be organized. This possibility will be developed in detail later.

From the point of view of the air, the Soviet Union has a considerable offensive and defensive capability. The tactical air force has 4,500 aircraft and the transport air force has 1,500, to which must be added more than 2,000 helicopters of all types. The modernization of these aircraft gives them an offensive capability and technological characteristics practically on a par with those of the NATO air forces.

## The NATO Situation in Central Europe

In previous chapters we have dealt with most of the problems arising from the European partners of the Alliance and have examined the value of their respective contributions. It therefore seems sufficient now to make a brief summary of the essential characteristics of the NATO forces in this theater:

- *a present deployment which is unsuited and incapable of coping with a sudden surprise attack* because of the often considerable distances between the peacetime garrisons and the planned wartime deployment positions in application of the forward strategy. Redeployment times vary from a few hours for the cover forces to several days for the divisions based outside German territory;

- *a continued erosion of conventional forces* resulting in serious shortages of troops, a lack of permanence in war preparedness, inadequate training, overstretched defense sectors, the absence of immediately available reserves and matériel intended for combat loss replacements;

- *a conscript service time far inferior*—in a ratio of one to two—to that of the Warsaw Pact forces;

- *an inadequate mobilization system*, the time required for mobilizing major reserve units being prohibitive if the rhythm of operations is extremely rapid or if political decisions are not taken in time. This is particularly serious in the case of reservists, to bring numbers up to strength or to replace untrained units, who have to be transported to the garrisons in the East;

- *the regrettable absence of standardization of equipment* which leads to enormous waste and operational inflexibility preventing interchange of forces and flexibility of maneuver;

- *the total dependence—except as regards France—on the ultimate decision of the president of the United States* on the use of nuclear weapons, tactical or strategic;

- *a cumbersome and probably long procedure* at the political level for making decisions permitting improvement in deployment, in bringing troop numbers up to strength, or having recourse to nuclear weapons. These political warning times are of vital importance for implementing the defense plans; and

- *insufficient motivation*, this phenomenon being due to the spirit of the times, to the destructive effects of insidious propaganda, to the impact of a détente which is more a matter of words than fact, to the lack of information directed at public opinion, the naive belief in the "impossibility" of war, and the blind and unjustified confidence in the American nuclear umbrella, as well as in the automaticity of United States intervention.

In numerical terms, the Warsaw Pact would be capable of committing 26 Soviet divisions—including 10 armored divisions—and about 15 satellite divisions to a *first wave* attack (including the 6 East German divisions of the GDR and half of the 15 Polish divisions). To these figures must be added some of the 13 Czechoslovakian divisions and Soviet airborne divisions as well as 2,500 fighter aircraft.

The *second wave* of about 60 divisions stationed in the European part of the Soviet Union could be brought into action five or six days after the first. On its side, NATO is capable of bringing 22 divisions (not including the two French divisions in the FRG) and about 2,100 aircraft into action. From these 22 divisions must be deducted those which are not on the spot and whose usefulness in a rapid and offensive surprise operation would probably be nil. In addition, the value of the divisions would be reduced by a coefficient relating to their state of combat training and the actual troop number situation.

In real terms, we must probably estimate at 15, or at a maximum 16, the number of divisions on which SHAPE could count in the first few days of the crisis. Reinforcements from overseas could only reach the continent after delays of a few days to a month. Under these conditions and comparing the capabilities of the two blocs, it is apparent that the conventional resistance capability of the Alliance would be limited to a few days at the most[10] and that the West would be rapidly faced with the following alternatives:

- either, because of shortage of conventional forces, to have premature recourse to nuclear weapons, to begin with tactical and then strategic;
- or, to accept the fait accompli of the partial or total conquest of Western Europe.[11]

### Is a Soviet Agression against Western Europe Conceivable?

This preliminary question is linked with another just as important. It concerns the justification for the establishment by the Soviet Union of a formidable war machine with an offensive capability absorbing from eleven to thirteen percent of its gross national product when it openly proclaims its peaceful intentions and claims to be the champion of détente.

Is the purpose of the Soviet war machine to prevent armed aggression against the Communist bloc, to consolidate its domination over the satellite states, or to support the hierarchic structure of the party and to use the armed forces as the vehicle for the ideology and as the tool for the homogenization of the immense empire? Is it to associate force with its foreign policy initiatives in order to increase its influence, to apply diplomatic blackmail through intimidation, or to create the tool permitting it to move to direct offensive action?

The first two assumptions hardly stand up to analysis at all. The most impartial observers agree that the present size of the Soviet armed forces is by far greater than that needed to discourage any aggression or "to maintain order in Warsaw." We do not have to add to this its impressive strategic nuclear potential, when facing a China which is still in the first stages of its development in this field or a Germany deprived of any nuclear capability. The ideological argument and the role of unification and "coagulation" of the various ethnic groups through two years of military service seem to me to be more convincing. But they do not explain the vast sums of committed money in an environment of chronic austerity with a standard of living far inferior to that of the West.

There remain the last two assumptions, both of them equally plausible either if the Soviets choose the indirect approach or if they decide on direct confrontation, deliberately or resulting from the escalation through contingent circumstances. In both cases, Europe—*the whole of Europe*—would lose its independence and even its freedom. "What can be said is that, in such a situation, the choice of the French would no longer lie between independence and extermination since, *in a Europe conquered up to the Rhine, their independence would in any case have sunk without a trace.*"[12] (My emphasis.)

In his book, General Steinhoff analyzes five assumptions, or rather options, open to the Soviet Union in the case of an aggression against the West.[13] Putting himself in the adversary's shoes, he notes their risks, advantages, and disadvantages, comparing the respective capabilities of the two blocs and the probable reactions of both the attacker and the defender.

The spectral analysis extends from the surprise and limited attack in Central Europe to the nuclear offensive, either on a continental scale or geographically limited, going from limited conventional aggression on the flanks of the Alliance to a large-scale conventional attack in Europe after massive deployment. In summary, he only considers likely the limited surprise offensive—the "lightning-war" in Central Europe—and action on the flanks, the two operations conducted solely by conventional forces without initial recourse to nuclear weapons. The other options would, a priori, involve risks too great to be treated as probable.

This opinion is shared by Ambassador François De Rose whom we quote in extenso:

> A general atomic attack and a massive conventional attack can be considered very unlikely in view of the risk of nuclear reprisals. In consequence, the most rational operation would be an offensive against a limited sector, using the means immediately available and not requiring preparation giving any warning and which in a few hours would be capable of establishing a fairly localized bridgehead, preventing the probability of

opening the nuclear Pandora's box, but whose loss would involve the allies in negotiations under the worst possible conditions: those in which the defeat of their will had been established. The deployment of conventional forces capable of preventing the execution of such an operation must therefore be the objective of the West.[14]

We should note that his judgment is similar to that of former Secretary of Defense Schlesinger who wrote in his report to Congress:

> However unpredictable the course and outcome of conventional conflicts, we probably understand them better than the risks and consequences of a nuclear campaign. If military force finally seems in order, familiar force is what is most likely to be used. Once the decision to commit conventional forces is made, surprise, shock, speed and the rapid acquisition of territory tend to be even more seductive to the non-nuclear attacker than to the operational planner of a nuclear assault. In fact, in the nuclear era, there may be a special premium on surprise and rapid advance; they permit the achievement of valuable objectives before the agonizing nuclear decision can be made.[15]

In the second section of this chapter we shall examine how the Soviets would design and prepare their plans for a surprise attack against Central Europe. Such an operation, the most likely and also the most dangerous to the Alliance, carries with it such political and strategic consequences that it deserves to be studied in detail.

## THE PREFERENTIAL ASSUMPTION

Examination of the political and strategic situation of the two blocs leads us to the conclusion that a Soviet offensive against the West, although it appears unlikely in the present international context, is potentially feasible. The state of armed peace existing in Europe cannot be considered a permanent factor. Its maintenance or its disappearance depends entirely on the political aims of the Kremlin.

The only problem is to prevent the use of force in their achievement of these aims. Stanley R. Resor, at one time secretary of state of the United States Army, expressed himself as follows on the same subject:

> We do not assume that the intentions of the Warsaw Pact are certainly aggressive. But based on past experience, we cannot with certainty conclude that they will always be peaceful either. We may be convinced that the Soviets have no present plans for military action against the West, but

could we be sure that the Soviets would not respond to an opportunity to spread their influence by military means if the occasion presented itself?[16]

There are two essential conditions for the success of the undertaking. They are *surprise*, both strategic and tactical; and *speed and shock effect*, with a view to taking possession of specific objectives in less than forty-eight hours in order to prevent the nuclear reprisal and escalation of the conflict.

The most probable type of action would therefore be limited aggression without the use of nuclear weapons. According to General Beaufre, an operation of this type would aim at total success under the protection of the strategic forces facing each other; in a very short time this kind of aggression would lead to the moral collapse of the adversary and would force him to negotiate after facing him with a fait accompli.[17]

Under these conditions, what might be the Politburo's concept?

## Politico-Strategic Concept of an
## Offensive against Western Europe

Within the framework of the expansion of world Communism, Western Europe must be integrated into the Soviet sphere of influence. Bearing in mind the inherent danger of a large-scale military action, this goal must be achieved step by step, i.e. in two stages.

The first step is aimed at the dissolution or at least the weakening of the Western Alliance by forcing it to accept a demilitarized and denuclearized zone in Central Europe, which as a consequence would lead to a withdrawal of all or part of the foreign contingents in Western Europe and oblige the Federal Republic to withdraw from NATO. To this end, an objective in Central Europe must be conquered. It will serve as currency to force NATO to negotiate from a position of inferiority. The territory conquered will be evacuated if the West acquiesces to the conditions laid down. On the basis of the newly established situation, the second stage is the satellization of Western Europe, either indirectly through political pressure on the divided Western nations or directly by military action.

The extension of Soviet military influence to the whole of Europe will mean the unilateral implementation of General de Gaulle's concept of a "Europe from the Atlantic to the Urals." It will enable the essentials of the Kremlin's goals to be achieved. The Soviet position as the potential leader of world Communism will be strengthened as a result.

The reduction of the threat in the West will permit the demobilization of part of the armed forces and the allocation of the manpower thus freed to the economic sector. Sufficient forces will be maintained to contain China on the Far Eastern front. If an unduly strong reaction on the part of the West were to force the Soviet Union to abandon the terrain conquered without reaching the objectives specified beforehand, a systematic dismantling of all the existing military infrastructure would be carried out in order to annul the results achieved after many years of NATO existence.

It is absolutely essential that the initial action succeed. Everything must be done to ensure that the military aggression keeps the conflict below the nuclear threshold and does not incite the Americans to extreme reactions. By means of a rapid and decisive action, NATO must be faced with a fait accompli.

No military action is planned against Denmark and Norway. These countries do not constitute an immediate threat to the USSR; they are only defended by small numbers of troops and no atomic weapons are stocked on their territory. They will be forced into neutrality by adequate diplomatic pressure. The member states of the Alliance on the southern flank of NATO are already too much absorbed in their internal problems to be in any condition to react.

Because France will probably want to retain its freedom of action, nothing will be undertaken against its territory and efforts will be made to keep it out of the conflict through diplomatic channels. It is also very unlikely that the United Kingdom will take the initiative to use nuclear weapons if its vital interests are not directly threatened.

In order not to drive London, Paris, and even Washington into extreme reactions, the buffer zones made up of the Benelux states will not be attacked with the exception of a few sabotage actions. Through their neutrality, Austria and Switzerland seal off the southern flank from the Central Europe theater of operations.

Accordingly, from the diplomatic point of view, the attitude of the Soviet Union might be as follows. Before launching the military operation, a policy of goodwill, détente, and peaceful coexistence would be conducted with the Western countries. Specific concessions might be announced. During the military action, all diplomatic efforts would be aimed at achieving the following objectives:

- preventing the use of nuclear weapons;
- keeping a series of states—both neutral and members of NATO—out of the conflict;
- taking the conflict from the operational field to the conference table in as short a time as possible;
- justifying the legitimacy of the military action undertaken to world opinion and stressing the limited nature of the armed engagement.

Having reached this stage of the concept, it is necessary to convert the war aims into strategic objectives, to set the limits of the operation, to determine the political and military constraints, and to justify the armed intervention. These various requirements would be the subject of politico-strategic directives to the Warsaw Pact supreme commander.

### The Prior Conditions Imposed on the
### Warsaw Pact Supreme Commander; General Strategic Concept

Should the Federal Republic of Germany continue to increase its military potential and claim the right to nuclear independence or full participation in the use of nuclear weapons, thus compromising the very security of the socialist countries, it would be possible that the armed forces of the Warsaw Pact would envisage a preventive and limited action in the Central European theater. (There may be many variations in the basic assumption. As such, the plan is applicable *immediately* as soon as the favorable circumstances come together.) The declared aim would be to force NATO to accept a demilitarized and denuclearized zone in Central Europe.

To this end, an objective in this zone must be conquered to act as a bargaining tool. A major portion of the NATO shield must be rendered ineffectual by the actions undertaken. The choice of objective and the speed of execution must be such that NATO is faced with an accomplished fact before it has been able to make a decision about the use of nuclear weapons. For political reasons it would be advantageous if the Ruhr area fell into Soviet hands. The operation will be conducted exclusively with conventional means; however, the use of nonlethal chemical agents could be envisaged.

The northern and southern flanks of NATO, as well as the French and British territories will not be attacked. The same will apply to the Benelux countries. During the military operation, the number of civilian victims and damage would be limited to the absolute minimum. The action against the Americans will be conducted in such a way that it cannot unleash extreme reaction.

With regard to China, they would stay on the defensive if the policy of rapprochement has not achieved the success counted on. As regards the action against NATO, minimum use will be made of non-Soviet armed forces. The satellite countries will only be informed about the planned operation at the very last moment. Proposals for obtaining additional equipment and the adjustments considered necessary to existing infrastructure will be put forward in due time.

### The Supreme Commander's Concept

After receiving the directives of the politicians, the Warsaw Pact supreme commander carries out a first analysis of the problem. If NATO has sufficient warning time, it can conduct a relatively coordinated defense for a certain length of time (this is a controversial question). The battle must stay below the nuclear threshold which in fact means a question of timing, and the operation must be completed before NATO has reached a decision on the use of nuclear weapons.

In view of the probable time required for decision-making, the whole thing must be completed within forty-eight hours. (The uninitiated normally have no precise idea about this; it seems however that the time required can be assessed at between twenty-four and forty-eight hours.) The operation must therefore be carried out at an extremely rapid rate. In view of the prohibition about using nuclear or lethal chemical weapons and that the objectives must be deep in NATO territory in order to dismantle most of its organization, a first possibility would consist in a massive attack with conventional forces.

This cannot be carried out without NATO discovering the large-scale preparations necessary for such an operation which would last more than forty-eight hours and might bring down reprisal measures, including the possible use of nuclear weapons. Furthermore, such a confrontation would cause considerable civilian losses and damage and this would run counter to the political directives. Finally, the probable long duration of such an operation would increase the escalation risks in proportion.

The second form of possible action would consist in carrying out a *surprise attack with limited forces* in order to dismantle the NATO shield before coordinated defense arrangements could be organized. Surprise and rapidity of execution are the vital conditions for the success of the planned operation.

The supreme commander would order the formation of a planning staff consisting of representatives of the various forces. In order to guarantee the most complete secrecy, this staff would be very small and consist solely of absolutely reliable individuals. (In fact, it is likely that plans for such an action already exist and are continuously brought up to date.) Its task would be to carry out a detailed study of the planned offensive, to set the requirements, and to determine the possible courses of action after the conquest of the objective.

## THE SURPRISE OFFENSIVE AND ITS PLANNING

### Surprise

Although only dealing with the main outlines of the operational plan, we must nevertheless say a few words about the way of achieving a condition of paramount importance: *surprise*.

An essential factor in all military operations, surprise is absolutely vital in the particular case of a limited aggression against the West if it is desired to gain a determinative political advantage without, as a result, unleashing nuclear escalation.

But how can it be achieved and can it be hoped that the movements of the attacking divisions will not be detected by the adversary's intelligence system? Must priority be given to the attack by land forces so that they can advance at maximum speed toward their final objectives, or should it be given to the offensive by the air forces with a view to neutralizing any reaction by which NATO might be able to hinder the progress of the army columns? There are numerous questions to be answered before going on to detailed planning.

From the outset, it is clear that a concentration of all the forces available involves large-scale movements of divisions stationed in Poland and the Soviet

Union. These huge movements of troops over considerable distances take time and would inevitably be detected by the adversary, thus giving him sufficient time to carry out his defensive deployment, to build up troop numbers, and to alert reserves.

It is therefore necessary to be satisfied with the forces already on the spot, i.e. the divisions stationed in East Germany and on the Czechoslovakian border. The movements of these units must be plausible and carried out under the cover of large-scale maneuvers in an area close to the demarcation line between the two Germanys. This method is the only one which can mislead the enemy vigilance or leave uncertainty about the real intentions of the opponent.

### Timing

Another essential factor in the achievement of surprise–timing–depends on many variables. But the date and time must be chosen after careful reflection. The most favorable time of year is that of the summer months, preferably July and August, when annual leave reduces NCOs and troops to minimum numbers and when the great tourist migrations might have a considerable hindering effect on NATO's deployment.

D day must be on a Sunday or holiday when the units have only limited numbers on duty and routine guards in the depots and barracks. (The attack on Pearl Harbor and the landing in North Africa [Operation "Torch"] both took place on a Sunday. As Admiral Castex said: "The great social upheaval started on a Sunday morning. . . .") Finally, the time should be such that vigilance is reduced and the roads are nearly clear. In order to conceal some of the movements of the major units, the attack should take place at dawn, and the operation as a whole should be completed within forty-eight hours.

## The Objectives and the Axes of Advance

The principle objective of the offensive is the Rhine from Frankfurt to and including the Ruhr (see Fig. 9.2). Protection of the northern and southern flanks demands the conquest of two secondary by equally important objectives, the Bremen-Hamburg area and the Nuremberg-Regensburg area.

The American troops could be encircled by means of a thrust from Frankfurt towards Karlsruhe. A subsequent thrust to the West of the Rhine and the Ems is provisionally not planned since it carries serious risks of nuclear reprisals and might incite extreme reactions from the French and the British. However, from the very beginning of the operation, bridgeheads must be established on the Rhine with a view to preventing the arrival of enemy reinforcements and resupplies, and isolating the area of action in depth.

At the same time as the conquest of these major objectives, a whole series of less important objectives, some civilian and other military, must be neutralized

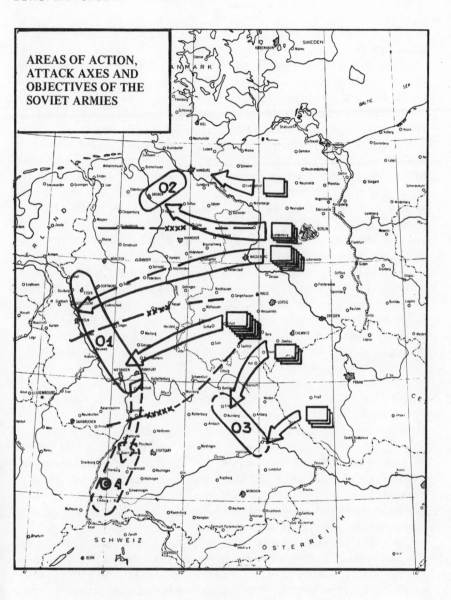

AREAS OF ACTION,
ATTACK AXES AND
OBJECTIVES OF THE
SOVIET ARMIES

*Fig. 9.2.*

in order to facilitate speedy progress toward the Rhine and to paralyze the adversary's communications and defense system.

The radio and television stations, the civilian airfields, the major rail junctions and the political decision centers are all top priority objectives. The various NATO headquarters—SHAPE, Central Europe—and major formations such as army corps or divisions, the barracks of the cover forces and combat battalions, as well as the radar installations are all second priority objectives.

The *attack axes* are determined by the geography and the road network. In the north, the most direct route to reach the Ruhr area goes from Magdeburg towards the Cologne-Duisburg area via Hannover, Bielefeld, and Dortmund. The terrain is suitable for armored formations; it is about 300 km. deep and the advance must cross a river obstacle, the Weser. To the south, the Erfurt axis via Eisenach goes directly from Frankfurt to Mainz. It is relatively short—180 km.—but the concentration of enemy forces is denser in that area. These two axes, north and south, each include a motorway.

The *allocation of tasks* is a delicate problem. How many divisions must be provided in the north, how many in the south and on the flanks, what targets should be neutralized by the helicopter-borne and airborne troops, and which should be entrusted to the fifth column? Furthermore, it is certain that all the secondary targets will not be attacked simultaneously. Selection is necessary on the basis of specific criteria with a view to achieving surprise and speed of action.

## The Specific Tasks

There is no question that East Germany is the ideal starting point for the main offensive. The twenty Soviet divisions, possibly reinforced by six East German divisions, make up a total force of twenty-six divisions responsible for the main effort. Three or four Soviet divisions stationed in Czechoslovakia would be responsible for the pinning down and protection action on the southern flank. The Polish and Czech divisions are not involved in order to maintain the most absolute secrecy and because of the large distances to be covered.

These relatively limited forces are not adequate for successfully carrying out such an operation if surprise is not achieved and if the NATO forces have been able to carry out their forward deployment movements in sufficient time. But if the NATO forces are surprised in their peacetime barracks and paralyzed in their initial movements, they are no longer in a position to mount a coherent defense against the brutal and speedy advance of the Soviet divisions.

Accordingly, the general deployment of the Soviet attack forces would be as follows:

- an army of five divisions responsible for the conquest of the Bremen-Hamburg port area;

- an army of six divisions with the industrial area of the Ruhr as its main objective;
- an army of six divisions directed against Frankfurt;
- an army of four divisions to ensure protection of the southern flank against a possible reaction by the American Seventh Army; and
- a reserve army of two divisions.

These forces would make up the *northern front*, responsible for the main effort with a total of twenty-three divisions. The *southern front*, with six divisions, would be responsible for the pinning down operation in the Nuremberg-Regensburg sector.

### The Dynamics of the Operation

A vital question now arises. Is it reasonable to assume that an imposing mass of twenty-nine divisions—i.e. almost half a million men and tens of thousands of vehicles—can advance westward and cross the iron curtain without firing a shot and without the alert being immediately sounded throughout the NATO forces?[18]

This problem deserves detailed examination. To begin with, let us consider the present stationing of the Soviet and East German divisions on the territory of the German Democratic Republic and let us agree that they are distributed uniformly throughout the country (Fig. 9.3). We immediately note that, from west to east, there are three echelons, three "waves" of divisions, and each is situated in a band of about 100 km. width. Schematically, we can agree that the centers of gravity of each "wave"—let us call them A, B, and C—lie respectively at 60, 160, and 260 km. from the demarcation line or iron curtain.

Let us use *M hour* for the time at which the divisions start their *movement westward* toward the iron curtain. Bearing in mind that this M hour will be during a period of lessened vigilance—for example during a weekend night—and that the movement does not take place during major maneuvers, it is reasonable to estimate that, by M + 2 hours, NATO headquarters would be aware of the unusual extent of the movements and of the imminence of attack. This information would be collected either by satellite or from normal intelligence sources. Time would still be required to process the intelligence, compare it, interpret it, and draw the correct conclusion and pass it on to those directly involved, i.e. the combat units.

The alert is given and, if everything happens normally, it can be expected that the last combat unit or at least its night duty component will be alerted by M + 3 hours. The air forces, on the other hand, being equipped with an almost instantaneous alert system would probably be at immediate readiness by M + 2 hours.

If the movements are incorporated in major Warsaw Pact maneuvers, a doubt may exist as to the real intentions of the adversary. Checking the intelligence

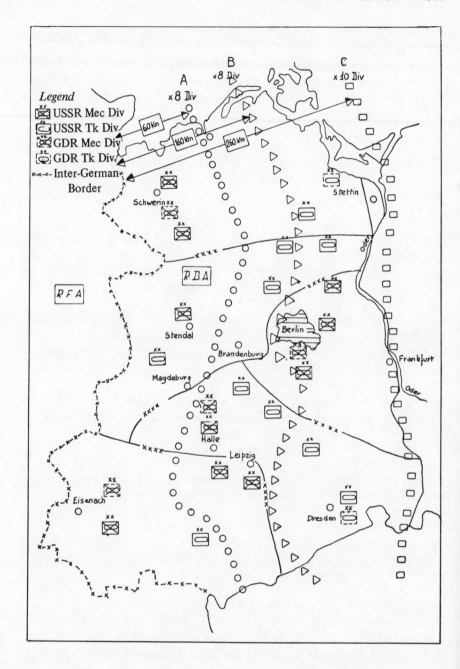

*Fig. 9.3.* Deployment of Warsaw Pact armed forces in East Germany.

and more delays will probably result in the alert not being issued until M + 3 to M + 4 hours at the earliest.

What would the Soviet divisions have been able to do during this time? The first "wave" of eight to ten divisions, deployed on average sixty km. from the iron curtain, would have been able to reach the demarcation line at M + 3 hours. Indeed, the fairly dense road system would have allowed three itineraries to be allocated to each division. Moving by night, without lights and at a cruising speed of twenty km. per hour, the leading units will cross the iron curtain three hours after the start of movements (*H hour*) and will attack the light units of the "Bundesgrenzschutz" (frontier guard unit of the Federal Republic) from columns on the march.

The second "wave," consisting of six to eight divisions, will cross the demarcation line at M + 10 hours and the third, identically composed, at M + 16 hours.

On the NATO side, under the best possible assumptions, the cover forces stationed near the iron curtain would be alerted at M + 2 hours. If they are neither hindered in their movements nor submitted to harassments by partisans, they will leave their barracks between M + 3 and M + 4 hours, and might be deployed to their combat positions between M + 4 and M + 6 hours, bearing in mind the varying distances to be covered.

The other NATO units, whose peacetime barracks and garrisons are widely dispersed in depth, would be alerted at between M + 3 and M + 4 hours. The men must be woken, combat vehicles taken out of the garages, equipment prepared, and ammunition loaded. Depending on their state of preparedness, a minimum of four to six hours is necessary before the combat units start their movements eastward and this brings an average time delay of M + 9 hours. *In the most optimistic terms*, these nine hours represent the reaction time difference between the opposing movements, Soviet and NATO.

If the NATO brigades advance at an average speed of 25 km. per hour—a generous estimate in view of present conditions and shortage of personnel—those nearest to their combat positions might reach them by M + 10 hours and start their defensive deployment. But a brigade 50 km. from its position would only arrive at M + 11 and would not be deployed until M + 15 hours.

In the most unfavorable case, the Netherlands Corps which has to cover more than 300 km, it is out of the question for it to be deployed before M + 25 or M + 30 hours.

In conclusion, the combat positions imposed by the "forward strategy" could only be occupied between M + 10 and M + 30 hours (under the most favorable conditions to NATO) using intervention and movement times appreciably more optimistic than those which would apply in reality. We should add that we have not taken into account the actions of the fifth column or of the helicopter-borne units which would have the effect of appreciably increasing the intervention time or, at the worst, actually paralyzing the units in their garrisons. We shall come back to this.

## TIMING FOR THE HELICOPTER-BORNE AND AIRBORNE TROOPS

At what time should these troops intervene to paralyze the NATO units and nerve centers? Detailed study of these operations will be undertaken later but it is clear that, in order to surprise the cover troops and therefore facilitate the crossing of the iron curtain as well as initial advance, the attack must be made *before* M + 2 hours.

Indeed, we have agreed that the alert would be given at that time by the duty staffs. But the sight of helicopters flying over the iron curtain will alert the frontier guards. This overflying must therefore take place when the leading regiments are no more than twenty km. from the demarcation line. Further west, the probable encounter between the helicopter forces and the units in their peacetime garrisons might occur between M + 4 and M + 6 hours.

The success of the helicopter-borne operation against the cover troops will have important consequences. The neutralization of these advanced units which constitute the only shield for the mass of NATO divisions during their movement, will permit a very rapid advance on the part of the Soviet divisions along axes which, as we have seen, would not be occupied by NATO troops before M + 3 to M + 9 hours.

With the speed of advance of 30 km. per hour, the leading units of these divisions could be 180 km. west of the iron curtain nine hours after starting their movement (M + 9) and six hours after crossing the demarcation line (M + 6). At this time, Frankfurt would be within immediate range and the troops responsible for attacking the Ruhr would have already passed Bielefeld, if everything goes according to pre-established plan.

# TIMETABLE OF OPERATIONS

From the foregoing, we can deduce the main outline of the general plan and the timetable of operations. The plan is based on two combined and almost simultaneous actions, the paralysis of NATO's combat capability; and the attack itself.

The first involves helicopter-borne and airborne troops, the fifth column, and the air force against a whole series of military and civilian objectives to the east of the Rhine before the land forces have reached the iron curtain.

The second is carried out by the divisions stationed in East Germany. The *movement* starts at M hour in the second half of the night with a view to crossing the demarcation line three hours later, advancing westward to reach the Rhine and the selected objectives as early as possible, and linking up with the helicopter-borne troops in the shortest possible time.

The precise *timetable* depends closely on the achievement of *surprise*, the limited use and the maximum efficiency of the troops engaged. As far as possible, the movement of the leading divisions must take place at night; the attack by the land forces must start at sunrise, i.e. about 0430 hours, in order to take maximum advantage of air support. The helicopters will land near their targets under minimum visibility conditions and the air force operations must be synchronized with the moment when it is assumed that NATO moves to the general alert.

Priority is given to the helicopter-borne attack which must completely surprise the static garrisons, and, in particular, those of the NATO cover forces. The landings will take place between 0330 hours and 0350 hours, assuming a flight time of twenty minutes to reach the garrisons lying at an average distance of 50 km.

Allowing an additional security margin, the attack should take place at 0400 hours.

Accordingly, the general movement of the divisions cannot start before 0200 hours (*M hour*), enabling them to cross the iron curtain at 0500 hours (*M + 3 = H hour*). From 0400 hours, the NATO and Central European headquarters could receive the first information about the attack against the cover troops but the army corps would not be alerted before 0430 hours. At this time all the helicopters should have reached their targets and the tactical air force could go into action to achieve its first results at 0515 hours. It is then that the air transport fleet can fly over West Germany. After thirty minutes flying time, it reaches the civilian aerodromes near the Rhine. A parachute unit—at battalion strength—can take possession of a civilian aerodrome in thirty minutes so that, at 0615 hours, the first aircraft carrying equipment and personnel for the airborne divisions could land without encountering major opposition.

As to the timetable for the advance of the land troops, only a general opinion can be given. If the neutralization action is crowned with success, the advance could take place at 30 km. per hour. (The T-62 tank is capable, even in formation, of advancing at 60 km. per hour. This was achieved during the invasion of Czechoslovakia in 1968.) Theoretically, the link-up with the airborne troops could take place on the Rhine in the late afternoon west of the Ruhr (300 km.) and at about noon at Mainz (180 km.).

Taking adverse or unforeseen circumstances into account, including a partial or total failure of the vertical envelopment, and vigorous reaction by the allied air force, it may be agreed that in the circumstances accepted at the beginning, the surprise attack against the West will have achieved all its objectives in less than *48 hours*.

## CONCLUSIONS

When this study was circulated to the international press in March 1976, numerous objections were raised, mostly founded either on established doctrine or on assumptions which were wrong from the beginning. We have already answered one of them, the impossibility of undertaking movements of such dimensions without their being immediately detected. Between the receipt of intelligence and its implementation by the combat units, there is a major time gap resulting in considerable delay, and this is what we have tried to demonstrate. Even accepting the instantaneousness of the arrival of the intelligence from the moment when the first Soviet tank starts moving—which is in any case illusory—the forces of the Alliance will still be nine to fifteen hours behind their presumed enemy. The second objection treats the assumption of an attack without prior warning as senseless and only accepts the probability of a massive offensive allowing the Alliance to deploy its forces over a comfortable period varying from nine to fifteen days.

It appears that such an attitude stems from the illusion maintained by the fear of having to consider the most dangerous assumption which is precisely the one we have described. Why should the adversary—if he has decided to undertake offensive action against the West—choose a form of action putting the Alliance in the best possible conditions and exposing himself to a maximum risk of nuclear reprisals?

There is also a third objection which denies plausibility to any surprise offensive action against the West. If there is no possible chance of this assumption becoming a fact at any time, why have the strategic as well as the tactical nuclear forces developed a radar protection network of such an extent as well as countermeasures of such effectiveness that they are able to reply to a first atomic strike within a few minutes?

The air forces, in their attempt to avoid destruction on the ground by enemy air attack day and night, have warning radar sets operating and aircraft ready to take the air in a few moments. Strategic Air Command maintained aircraft in flight. All these precautions—whose soundness and usefulness are unquestionable—have been taken with a view to avoiding strategic surprise in the case of local or limited nuclear aggression. Such an undertaking is infinitely less plausible than a conventional aggression. Accordingly, is it not illogical and foolhardy to neglect the most elementary precautions to parry the assumption of a surprise attack on NATO land forces?

The strengthening of units, their movements, and advanced deployment within the context of the forward strategy are all linked with *political decisions* whose organizational complexity makes it likely that the measures will not be taken in due time. The present strategy neglects the support of a paramount factor. *Popular deterrence* (if it were applied imaginatively and effectively) would be likely to discourage an undertaking of the type we have described and would increase the value of the deterrent, the supreme aim of the Alliance. We shall come back to this subject when we deal with the positive measures to be taken so that the security of the West does not lie at the mercy of an unforeseen "coup de force." (See Chapter 11.)

We must first measure the vastness of the stake involved and reflect on the incalculable consequences which a surprise offensive crowned with success could have on the balance of world power. This will be the subject of Chapter 10.

# 10 48 Hours That Could Throw the West into Confusion

In barely two months and against all expectations, the armed forces of the Third Reich brought to its knees a Europe whose moral and material unpreparedness, internal differences, lack of political will, and naive belief in the good intentions of the adversary had already sealed its destiny.

The Allies of the time, however, had raised considerable forces, mobilized their reserves, and completed their forward deployment. (They had a total number of divisions greater than those sent into action by Germany.) They had spent much money on defensive works (of which the Maginot Line is the most famous example) and had, at the very last moment, tried to overcome their relative backwardness, resulting from many years of negligence.

Defeated separately, surprised strategically and tactically, incapable of inspiring their forces with the unflinching will to resist and the fighting spirit which could have saved them, they suffered years of enslavement and restriction, having from one day to the next lost everything gained during a long period of freedom.

This fate could be Europe's if we refuse to face reality and allow the security of Europe to be based on assumptions suiting our wishes, rather than on obvious truths consistent with the lessons of the past. There is only one difference between the experience of more than thirty-eight years ago and the future perils. Our fate would be determined for a long time to come in a confrontation which will be infinitely shorter than that of 1940. Technological progress, conquest of the third dimension, the weakening of our fronts due to dwindling troop numbers, fire power, and the instantaneity of decisions supported by an immense communications network make a lightning operation both possible and likely.

In the particular circumstances, recourse to nuclear weapons would be in vain; it would cause greater destruction among those it was designed to defend than among enemy forces.

Through our incompetence, we will have sabotaged the strategy of deterrence, increased the risk of conflict, killed all hope of uniting Europe, and cleared the way for the triumph of world Communism. It is a very gloomy picture, but one consistent with reality. If such a scenario is feasible, how would it take place from the strategic and political point of view and what would be the long-term consequences of a lightning offensive directed against the West?

## THE THIRD DIMENSION:
## HELICOPTERS AND AIRBORNE FORCES

Can we be certain that the use of the third dimension would enable the Soviets to paralyze the defensive capability of NATO in the Central European theater, enabling them by that very fact to reach their objectives in record time? Speed and flexibility of action are the essential characteristics of this type of operation.

The Soviet Union has an enormous transport helicopter capability assessed at 1,000 helicopters of various types; the best known are the MI-6 (or Hook) and the MI-8 (or Hip).[1] The first of these can carry sixty-five men over a distance of 650 km. at a speed of 250 km. per hour, the second, twenty-eight men over 460 to 480 km. at 180 km. per hour (Fig. 10.1). The Soviets have recently undertaken the construction of the MI-12 (Homer), the largest helicopter in the world, capable of lifting more than 30 tons.

This enormous potential, used at only two-thirds of its capacity, would be sufficient to attack a whole series of targets, including the peacetime barracks and the cover troops. Independent of these main targets, they could also deal with the Rhine bridges, the NATO radar stations, and various headquarters.

Two objections immediately spring to mind when an attack of the NATO barracks is proposed for the initial phase of the operation. The first is the vulnerability of heavy helicopters to air attack during the flight of an armada of this size over German territory. The second points out the disproportion of

*Fig. 10.1.*

forces between the helicopter-borne assault detachments and the personnel in the NATO garrisons. Indeed, in the barracks, there are troop numbers the size of several combat battalions with heavy equipment (tanks, armored personnel carriers, self-propelled artillery, and so forth).

To answer the first objection, we should remember that this enormous operation would have the advantage of *complete surprise* and that, in view of average cruising speed, reaction time would lie between 20 and 90 minutes if it is accepted that the departure line lies some 50 km. east of the iron curtain.

Initially dispersed and flying at low level to escape radar detection, the helicopters would cross the demarcation line at first light, i.e. at about 0330 hours. At this precise moment, the iron curtain between the Elbe and the Main would be crossed by 450 helicopters or, on average, 3 helicopters for every 2 kilometers of frontier. At 0430 hours, all the NATO garrisons in depth would be attacked and the activities of the Soviet air force could start to counter adverse reaction and ensure air superiority.

Concerning the disproportion between the forces of the attacker and those of the defender, it must be stressed that the operation takes place under conditions of complete surprise against reduced garrisons and troops who at that time are asleep in the barrack rooms. The helicopter-borne troops are perfectly trained, combat-hardened, strongly armed, and readied for the most minute details of the targets to be attacked and neutralized. (On May 10, 1940, 71 German parachutists who had undergone intensive training forced the capitulation of the biggest and most modern fort, Ebenemael, which had a garrison of 700 men. This famous operation took place *after* the alert had been given and when war was imminent.)

The absence of antiaircraft defense positions in the garrisons of the NATO forces would enable the helicopters to land very close to the barracks and even—when possible—inside them. The guard posts would quickly be eliminated. Each member of the assault group would be fully aware of his specific task: to prevent the sortie of the troops, to ensure control of an ammunition depot, to occupy a guard post, to destroy major equipment, or, better still, capture it. Under the conditions most favorable to the enemy, it can be expected that the whole garrison will be destroyed or neutralized. If unforeseen circumstances have upset the plan, there will be considerable time before the NATO units can regroup, eliminate their adversaries, and finally start their movement eastward to occupy advanced combat positions.

Every hour lost increases by the same amount the time available for the advance of the Soviet divisions in open terrain at a rate which can reasonably be estimated at 30 k.p.h.

## Forces Required for Such an Operation

For the first attack, approximately 14,500 men would have to be transported, i.e. the personnel of an airborne division reinforced by three commando brigades. There is nothing to prevent them from being brought to their departure point under the cover of maneuvers. (The "Reforger 1976" maneuvers brought into action the whole of the 101st U.S. Airborne Division, transported from the United States to Germany with its complete equipment including, in particular, nearly 400 helicopters.)

Another procedure would be to make a considerable increase in the allocation of helicopters to the tactical air forces or even to the armies stationed in East Germany.

We shall not go into tedious detail about the allocation of troops to each individual target. It appears that five helicopters carrying a total of 325 men should be sufficient to attack and neutralize the combat battalions of a brigade if surprise is achieved under the conditions we have defined.

On completion of the first stage, the helicopters can return empty—provided that a reasonable level of air superiority has been achieved—and repeat this type of operation for the attack divisions or against secondary targets. The deployment of 500 helicopters, used on a massive scale and in the context of complete surprise, could thus compromise the defense plans of NATO and constitute a decisive factor in the strategy of the "fait accompli."

### The Airborne Divisions

The helicopter-borne operation we have just described would very likely be backed up by an airborne action using one or more of the seven Soviet divisions of this type.

The transport fleet is capable of carrying two complete divisions in a single sortie (250 aircraft transported a complete division to Prague in August 1968). An essential condition must however be realized beforehand—the seizure of the airfields capable of accepting the huge aircraft carrying the heavy equipment.

Helicopter-borne attacks associated with fifth column activities would have the task of taking control of the main airports near the Rhine bridges: Frankfurt, Wiesbaden, Cologne-Bonn (Wahn), and Düsseldorf. Another procedure similar to that used in Prague on August 21, 1968, consists of the use of civil aircraft, of the Tupolev-114 type for example, carrying 200 parachutists responsible for speedily gaining control of the airfield. Five or six regiments of parachutists would be sufficient to conquer all the targets.

### Fifth Column Activities

It would be inconceivable that a surprise offensive did not try to take maximum advantage of fifth column activities, using infiltrated agents or local partisans.[2] It is estimated that there are, at the present time, between 16,000 and 20,000 Soviet agents working in the Federal Republic. (These figures have been mentioned on several occasions, particularly during the famous "Guillaume Affair" which led to Chancellor Brandt's resignation.)

If the operation takes place during the tourist season, their numbers would probably be greater without, however, exceeding an alarm threshold which might compromise the surprise effect.

The execution of the fifth column plan requires meticulous preparation which might extend over several years. Each agent will be well aware of his mission, but will only act on express orders, without knowing anything about the tasks of other agents or the plans for the surprise offensive. The maintenance of secrecy requires perfect segregation without the possibility of leaks.

The targets of the fifth column are disorganization, even temporary, of telecommunications; seizure of important radio or television stations; sabotage activities against NATO headquarters; destruction of the warning radar system; neutralization of high-ranking political or military individuals; and attacks against nuclear depots (in short, anything which can assist in hindering or paralyzing the Western defense system).

In this context, it can be accepted as plausible that the neutralization of all the commanders of the major units stationed in Germany—from army corps to brigade—would be part of the internal subversion plan. Their residences are known and the action only needs small numbers of well-trained personnel—a few hundred agents. The consequences for command cohesion and implementation of the defense plans would be incalculable.

Let no one question their assumption. We are living daily in an age of violence in which kidnappings, illegal imprisonment, skyjacking, and sabotage have become commonplace. We also should not doubt the formidable effectiveness of this type of operation. (Remember that two explosive charges, put in two Rome telephone exchanges by night, paralyzed nearly one-quarter of the whole telephone system of the city for several weeks.)

In these times of relaxation of authority, audacity and violence pay off. In order to support offensive strategy, the adversary would not hesitate for a moment to put into effect tactics which have already fully demonstrated the considerable results they can achieve at very small cost.

## INTERNAL AND EXTERNAL
## PSYCHOLOGICAL ACTION

The permanent doctrine of the Soviet Union was clearly expressed in the 1931 statement by Dimitriy Manuilskiy, the former leader of the Comintern:

*Total war between Capitalism and Communism is inevitable. Naturally, we are not yet strong enough to undertake it at the present time. We must still allay the mistrust of the bourgeoisie and, to this end, we shall set in motion the most spectacular pacifist movement which has ever existed. We shall make fabulous proposals and concessions. The decadent and credulous capitalist countries will rush to accept our offers of friendship and, in so doing, will contribute to their own destruction. As soon as their vigilance has been lulled and they have lost their protective shield, we shall destroy them with our powerful fist.* (My emphasis.)

*Internally*, the Kremlin wants above all to maintain the internal cohesion of the system, to strengthen the ideology, and to consolidate its hold over the East European countries. From that stems its reticence about implementing the liberal measures of the Helsinki Conference, aimed at promoting the free exchange of men and ideas, and the pitiless elimination of any internal opposition and the refusal to consider "peaceful coexistence" as putting an end to the ideological competition between the two opposing systems. To admit it would mean confirming the end of Communism, crushing its internal stimulus, and losing that powerful psychological level (the Marxist-Leninist ideology, the only custodian of the ultimate truth).

The indoctrination of youth, the refusal of free expression to critics of the regime, whatever their intellectual level or their scientific authority, the tight hold on all means of circulating ideas through censorship on the grounds of reasons of state, all these contribute to making it easier to condition the masses, trained from their earliest years to accept as final the truth dictated by the Party. Accordingly, it will be relatively easy to mobilize public opinion by means of the well-worn slogans "Western Imperialism," "German Revanchism," or "Capitalist Subversion" which represent the undermining of the system and the compromise of the security of the socialist world or demonstrate the apparent imminence of the triumph of Marxism-Leninism over a decadent Western world.

In this context, the armed forces constitute the most important vehicle of the ideology. We can rest assured that an operation of the type envisaged would encounter absolutely no opposition, either open or hidden, among the ranks of the Soviet units. The Russian soldier is accustomed to unconditional obedience and is subjected to rigid discipline. If we remember that the security of the union is based on an offensive strategic doctrine, there is no doubt that an operation of this kind could be presented as a preventive action intended to nip a threat of Western aggression in the bud. The examples of the invasion of Czechoslovakia in August 1968 and, earlier, the repression by Soviet troops of the Hungarian Revolt in 1956 are adequate proof that there can be no hope of a "conscript uprising" or of splits in the military apparel if the offensive against the West were to become a reality.

*Externally*, it may be said that psychological warfare has been waged unceasingly. The "Agit-Prop" section of the KGB has ramifications throughout the world. Its activities may vary according to the ideas of the moment; they are, however, never stopped.

Whether it is through local Communist parties, pacifist movements—often strong on idealism but unreceptive to objective and realistic arguments—agents infiltrated at various levels of society, or through direct propaganda action, Moscow exercises an undeniable influence on Western opinion, whose most spectacular example is the striking success of the idea of détente. Clever at taking advantage of all the psychological stimuli of Western opinion, turning dissension to its own use, exploiting scandals, fermenting troubles against authority, holding out prospects or threatening with the bogey of nuclear apocalypse or of Western warmongering, allaying mistrust or claiming to be the champion of unconditional pacificism, the Soviet Union has, at all times, a unilateral advantage of exceptional importance. It is capable of acting from within and of sapping the will to resist and the sense of security of an over-credulous and easily fooled Western opinion.

On our side, can we claim similar successes within the Communist bloc and do we have recognized outlets for information which are subsidized by the State and tolerated with a naive indulgence? It is easy to see how unequally matched the two sides are in this vital area of the struggle for ideas and the conditioning of the masses.

*The theme* chosen by the Soviet Union to justify or explain its aggression in the eyes of Western public opinion would include a clever mixture of promises and threats, peaceful affirmations, and firm proposals which many people would be only too happy to accept provided that the specter of nuclear conflagration was withdrawn forever.

As an example, we have chosen to compose a brief text—probably far from perfect—which might indicate the way in which the Soviet Union would try to rally the support of Western opinion.

From 0800 hours on the day on which the operation is set in motion, the transmitting stations of the Soviet Union start broadcasting to the populations of the entire world. The broadcasts stress, once again, the preventive and limited nature of the attack, considered necessary to save the world from a nuclear holocaust and to save youth and future generations from certain destruction. They repeat that the Soviet Union is a country enamored of peace but forced by NATO's aggressive policy, to undertake a preventive action to save humanity. Everything possible will be done to limit the number of victims by refusing to have recourse to nuclear weapons.

Moscow gives assurance that the creation of a demilitarized and neutral Federal Republic of Germany will serve world peace by eliminating the last obstacle to the definitive settlement of the East-West dispute. The Soviet Union states that it is ready to negotiate immediately and promises to do everything possible to avoid a nuclear escalation.

The youth of the world are invited openly to manifest its unshakable opposition to the use of nuclear weapons by organizing mass demonstrations in front of the United States embassies.

Thus the use of the mass media to condition Western public opinion would play a major role in the development of the surprise attack. The aim would be to establish the "fait accompli," to prevent the escalation of the conflict, to paralyze government action, and to prepare the way for the future. Even so, the strategic and political impact would have to be such that the disorganization in the West could be considered secured.

## THE STRATEGIC REPERCUSSIONS
## AND DOUBTS ABOUT NUCLEAR REPRISALS

Let us take a brief look at the chronological sequence of events on both sides.

On D Day between 0040 and 0140 hours, more than 400 heavy, medium, and light helicopters land in their concentration area 50 km. east of the iron curtain, on completion of major Warsaw Pact maneuvers. At 0200 hours (M hour), the divisions start moving. At 0240 hours, the parachute units and commandos board the helicopters. Between 0310 and 0318 hours, 270 light helicopters, 88 medium, and 105 heavy helicopters take off and start forward at low level. At 0330 hours (H minus 1.30), the helicopters cross the iron curtain. Some of them are sighted and identified by units of the "Bundesgrenzschutz" whose command posts are alerted within ten minutes.

The cover forces are attacked from 0400 hours by commandos and parachutists who have landed near the barracks between 0342 and 0350 hours. Neutralizing gas granades are thrown into the guard posts and the barrack rooms; the combat vehicles are destroyed or neutralized. Some garrisons are alerted in time and are able to contain or throw back the helicopter-borne troops.

The communications system, sabotaged in places, is partially out of action and the interallied headquarters are attacked by partisans. The technique is simple—elimination of the sentries or guards and attack and destruction of the communications center. As a result, disorganization of the chain of command is inevitable and there are considerable delays in the transmission of the alert.

At 0400 hours, the light helicopters responsible for destroying the advanced radar stations cross the demarcation line and engage their targets with mortars from 0415 hours. Most of the garrisons are surprised while still asleep; others try to assemble their men and evacuate the combat vehicles.

The attack by the Soviet air force starts at 0430 hours. Violent engagement with the NATO forces take place throughout the air space with a view to gaining air superiority.

From dawn, 0400 hours, the first units of the army divisions are near the iron curtain and their speed of advance is increased. Between 0430 and 0500 hours, the first fighting starts with the thinly scattered detachments of the Bundesgrenzschutz. From 0630 hours, and despite radio appeals, the first West German refugees cross the Rhine bridges. They rapidly increase in numbers and, by about 0800 hours, the roads to the west of the river are congested with civilian vehicles, creating major traffic jams which hinder military movements eastward.

During their advance toward the Rhine, the leading Soviet units initially encounter little resistance. The small number of cover units which have been able to oppose the helicopter-borne troops successfully left their barracks about 0500 hours and, despite continuous harassment from enemy tactical aircraft, have continued moving and have deployed eastward with the aim of slowing down the advance of Soviet divisions. It is clear that their action has only a limited effect on the speed of advance since only uncoordinated operations by isolated units are concerned. It would be tedious to go on describing the fighting hour by hour. In the circumstances we have described, it may be considered certain that during the first few hours of the morning, the situation of the NATO forces would be seriously compromised and that it would be impossible to implement the preestablished plans.

We must now discuss if recourse to tactical nuclear weapons, the first stage of the escalation, would still be possible.

## The Agonizing Dilemma of Nuclear Response

It is reasonable to think that the president of the United States, the custodian of the decision to use the nuclear weapon, would be informed of the aggression about an hour after H hour (i.e. about 0600 hours European time). At this time, it is the middle of the night in Washington. In a few moments the Pentagon is in full activity. All the American forces throughout the world are immediately alerted; the intercontinental missiles, the Polaris submarines, and Strategic Air Command move to the highest degree of readiness. The whole strategic organization is ready to intervene as soon as it receives the order.

But it is the president who will decide on this order. His military and civilian advisers are immediately summoned. However, in view of the fact that it is a weekend, a holiday period, and the middle of the night, this process will take several hours.

In the meantime, the emergency evacuation arrangements are put into operation. The government decision center is transferred to its alert site; the operational strategic command on board a B-52 is airborne and is capable of taking over the case of a nuclear strike by the adversary. The whole complex system of atomic reprisal is ready from Colorado Springs to the ballistic submarines dispersed throughout the oceans of the world. In their cells seventy feet underground, the young air force officers are ready (on receipt of the presidential order) to start the firing sequence for the Minuteman intercontinental missiles and they wait in front of their firing consoles.

At 0630 hours, the Kremlin, contacted over the Red Telephone, answers with a dilatory message repeating the main points of its broadcast communication. From that moment on, the destiny of the free world is in the hands of the president of the United States.

An hour and a half of feverish waiting and complex discussions goes by, with attempts to clarify a situation whose gravity no one is fully aware. At 0800 hours, radio and television give news of the aggression to a stupified world.

By then, the Soviet armored and mechanized columns have already penetrated deeply into the Federal Republic. They have made their first link up with the airborne troops; whereas the NATO forces, at least those which have not been completely neutralized or decimated, are trying to act on their own initiative in the absence of any general coordination. Panic spreads progressively throughout the populations of Western Europe and the United States. Very quickly, the roads in Benelux and France are blocked with refugees from the Federal Republic. The police and the gendarmerie try in vain to reroute them onto minor roads. The chaos caused by this human tide further increases the disarray of the military, whose columns are unable to move.

At about 0800 hours, after passionate discussion, the president of the United States appeals to the Kremlin, asking it to put an immediate end to its aggression. The message contains an unambiguous threat of nuclear reprisals should the hostilities be continued. Moscow declares itself ready to interrupt the operations provided the United States accepts its conditions. In their turn, the Soviets threaten to use nuclear weapons to an extent equal to that of the possible American atomic reprisal.

Faced with this situation, what is the attitude of the president of the United States after the failure of any attempt at reconciliation? On the one hand, he is the supreme arbiter of the discussions setting the "doves" against the "hawks" in the White House, the Pentagon, and Congress. Furthermore, it is extremely difficult for him to have a clear and complete picture of the real military situation in Europe. The messages received from SHAPE by the American Seventh Army are confused and often contradictory; unconfirmed rumors circulate in the corridors. All communication with Central Europe is cut. The NATO Secretary General, with whom contact has just been made, can only give a laconic answer—the Council will only be able to meet at the beginning of the afternoon at the earliest. The situation is extremely confused in the Northern Army Group sector, whereas in the Central Army Group sector no major action appears to have taken place, except in the extreme east of the sector.

In the meantime, several nonaligned States, as well as the president of the European Communities, have been in touch with Washington to ask the United States government to consider the Soviet proposal. In their estimation, recourse to tactical nuclear weapons under present conditions of disorder could only aggravate the fate of Europe by causing useless and probably irreparable destruction. Identical appeals are sent to the Kremlin.

Trying to forecast what the decision of the president of the United States might be in such a combination of circumstances would be playing a very long shot. He could try to play for time or be inclined to open negotiations with Moscow in order to save what still could be saved. He could tend toward the "hawks" and follow the hard line suggested by the Pentagon.

He could decide either to reinforce the conventional forces in Central Europe, or to make selective or massive use of nuclear weapons after, or without, consultation with his NATO partners. In its parleying, the United States would recognize that it is not in a position to dominate the conflict. It would lose face in the eyes of the other NATO countries and would justify the conviction of those who consider that the United States is not prepared to put its very existence in the balance when the defense of the European continent is endangered. The strategy of the flexible response would be discredited forever, and the very principle of nuclear deterrence would be put to question, opening the way to almost any possibility.

The result would be an enormous loss of prestige for the United States and a considerable reduction in its influence in Western Europe which would lead to the breakup of NATO. Furthermore, from the military point of view, any shilly-shallying would give the Soviets the necessary time to reach and consolidate their objectives.

What should be thought at present about a *purely military solution*, either conventional, through reinforcement of the theater with additional forces, or nuclear, through recourse to tactical or strategic weapons? The conventional reinforcement forces would not have any direct influence on the course of operations, since they would only arrive in the area after prohibitive delays. Furthermore, the American reinforcements destined for the Central Army Group would have to pass through France, whose attitude might be rather hesitant in view of the circumstances. It is fair to think that the Soviets, as soon as they were informed of the presidential intentions, would take advantage of their favorable strategic situation and their numerical superiority to finish off their offensive and achieve the comple encirclement of the Central Army Group. Cut off from their bases and their lines of communication, it is difficult to see how these forces could escape surrender or annihilation.

## Recourse to Nuclear Weapons

Would the president decide on the use of nuclear weapons after consultation with the other member states of NATO? There would probably be long delays before the plenary meeting of the Council and an even longer time before a positive decision was reached. We would have to consider the attitude of the countries whose forces had been involved in the action but whose territories were not directly threatened (the Benelux countries and the United Kingdom). We would also consider Germany's reaction, faced with the choice between a negotiated solution and unprecedented destruction of its country and its population.

If the president of the United States ignores the opinion of the Council, he alone would assume responsibility for the decision which decided the fate of humanity. Accordingly, we find ourselves in an area of the irrational in which nobody can foresee the mysterious play of action and reaction, the impact of personalities, the weight of the prestige of empires, or the strength of their determination to carry the race to its bitter end. It is the "chicken game" described by Raymond Aron in his masterly work, *Le grand débat*.[3] Will it be too late to stop the monstrous machinery that can sow death and destruction throughout our planet? Without going further into these extreme situations, we must examine the controversial problem of *"selective" or "massive" response and the choice of targets*. In the first case, "selective" response (a kind of warning nuclear firing intended to demonstrate the will of the United States and the credibility of its support) we may wonder about the true effectiveness. At the time of the monopoly or of even marked superiority in the nuclear field, there was no doubt that the warning shot would have produced the expected effects. Now that there is overall parity, the Soviets may immediately reply with an identical or more powerful weapon on a "selected" target of their choice, almost certainly European. As a result, we are brought back to the previous case or uncontrolled escalation. Because of the reprisal capabilities of the enemy bloc, it seems that the "massive" response must be excluded.

In the case of an intermediate solution, the points of impact must be decided. They are, without any doubt, military targets. How can the Soviet concentration be determined accurately when the troops would be intimately mingled with the civilian population and would thus suffer the most serious losses for an uncertain military result?

Could the Soviet lines of communication be cut by hitting the major terrain obstacles in the satellite countries? This attitude would undoubtedly lead to a reprisal against the Western European countries, causing greater damage to the West in view of the high population density and without positive results from the overall strategic point of view.

The military operations in the Federal Republic of Germany would not be interrupted as a result, because of the self-sufficiency of the divisions and the major logistic facilities sited at a maximum distance of 500 km. from the Rhine.

The problems that the president of the United States would have to face are so complex that it may reasonably be thought that a decision to use the nuclear weapon—if there is one—could only be taken thirty-six to forty-eight hours after the start of the conflict.

By that time the die would have been cast and the fate of the West settled for a long time, as we will show by an examination of the political situation.

# THE POLITICAL IMBROGLIO AND THE
# SHORT- AND LONG-TERM CONSEQUENCES

After describing the sequence of operations on the Soviet side and the reactions of NATO faced with a crisis situation resulting from total surprise, it seems necessary to give an idea of the political confusion of a Western world in disarray. We shall stress the problems which will confront the governments of the European members of the Alliance faced with divergent interests, internal pressures, and the paramount concern to safeguard their independence of action in a divided Europe which will have suffered a relentless blow from Soviet aggression.

The Warsaw Pact's attack catches the Western world in a state of blissful unawareness and presents it with a fait accompli. Two-thirds of the territory of the Federal Republic and almost the whole of its industrial potential are in the hands of the Soviets. NATO finds itself in total disarray. Most of the forces of the Northern Army Group and some of the Central Army Group are destroyed or threatened with encirclement.

Only a very limited number of the troops engaged have been able to withdraw West of the Rhine. The Soviets have established three bridgeheads on the river giving them an adequate base for starting a possible offensive further westwards.

The American and German forces of the Central Army Group are pinned down by the southern front offensive. Their airfields are unusable. The air forces of the Warsaw Pact have achieved air superiority, thus preventing any freedom of action for the American Seventh Army and the German Second Corps in this area. Furthermore, the allied forces run the risk of being encircled if the Soviet army starts an envelopment operation from the Frankfurt region toward the Black Forest. The forecasts of reinforcements for the Central European theater are far from encouraging.

In Belgium and the Netherlands, mobilization was decreed on Sunday evening. It takes place more slowly than planned because many of those recalled are on vacation during the month of August. It cannot be expected that the first Belgian and Netherlands reinforcements will reach the Rhine before D + 4 or D + 5, at the earliest.

Up to the present, no American or British force has been able to reinforce Western Europe. An airborne division of three infantry brigades and a parachute brigade could arrive from the United Kingdom, but not before D + 6 or D + 8, under the most optimistic forecasts.

As regards the Americans, they have an additional problem to face. The equipment and matériel of the three divisions destined for the reinforcement of the Seventh Army are pre-positioned in depots east of the Rhine. Accordingly, not only must the personnel of these divisions be sent from the United States to Germany but also their heavy equipment. In addition, these units will have to be routed to the Rhine after landing in the United Kingdom, Belgium, or the

Netherlands, which implies emergency plans which must be drawn up at very short notice.

The possibility of the arrival of American reinforcements within a reasonable time appears therefore to be seriously compromised. For their part, all the members of the Warsaw Pact decreed general mobilization on Sunday morning. Since Monday morning, reinforcements are on the way westward across Czechoslovakia. Ten divisions will reach the Dresden-Prague area on D + 4.

## The Attitude of France

Would France authorize the passage of American troops across its territory? The Soviet Union could consider this attitude an act of hostility which would immediately plunge France into the conflict. Either France must remain apart in the way Soviet diplomacy is encouraging it to do, or it must fight alongside NATO (of which it is still a member from the political point of view).

The answer would not have been in doubt if events had followed a normal course, and if the Central European forces had been able to carry out a coordinated deployment, progressing from one alert stage to another as the political tension increased. This has in no way been the case and, accordingly, it is particularly difficult to forecast what France's reaction will be, knowing that it intends to maintain complete independence about its decisions. Perhaps it will propose that it should act as mediator, or it will side with the Americans since two of its divisions are stationed in Southern Germany. It seems that, in the case of a surprise attack crowned with success, Paris will take time for reflection before deliberately committing itself to action. Its delayed intervention would, moreover, no longer have any decisive influence on the course of the battle.

## Diplomatic Activity Carried Out by the Soviets

Let us go back forty-eight hours and try to follow the sequence of events.

One hour after H hour (i.e. at 0600 hours), the Soviet diplomatic machinery gets under way. All the capitals, as well as the United Nations, are informed of the situation by means of a note addressed to the various governments and the Secretary General of the UN. In it, stress is laid on the urgency and need for preventive action to eliminate the growing danger of a nuclear confrontation in Europe. The militarization of the Federal Republic, its growing weight in the nuclear decision-making process, its role as the political and economic leader of a Europe resolutely hostile to the socialist countries, and its subversive maneuvers aimed at rallying support from eastern European countries are all considered tangible signs of irrevocable opposition to the principles of the Helsinki Conference and the spirit of détente.

Furthermore, the occupation of German territory will only be temporary; it will be ended as soon as the West is ready to accept the creation of a denuclearized and demilitarized zone in Central Europe. If this plan were to be applied successfully, it could be the forerunner of much wider agreements leading to general disarmament and an era of peace, for which the Soviet Union has always been the most ardent protagonist.

Stress is also laid on Moscow's intention not to engage in a nuclear conflict. However, if the member states of NATO use atomic weapons first, the Soviet Union will not hesitate to envisage their total destruction.

The note finally emphasizes the need to start negotiations at the earliest possible moment. The Soviet Union states that it is ready to do so immediately. The abrogation of the military pacts and the withdrawal of foreign troops from European soil are two essential conditions for the success of a future agreement.

In a special message to the French government, Moscow undertakes not to violate the territorial integrity of France under any circumstances, not to compromise its economic interests, and scrupulously to refrain from any interference in its political regime, complying with the agreements reached at Helsinki. No attack will take place against the French troops and installations in the Federal Republic, provided that they do not interfere in the conflict and that France does not open its territory to the armed forces or logistics system of NATO.

Denmark and Norway are threatened with immediate invasion and reprisals if they allow foreign troops, or the siting of nuclear weapons, on their territory.

Painted in very broad strokes, this might be the situation of the Western world immediately after the surprise offensive by the Soviets. In the long term, it seems certain that no European state, even if not directly affected by the operations, would be in a position to maintain its independence of decision or its sovereignty intact. Their situation would be similar to that of Finland after the Second World War, when the Soviet divisions were stationed a few dozen kilometers from Helsinki and the Russian fleet was cruising in the Gulf of Bosnia. None of the countries of the West is capable of ensuring its defense by itself against the Soviet military potential.

*There is absolutely no safety outside the Alliances; there is no militarily viable solution without close and total association with the defense of Germany, the advanced bastion of European defense.* This is what we have tried to demonstrate in analyzing the possible scenario for an operation directed against the West. Another consequence of the sequence of events, ending at some specific moment with the agonizing problem of the nuclear decision, is *the total dependence of Europe on the president of the United States for its future destiny.*

In the case where the lightning strike has achieved its objectives, nuclear weapons may be used, or their use may be renounced. In the first case, as we have seen, the response may be *selective* or *massive*, i.e. the destruction or the safety of Europe lies entirely in the hands of a head of state who, however favorable he may be to Western views, is not a European and represents world interests, some of which may be appreciably different from ours.

It is absurd to think that, for many years, this has been the only alternative we have been offered, the only one considered valid and which is wholly expressed in the unequivocal slogan "Better dead than Red." If Germany—the cornerstone of any European construction—were subjugated by the Soviets, who could think for a moment that the Europeans would coolly envisage nuclear reprisals, of which they would be the first victims?

In this context of disarray and disorder, we must think about the meaning of "superiority in tactical nuclear weapons" which the Alliance claims and with which "our ears have been bashed" for years and years. We must consider the possession of 7,000 tactical nuclear warheads against the 3,500 of the Soviets, and if this means, in the case of the selective response, only two or three devices are to be used, followed by a Soviet broadside of the same dimension. In the case of the "massive" response, what does our apparent "superiority" mean when the use of one-tenth of this potential would leave Europe bled to the bone?

We can see how easy it is to fall into the trap of fallacious reasoning from the moment when the land situation is irretrievably compromised, when the supreme decision is no longer ours, and when the other camp has a destruction potential which is equal, or at least equivalent, to that available to us.

Is there, therefore, no answer to this tragic dilemma of capitulation or destruction and must the Europeans give up any hope of taking their own destiny in their hands, relying (as in the past) on the cooperation and support of their natural ally, the United States, but without giving somebody else the responsibility for deciding their future fate, their survival, or their annihilation?

Some people claim that there is no way out and that it is not within the power of Europe to maintain an independent defense effort enabling it to counterbalance the Soviet conventional forces. This is a debatable statement as we shall see later when we analyze the present resources of a *politically and economically united Europe*, but it is a reasonable point of view in the present context of shortages.

Accordingly, in order to escape the agonizing question of "all or nothing," the present strategy must be given a new dimension, making use of a fourth factor, "popular deterrence." This needs a word of explanation before being analyzed in greater detail in the next chapter.

At the present time, the NATO forces maneuvering in Germany operate in an environment which could be called one of indifference, because no cooperation exists between the allied units and the German people. However, in the smallest village as much as in the most highly populated city, the FRG has thousands of trained men who have only recently completed their military service in the ranks of the Bundeswehr. All this formidable capacity is partially untapped. As we shall see, the organization of small, instantly mobilized groups centered around an ultramodern antitank weapon, with their weapons and personal equipment at home and raised on a regional basis, would markedly and probably decisively increase the operational capability of the NATO divisions. Working in close partnership with the latter, these formations could take on many of the tasks which the highly sophisticated NATO divisions can no longer undertake for fear of squandering their own resources.

They would form a network into which the maneuvering of the allied armored and mobile forces would fit. Through their harassing activities on the rear and on the flanks of the enemy, they would represent a difficult if not insoluble problem for any Soviet operation of the type we have described. A people under arms would meet the aggression with a mass uprising. This is the meaning of "popular deterrence," which would not only allow us to escape from the monstrous nuclear dilemma whose long-term consequences we are incapable of rationally estimating, but would give us back the responsibility for our own destiny and would add an element essential to the prevention of a war we do not want.

I consider this solution to be the only realistic one, the only one which takes the logic of defense into account, the only one which can be set in motion without demanding exorbitant sacrifices which are incompatible with the economic condition of the European countries. It is the only one which offers sufficient guarantees against the possibility of a lightning war. We shall therefore examine it in greater detail in a later chapter.

We have spent a long time developing our analysis of an assumption which seems to be both the most dangerous and the most probable should a direct confrontation between East and West ever come to pass.

Some people will object that, under the conditions described, it is hard to believe that the Soviets have not taken the initiative and gone into action years ago. For those people I must once again state some common truths.

- The achievement of strategic nuclear parity or equivalence is relatively recent. The American atomic monopoly prohibited such an undertaking until recently.
- The growth of Soviet air, land, and sea military potential has developed during the past five or six years, in parallel with the erosion of NATO's conventional forces.
- Politically, there is no reason for launching an operation of the kind. On the other hand, no one can forecast with certainty when the combination of unforeseeable events will make it probable if not certain. A valid security policy is not founded on the good intentions of an adversary with such an impressive aggressive arsenal whose characteristics are based on the offensive.

- *The ultra conservatism of the Europeans*, the internal problems of an Alliance which seems to be more divided than ever, and the incapability of its members to make the choice between effort and the easy way out all favor the indirect strategy of the Soviets and enable them, without running major risks and at minimum cost, to achieve positive if not spectacular results in the extension of their influence and the consolidation of their conquests.

What we must fear is that a growing indifference to the problem of European security, the reappearance of national egotisms to the detriment of real cooperation, a more and more marked tendency to reduce the conventional component of our strategy, and the hardening of our methods and conceptions, may drag us into a state of imbalance that represents a more and more powerful incentive for the launching of an open conflict whose risks appear minute compared to the stake involved.

We cannot be satisfied with reassuring declarations that are not corroborated in any way by reality, with empty formulas such as, ("The training of the NATO forces and the quality of their equipment adequately compensate for the imbalance in numbers.")

The *training* of a large number of NATO units is *inadequate*. How could it be otherwise with a conscript service time of less than half of that of the Warsaw Pact forces? There has been insufficient attention paid to the actual number of weeks devoted to training out of eight, nine, or twelve months of service?

We are unable to take seriously the argument about *qualitative inferiority* of Soviet equipment when we see in the international press that the characteristics of the Soviet MIG-25 have no parallel among the aircraft with which the air forces of the Alliance are equipped. (See some of the various contradictory articles which appeared after the landing of a MIG-25 in Japan.) We furthermore do not believe that the T-62 or T-72 tanks, the BMP (armored personnel carriers) equipped with 76 mm. cannons, and the SAMs or the Soviet rocket launchers are so inferior to their Western opposite numbers. This would be absolutely deluding ourselves, falling back into the bad old ways before 1940: "We shall win because we are the strongest!" We cannot live with our illusions and make a pretense of believing in unjustified statements which no longer fool anybody.

It is time that public opinion is made aware of the facts and takes a closer interest in two vital problems which concern it directly. *Are the armed forces which the country raises really able to carry out their fundamental task, i.e. maintaining the security of Europe and its own security? Are the funds voted for the defense budgets used for this purpose with concern for maximum effectiveness and operational capability?*

The future fate of Europe depends on the answers to these two questions and the measures which will be taken. In the meantime, if the European members of the Alliance do not agree to make a serious effort to ensure their security and take their own destiny in their hands, they may alienate the United States guarantee and support, as is made clear in the *Congressional Record* of June 8, 1976. On that date Senator Taft (on the basis of a study undertaken by the author and on the basis of the book by General Steinhoff) drew the attention of his colleagues to the vulnerability of NATO to a surprise attack by the Warsaw Pact.[4] Posing the question of the viability of the Alliance, he considered that the first and probably the only important responsibility for raising the land forces capable of reacting immediately must be assumed by the Europeans.

Listing measures to be taken to revitalize the Alliance, he proposed a condition for the continuance of United States participation. Quoting an article by T.R. Milton,[5] a former collaborator of General Steinhoff in the NATO military committee, Senator Taft requested the inclusion of the text in the record and said that the author's conclusions were also his own. The most important part states that *"Since there is no point in the U.S. participating in an Alliance that cannot react to a Soviet attack—NATO's only real purpose— perhaps our next President should lay down some conditions for our continued participation."*[6] (My emphasis.)

It remains for us to see what might be the strategic, political, economic, and psychological measures to take to discourage any aggression, to ensure full participation by the United States in the defense of Europe without, as a result, the Europeans being totally dependent on American protection; and to obtain full value from our defense effort through increased cooperation and integration. This is the subject of the next chapter.

# 11 The Defense of Europe: Capabilities, Achievements, and Political and Strategic Prospects

The present defense of Europe stems from the existence of the North Atlantic Treaty (April 1949). The evolution of strategic concepts since 1945, the nuclear parity achieved by the USSR in its competition with the United States, and the relative decline in the conventional forces of the European theater in the face of the continuing growth of the Soviet potential have led to an examination of European defense in new terms.

While maintaining the framework of the Atlantic Alliance, the indispensable guarantor of the security of Europe, it is desirable to strengthen its European bastion, to envisage its own defense policy based on increased cooperation and integration with a view to achieving maximum results from defense budgets and the cost-effectiveness ratio as well as increasing the operational value of the conventional forces.

From this point of view, a question arises about Europe's resources to launch such an undertaking. Is it moved in this direction by political motives linked with its attempts at unification, and what would be the specific tasks of the European partners of the Alliance (or in other words can a truly European strategy be conceived within an Atlantic framework)?

Resources, motivations, means available, and methods form the main part of this chapter.

## THE RESOURCES

Many criteria have been used in establishing the power of a state.[1] Let us remember that size, population, economic capacity, degree of technological development, and military capability are the essential ingredients of that power.

Accordingly, if we make a comparison between Europe on the one hand and the United States and the USSR on the other, we cannot help being surprised that with the considerable resources it holds (in most cases greater than those of the Soviet Union) Europe is incapable of insuring its own defense and must rely on others for its security:

- Population: 258.1 million against 211.9 in the US and 252 in the USSR.[2]
- Gross National Product: $836 billion against $1038.1 and $611.2 billion (i.e. three-quarters of the American GNP and 30 percent greater than the Soviet GNP). Per head and in dollars, this gives $3,257 for the European against $4,934 for the American and $2,467 for the Soviet.[3]
- Exports: $276.7 billion for Europe against $97.1 and $27.4 billion!
- Merchant fleet: 65.8 million tons against 14.8 and 17.4.
- Steel production: 154.9 million tons against 132 and 136.
- Vehicle production: 7.6 million against 6.1 and 1.0.[4]

Comparisons relating to cement, energy, and the production of electricity show differences of the same order. Finally, when we examine defense budgets, we find that the Europe of the Nine spends $42,099 million against $92,800 million for the United States and $103,800 million for the Soviet Union.[5] (See Appendix C.)

On this basis, how can we explain the disparity which exists between the forces of the Warsaw Pact and those of NATO? From a simple examination of the resources available, there appears no justification for claiming that Europe does not have the necessary means to undertake an adequate defense effort. "An economic community which alone represents 20% of the gross social product of the whole world, 41% of international trade and about 50% of world monetary reserves—cannot deny its world responsibilities in establishing peace and social justice."[6]

Once again we put our finger on the essential problem. The effectiveness of the defense of Europe of the Nine is *not* the sum total of its components. Duplication, waste, proliferation of headquarters, and absence of homogenization are the many weaknesses to which we have already paid considerable attention. On the other side, total centralization, standardization, continuity of views, and priority for the military effort which monopolizes brains and means, all permit the achievement of an efficiency and output which are infinitely superior to the West.

"If the Soviets believe it possible to snatch some advantages by the limited use of force without unleashing the apocalypse, then in this case, the best method of dissuading them is to give ourselves the means for denying them these partial aggressions without recourse to the arms whose use is terrifying to us all."[7]

The answer is obvious. We must repudiate forever the "national" defenses which are incapable of insuring the security of the states and commit ourselves resolutely to the road of "European" defense, the only one capable of giving us a world dimension. In order to achieve this, we must now work out the political structures of this Europe of defense.

## EUROPEAN DEFENSE–THE POLITICAL ASPECTS

There will be no political Europe without a European defense, and the establishment of the latter depends strictly on the political will to achieve it. This will does not seem to have been demonstrated by facts in the past. If we intend to make any progress in the defense of Europe dependent on the prior condition of a political union, we would be in a kind of a deadlock.

It seems that this is a false problem and that it should be possible and even certain to make considerable progress along the way with harmonization and perhaps *sectorial integration*, provided that we proceed rationally, carefully, and on a pragmatic basis. It is however essential that the general directives be political and that the common budget be planned in particular sectors.

This study deals with the political structures which should be established, the qualifications and responsibilities of the future European authorities for defense matters, the suppression or "cocooning" of existing bodies, and the possible timetable for the proposed reforms. In order to see this all clearly, we must briefly mention on the one hand what has already been tried and the causes of its failure; and, on the other, list the existing bodies, study their functioning, and make a critical analysis of the present system and propose substitute solutions.

### Attempts at a New European Defense:
### The Fouchet Plan

As we have seen in chapter 3, the failure of the European Defense Community was an extremely serious blow to the idea of European defense.[8] Any initiative in this area seemed condemned from the start and it was only in 1960, at a press conference given by General de Gaulle on September 5, that a relaunching appeared possible: "Ensuring the regular cooperation of the States of Western Europe, this is what France considers desirable, possible and practicable in the political, economic, cultural and defense fields. . . . This involves organized and regular consultation between the governments responsible and then work by specialized bodies in each of the common fields."

In February 1961, a meeting took place in Paris between the six heads of state. In July the foreign ministers met in Rome. This meeting was followed, in the same month, by one in Bonn at the heads-of-state level. The Bonn meeting then instructed a committee to study a statute for European political union and nominated the French representative, Mr. Fouchet, as chairman.

We shall discuss only a few essential points of the *Fouchet Plan*, a draft treaty of eighteen articles:

1. *The aims of the union*: to adopt a common foreign policy, to ensure the growth of the common heritage and the safeguarding of the values of the Western civilization, to contribute to the defense of human rights, the fundamental freedoms and democracy and strengthen, in cooperation with the other free nations, the security of the member States against any aggression, *through the adoption of a common defense policy*. (My emphasis.)

2. *The institutions include*:
   - *the Council*, which meets every four months at heads of state level and, in the intermediate period, at least once at foreign minister level;
   - *the European Political Commission*, made up of high officials of the foreign affairs' ministries of each member state. Its headquarters is in Paris;
   - *European Parliamentary Assembly* which consults, asks questions which the Council is required to answer within four months, votes recommendations, and annually discusses an annual report of its activities by the Council.

3. In its Art. 16, the draft provides for a revision of the treaty three years after it comes into force with a view to strengthening the political union, particularly by establishing a common foreign policy.

Nothing of note was achieved and disagreements appeared within the commission to begin with, and then at the meeting of foreign ministers in December 1961. At the second meeting of the commission in January 1962, there was no rapprochement, while the April meeting at minister level decided the final failure of the plan.

## The Harmel Plan

It was within a wider framework, that of NATO, that the Harmel Plan aimed at counterbalancing a military alliance dominated by the United States by means of a more flexible political alliance in which this predominance would be less marked.

At the December 1966 meeting of the North Atlantic Council Mr. Harmel, the foreign minister of Belgium, outlined his doctrine in a document titled: "Report on the Future Tasks of the Alliance." It related to the (political) achievement of a just and durable peace in Europe, i.e. a final settlement of European problems, at the center of which lay the German question. The substitution of the idea of peaceful coexistence for the principle of the cold war demanded the transformation of the long-term aims of the Alliance. It stated that the solution of the tendentious problems "will end the unnatural barriers between Eastern and Western Europe ... but the participation of the USSR and the United States will be necessary to achieve a settlement."

It remained understood, however, that the search for détente could not compromise security and therefore could not be conceived without the mainte-nance of defense and a certain balance of forces. On this point, I shall quote the lucid and clear proposals made by Ambassador de Staercke, the permanent representative of Belgium to NATO (Lecture delivered at the Belgian War College, 1970).

> Détente is not an end in itself, it is a consequence of defense and, although it is the proof of the success of deterrence, this very proof demonstrates its limits and its dangers—the limits of détente are that it cannot open the question of defense without the risk of destroying itself. . . . As regards the dangers of détente, these have a dual aspect. The first is false security, the permanent temptation for the West to believe that, because it is living in peace, the threat has disappeared, whereas it is simply contained and it would only need a relaxation on our part to bring it to the fore again. Much more, this relaxation would not even allow us to negotiate any more. To pursue détente without buttressing it by defense would be equal to signing a check without sufficient funds either now or for the future.
>
> The second danger of détente is that of ignoring the aims of the adversary. These are however so clear that it needs a remarkable compla-cency on the part of those who want an arrangement at any price not to be aware of them.
>
> The first aim of the adversary is to separate Europe and America in order to have the former at its mercy immediately and the second at a later date. . . .
>
> The second aim of the East is to stabilize the status quo by making it legally recognized.

## The Davignon Committee or the
## Draft of a Common Foreign Policy

Foreign policy and defense are inseparable. This is why it is essential to clarify the harmony achieved in the first field before making suggestions about the second.

It was on October 27, 1970 that the report by the foreign ministers or the "Davignon Report" (named after the director of policy at the Belgian ministry of foreign affairs, at present Vice President of the Commission of the European Communities) was finally adopted. Its main points are:

- *six monthly meetings of the six foreign ministers* with the aim of agreeing and harmonizing their points of view on foreign policy;
- the creation of a *political committee*, comprised of the directors of foreign policy of the six ministries (quarterly meetings); and
- the preparation of a second report on the pursuit of political unification.

## THE PRESENT DEFENSE SITUATION

### North Atlantic Treaty Organization

The North Atlantic treaty goes beyond the framework of European defense, but, at the present time, it is the only viable means of ensuring the defense of Europe in the absence of any political will on the part of the European members of the Alliance to contribute collectively to their own security.

The structure of the organization is well known and includes a *North Atlantic Council*, the supreme power of the Alliance, which meets continuously at the level of government permanent representatives and occasionally at ministerial level. Defense problems are dealt with by the *defense planning committee* (DPC) set up in 1963 which meets at the same level and almost as frequently as the Council. The *Secretary General* presides over the North Atlantic Council, the DPC, the nuclear defense affairs committee (twelve countries) and the nuclear planning group. He also directs the *international secretariat*. Also, there is a North Atlantic assembly which, although without any real legal existence, nevertheless fulfills a useful role as a forum for parliamentarians from both sides of the Atlantic. It has a much more limited role than the WEU assembly, which we shall discuss later.

From the military point of view, the highest authority is the *military committee* which is subordinate to the DPC and in principle consists of the chiefs of staff of the thirteen countries which participate in the NATO integrated military structure. Like the Council, it meets occasionally and has its permanent headquarters in Brussels at military representative level.

The essential aims of the organization are therefore multilateral political consultation and military planning. In addition, however, it permits attempts at cooperation between European allies.

We have already referred to the considerable and often preponderant weight of the United States of America in NATO in comparison with partners of unequal size who have in no way given up any of their sovereignty.

## Western European Union

What is the situation with the *Western European Union* (or WEU), born of the Brussels Treaty revised by the Paris Agreements?

The *Western European Union* is Europe's present voice on foreign policy and defense matters. Its powers are expressly recognized by the revised Brussels Treaty (1954). The WEU has a *Council*, consisting of the foreign ministers or their representatives, with its headquarters in London. Periodic meetings at ministerial level—in principle once a quarter—take place in a capital city of one of the member countries; at permanent representative level, meetings take place two or three times a month.

The *assembly* meets twice a year in Paris in ordinary session. It hears the Council's annual report and votes on recommendations, resolutions, and questions and answers addressed to the Council.[9] It is assisted by six commissions, including policy (general affairs), military (defense and armaments questions), and scientific.

From the military point of view, the major bodies are the *agency for the control of armaments*, with its headquarters in Paris, and the *standing armaments committee*, both directly under the Council.

The mission of the agency is twofold:

1. on the one hand, to check the levels of the armament stocks of the member countries on the continent of Europe;
2. on the other, to ensure respect of the commitments undertaken by the Federal Republic of Germany not to manufacture certain types of arms on its territory (in particular atomic, biological, and chemical weapons).

The *standing armaments committee* is linked directly with European cooperation on arms production. Bilateral or multilateral projects concluded or being developed between countries of WEU are communicated to it. It has an "ad hoc" group consisting of representatives of the army chiefs of staff of the member countries and sub-groups.

All this is the structural organization defined by the treaty. What, in practical terms, are its positive results?

Despite the prerogatives accorded to it, it must be recognized that in nearly twenty years of activity, results have been few and far between. There has never been any common will on the part of the governments to use WEU in the fields of foreign policy and defense in cooperation with the assembly.[10] This apparent indifference is due to the fact that in 1950 the WEU delegated most of its defense obligations to NATO under Art. 4 of the treaty proscribing duplication, and because the tensions within the Council have not allowed positive and concrete resolutions to be reached on most of the recommendations made by the assembly.

This same story of indifference is also found in connection with the standing armaments committee whose role, on the strength of its prerogatives, could have been determining in the standardization field. The 1970 "Report of the Council" states that in 1969, the standing committee met four times, the "ad hoc" group once, and its subgroups ten times. In fact, each European country followed its own equipment policy in complete independence; it was only within the NATO working groups that bilateral or multilateral attempts at cooperation in specific fields were developed.

Everything about WEU, however, is not negative. The assembly discussions are often of high quality and the reports it produces are of undoubted interest, relating to topical subjects as well as to the crucial problems of the Alliance and its evolution. We should also note that Article 5 of the treaty constitutes a categorical commitment since, in case of armed attack against one of its members, all the others would automatically go to war against the aggressor and would be legally obliged to aid and assist the aggressed by all means within their power, both military and other. (The provisions of the North Atlantic treaty are much less compulsive since the members will "take action as they deem necessary" to restore and maintain the security of the area. See Art. 5.)

Despite various discriminations which make certain governments of the member countries accept it with reticence, the Brussels treaty must be maintained, pending the definite establishment of other European defense structures. Otherwise the only legally competent instrument explicitly linked to European union in defense and foreign policy matters would disappear. We must now look for any signs that new structures can be set up.


## The Eurogroup

Both NATO and the WEU were born of legally precise structures. This is not the case with the Eurogroup, a pragmatic creation which came to life during the autumn of 1968 as a result of a British initiative on the part of Dennis Healey, then the British minister of defense.

Under his leadership, it was agreed that the European ministers of defense would meet among themselves at dinner on the evening before the Atlantic ministerial meetings in order to examine the agenda from the European point of view. "The infectious warmth of the banquets gave birth to a spirit of genuine camaraderie at the same time as some apprehension about going too far. These meetings were soon referred to as the Eurogroup. . . . There was no question of establishing a new institution, only at most to continue a new habit."[11]

But faced with the prospect of a reduction of the American presence in Europe, an agreement in principle was reached on a Healey-Schmidt proposal aimed at establishing a European defense improvement program. A billion dollars spread over ten years was the European contribution to the American effort for the defense of Europe.

Since that date, the Eurogroup has become a "de facto" institution; a program of work has been established aimed at harmonizing the opinions of the member countries. The Eurostaff group consists of the European military representatives to NATO in Brussels.[12] The European defense improvement program, the joint training projects, the health services cooperation, the harmonization of logistics, and the attempts at standardization by exchanges of national armament plans and cooperation in the weapons sector are all aspects of efforts at Europeanization within the Alliance.

Ten countries take part in it. France and Portugal are not members, like Iceland, which does not maintain any armed forces. It can immediately be seen that the absence of France constitutes a serious handicap for any initiative aimed at promoting a closer European identity in defense matters. It was partly possible to fill this serious gap when the EPG (European Planning Group) was set up in February 1976 and destined to encourage progress in standardization of equipment and its interoperability under the dual pressures of economic and operational necessity. France has agreed to take part in this work, whose results appear to be positive. The meetings take place regularly in Rome at armament director level but also at political level. Whatever the achievements of the Eurogroup or the European Planning Group, these are no more than embryonic bodies without political heads or the necessary permanence to ensure the continuity of a grand design.

We will now examine future prospects in the much wider framework of the European Communities.

## The Prospects of Political Unity and the
## June 26, 1976 Report by the
## Commission of the European Communities

In this very comprehensive but limited forty-three-page report,[13] defense occupies barely one page and only eight paragraphs (74 to 81). However their content is considerable and their implementation would involve profound changes in present structures. The essentials of this text follow.[14]

*The establishment of Joint defense by the Europe of the Nine cannot weaken the Atlantic Alliance and might even strengthen it.* Geographical and military reasons; considerable disproportion between the Franco-British unclear arsenal and that of the USSR making the United States nuclear guarantee essential; community of interests and values to be defended; and maintenance of the transatlantic dialogue and increased interdependence are the imperatives in favor of faithfulness to the Alliance while preparing a future military integration of the Nine.

The Atlantic Alliance plays and will continue to play a determinative role in the security of Western Europe, but the security of the Union, its long-term cohesion and the solidarity between its peoples could not be fully ensured if the defense problems were purely and simply left aside when the Union was created.

*"Potential" competence of the Community in defense matters* would need a special procedure assuming the assignment of powers and means of action in defense matters. In such a case, fundamental structural changes might take place more or less quickly—cooperation agreements with a view to developing a European "force de frappe" (we shall come back to this); harmonization of strategies and tactics; the creation of a European armaments agency in order to promote standardization, joint planning, and the pooling of human and material resources; progressive "Europeanization" of national headquarters sector by sector; and common logistics. All these matters would have to be featured on the agenda of a commission equipped with the necessary "powers and means of action." Some of these points are specifically mentioned in paragraphs 80 and 81 of the report.

*Maintenance of an open option regarding a European force de frappe* will be the subject of later developments.

Let us note for the moment that paragraph 78 of the report provides that "Since potential competence is concerned, the member states will be required not to undertake with third-party countries actions which might affect the security of another member state or compromise the long-term cohesion of the Union." As an example, the report expressly mentions the nonproliferation treaty and stresses that "the commitments stemming from this treaty should not pre-judge the rights of a future European Union."

*Interdependence of European defense and political union* is explicitly mentioned in paragraph 79: "A rapprochement of the positions of the member States in the field of defense remains desirable and may even facilitate the realization of the Union." Then a measure follows for practical and immediate application. "Among the measures which could be the first concrete manifestations of such a rapprochement, *in a properly European framework* covering all the member States, there could be periodic discussions on the problems of defense and on the effort to be undertaken to ensure it." (My emphasis.)

In terms of the *specific character of the future Western European Union*, paragraph 3 rejects the idea of "several independent and parallel organizations." In plain language this means that if the union were to assume its responsibilities in defense matters, WEU, after having carried out its task on a temporary basis, would disappear or would merge with the specifically European defense bodies of the union.

We realize the importance and implication of these declarations of principle, but it is not clear if they are pious wishes, laudible intentions, or a concrete program to be implemented in stages.

The Tindemans Report, which was decided on following the meeting of the European Council held in Paris on December 10-11, 1974, may perhaps give us more information on the future prospects of a European defense emerging from nothing.

## The Tindemans Report

This report to the European Council, dated December 29, 1975, deals with security, and recognizes that this problem "cannot be left aside from the European Union."[15] The concrete measures it proposes are regular *exchanges of views* on specific problems in defense matters and on the European aspects of multilateral negotiations on security; cooperation in the *manufacture of armaments* (setting up a European armaments agency for that purpose must be envisaged); and the continuance of political cooperation on the question of détente.

There is also a political proposal which seems important. This suggests that "Parliament should be able, from now on, to consider all questions within the competence of the Union, whether or not they are covered by the Treaties." A footnote points out that "the extension of the competences of the European Parliament to matters hitherto discussed in the Assembly of WEU leaves one to question the need to maintain the activity of the parliamentary institution of the Western European Union."

After this long review of the present situation and future trends, we must now propose a concrete solution based on some fundamental principles. They are:

— the avoidance of duplication at all costs and, if possible, the use of existing bodies, possibly adapting them appropriately;
— remembering the direct elections to the European Parliament in June 1979;
— consideration that the Commission of the European Communities and the Council are the nucleus of any future European union at executive level; and
— taking care not to go too far too quickly to avoid the failure of the EDC in August 1954.

Sectoral and pragmatic progress appears to be the most rational solution, but this does not exclude drawing inspiration from the revisions of the EDC treaty which could now apply.

## Preparing the Way for the Elected European Parliament; Taking Advantage of Existing Organizations

At the political level, a decision should be made to set up at short notice a *European working group*, responsible for carrying out preliminary studies on the future European defense organization. Its members would be taken from European personnel appointed to the NATO international headquarters or to national headquarters. It should not exceed fifty in number and would mainly consist of officers belonging to the European countries of the Nine (if Ireland and Denmark agree to take part). The European countries which are not members of the EEC could nominate observers. The headquarters of the working group would be in Paris and, to begin with, it would come under WEU, thus constituting an embryo European headquarters working for the organization. (We should point out that a similar working group had been established to develop the practical methods of application of the treaty creating a European Defense Community.)

Its tasks would relate to clearly defined sectors: Harmonization of tactics, proposals for a joint research budget, the development and production of standardized equipment, the structure and final arrangements for a "European Armaments Agency," standardization of conscript service time, common instruction and training programs, modernization of mobilization plans, procedures for inspection and tactical evaluation ("Tac Eval") of the conventional forces, improvements to the alert system, appropriate measures for promoting a European (and no longer strictly national) logistics system, and so forth.

The members of the *"European working group"* would be able to take advantage of the studies and work carried out by the Eurogroup, and various specialized NATO offices. The group would lay its conclusions before specialist committees of the Parliament within a maximum of one year. For its administrative support, it would use the existing secretariat and services of WEU and would come directly under that body. Later, it could be enlarged and constitute the nucleus of a *sectoral European headquarters*, initially limited to the fields of common programs for armaments, equipment, supplies, and infrastructure.

This process could be set in motion by the progressive reduction of the national bodies or specialized branches now dealing with these problems. A common budget proposed by the European Parliament and approved by the European Council—at minister level—should be planned. Initially this budget could represent a specified percentage of the investments allocated nationally for future programs. The European sectoral headquarters does not raise any insurmountable problem if the political will exists. It could be established during the six months following the approval of proposals at executive level.

## Building Up the Necessary Political Structures

This process needs a period of very careful study, political negotiation, the approval of one treaty, and the revision of another. The task is, however, far from being insurmountable if the political will is demonstrated here at European Council level.

The *preliminary studies* could be entrusted to a "European defense study committee," consisting of senior officials of the nine foreign ministries. Its program would relate to the political structures to be provided, and its work would be submitted within six months from when it was set up to the *political committee* or the *Davignon committee.*

After harmonization of points of view, the latter would, in its turn, submit the final report to the *council of foreign ministers* for final approval before ratification by national parliaments.

The structures envisaged might include a *European defense commission*, initially consisting of seven members. (This could be enlarged if Ireland and Denmark agreed to participate. Similarly Greece and Turkey, which are members of the Eurogroup, could be associate members.) Their status would be similar to that of the members of the commission of the European Communities. The chairmanship would rotate and an annual report would be submitted to the European parliament as soon as the latter had taken over the prerogatives and competences of the assembly of the Western European Union for defense matters. The commission would centralize all the powers relating to choice of equipment, their distribution, and their import or export.

The *European armaments agency* would become responsible for research and development on the European production of armaments and equipment. In a first stage, it would identify the joint production programs, case by case and in a rational way, with a view to maintaining and increasing the European potential while maintaining acceptable production costs. There would still be competition but it would be tempered by compensation rules; duplication would be eliminated. The agency would not be essentially technical but would include political, military, and industrial components.

The *council of European defense ministers* would meet periodically to harmonize points of view and adopt a common attitude prior to the plenary meetings of the Atlantic Alliance. Its work would be prepared by a *permanent secretariat* consisting of officials of national ministries and coordinated by a *secretary general.*

The bodies described above could progressively assume the functions of an embryo European ministry of defense, taking in specific sectors in which cooperation could be rapidly and effectively established but taking care not to include the sensitive areas of personnel and personnel budgets.

Concurrently, we must wonder about the need to keep these bodies in existence. We have already suggested the maintenance of the assembly of the WEU for a limited period until the European parliament is in a position to take on its prerogatives.

The *Council of the WEU* and its secretariat should either disappear or merge with the permanent secretariat of the council of European defense ministers. In any case, its headquarters should be moved from London to Brussels. The *standing armaments committee* should be dissolved, as should the *agency for the control of armaments*, whose prerogatives from the revised Brussels treaty should be taken on by the *European armaments agency*. It seems, solely from the political point of view, that the clauses of the treaty relating to limitations and the nonproduction of certain types of armaments must remain. In any case, it seems that the Treaty of Brussels should be revised, if it is accepted that the European parliament will take on the competences of WEU and if the suppression of certain specialized bodies is envisaged.

Similarly, the Treaty of Rome could be amended in order to increase the competences of the commission in defense matters. The European parliament can extend the field of its discussions to new matters, with the cooperation of governments.[16]

It remains to be determined whether the decisions taken by the European parliament will take precedence over the resolutions of the national parliaments. The European parliament should, as is the national rule, have a right to check and amend the common budget.

At a later stage, a *European coordination and nuclear planning committee* should come into being if appreciable progress is achieved towards the establishment of a European nuclear force. The existing constraints and the hopes which can be expected in this connection will be discussed in a later section of this chapter. In the immediate future, we can hardly expect spectacular results as long as political union does not become a reality. But even limited progress in the technological field or in the deployment of forces will need the creation of a European consultation body similar to that which exists at the Nuclear Planning Group level of the Alliance.

The establishment of the political structures for European defense will certainly involve a long, tedious, and complex process. Harmonization of points of view, revision of existing treaties, suppression of bodies which have become superfluous, and the establishment of European administrative machinery, working efficiently without duplication of what exists already, all assume political will, creative imagination, loyal cooperation, and firm decisions.

This is what the security of Europe costs. But before the new institutions become established, we must know what problems will arise from the military standpoint, as well as the solutions which can be applied.

## MILITARY MEASURES

It is worth summarizing what has already been undertaken and achieved from the military standpoint, even if the results seem modest.[17]

The achievements of the Alliance are far from negligible in the field of infrastructure—airfields, pipeline network, headquarters, advance depots—or alert systems, principally against a sudden air threat.

The NATO electronic air defense system (known as the NADGE system) certainly constitutes progress in this area for the security of Europe. Let us also mention the NATO integrated communications system (NICS) which extends the long-distance telecommunications system and independently links headquarters, command posts, and national governments.

The coproduction of weapons systems on a bilateral or multilateral basis has led to some major achievements. The German Leopard tank is used by six European members of the Alliance (Norway, Denmark, the Netherlands, Belgium, the Federal Republic, and Italy) and the Lance missile will be used by five countries.

For the air force the F-104 Starfighter, the Phantom, the Jaguar, the Transall transport aircraft, the Alpha-Jet light training aircraft, the MRCA multirole combat aircraft (or "Tornado") and, in the future, the American F-16 aircraft, will all be common to Denmark, Norway, Belgium, and the Netherlands.

Joint training is carried out during multinational NATO exercises on a modest scale through existing affiliations between units and battalions of different countries. It is quite normal to see Germans, the Dutch, Belgians, Americans, and even Frenchmen maneuvering alongside each other. This is a powerful contribution to closer solidarity between allied military men and to the practical harmonization of tactical doctrines and procedure. These exercises have recently been extended and increased in number with extremely positive results from energetic action by General Haig, the supreme commander in Europe (the "Reforger" maneuvers of September and November 1976 are a most spectacular illustration).

In this fundamental field, it may be estimated without fear of exaggeration that European and Atlantic cooperation at execution level is far in advance of the political level. Despite language difficulties, different equipment, and national procedures, a real fraternity has been born among the armed forces and is developing as more experiences are shared.

It is all the more regrettable that vigorous *political stimulus* is cruelly lacking, and that there is no hope in the near future for rationalization, harmonization, and standardization to the extent to which they exist in the Warsaw Pact.

## Operational Priorities Stemming from
## Forward Strategy and Immediate Availability

Chronologically, an attack against the West would involve cover forces responsible for protecting and permitting the implementation of the defense system of
Central Europe in the context of the "forward strategy." These forces must be
in a position to carry out their missions, upon which depend all subsequent
developments. They must be *immediately available*, sited as near as possible to
the iron curtain, and completely operational from both the personnel and
equipment points of view. They must be capable of intervening at extremely
short notice (a maximum of a few hours), and their vulnerability in their present
deployment area must be at a minimum.

But peacetime contingencies cannot be ignored; the personnel of the cover
forces also have a right to leave, free time, and periods of unavailability. It is
therefore essential that their numbers and equipment *be permanently raised to
130 percent* of their base in order to ensure an immediate presence and
availability at all times.

The intervention divisions sited furthest to the East must for similar reasons, but
with less urgency, have at least 110 to 115 percent of their wartime operational
establishment readily available in peacetime. They cannot be satisfied with the
complex, slow, and risky procedure of replacement of numbers from reinforcements in rear areas which would never arrive in time. This "replacement"
system, or "bringing up to establishment," can only apply to divisions sited on
national territory, outside the Federal Republic of Germany, and is a system
made possible by the proximity of depots and reduced traveling time.

We have said that *the battle for Europe* will take place in the forward area,
i.e. *on the territory of the FRG*, and its result cannot depend on optimistic
calculations about the arrival of reinforcements or additional forces whose
routing would involve prohibitive delays. All the commanders-in-chief of Central
Europe have supported this argument. General von Kielmannsegg,[18] General
Bennecke, and others again have stressed the vital importance of having troops
on the spot, fully operational, self-sufficient, and not dependent on political
decisions for their entry into action. From the diplomatic and political points of
view, there are obvious advantages in this. Let us assume that a crisis situation
arises and that precautionary and alert measures are applied. One of the first
measures will be to bring the troop numbers in the forward areas up to full
strength—all our security depends on this.

But then some diplomats say that these precautionary measures would be
considered by the Soviets as an act of hostility, as a proof of aggressive
intentions. Wouldn't the Soviets be inclined to unleash a preemptive action in
order to retain the advantage of superiority, shock effect, and surprise?

In order to get out of this vicious circle, there is only one valid answer: To
guarantee in peacetime the completeness of the operational forces stationed

along the eastern borders of the theater, i.e. to increase 130 percent and 115 percent, respectively, the troop numbers and equipment essential for effectively carrying out war missions.

Any other attitude (pruning of means available, reductions in establishment tables, withdrawal of units, deadlocks about logistics or equipment, arbitrary extensions of intervention times, acceptance of an extraordinary reduction in availabilities at weekends or during leave periods) leads to a proportionate reduction in the validity and credibility of the deterrence on which we base the prevention of a conflict.[19]

At the same time we are reducing in alarming fashion the yield from the capital invested. Let us illustrate this statement by means of a simple but topical example. During every weekend and leave period the barracks of the Bundeswehr, and to a lesser extent those of the allied contingents, are deserted by their military personnel, who have full freedom to return to civilian life. Has an estimate been made of the loss in *collective security for which the European taxpayer pays*? There are 104 days of reduced vigilance, 3 or 4 weeks of leave where personnel is reduced by 50 percent, holidays, and so on. More than 130 days, i.e. more than one-third of the year, is the period during which the investments allocated for defense are absolutely unproductive. This is a lot in a situation of imbalance of conventional forces, and in which exists the permanent threat that we have described.

This same principle of immediate availability should involve a revision of the stationing of certain allied contingents. One division of the Netherlands army corps should be permanently stationed on the territory of the Federal Republic of Germany. Refusing to do this would lead to doubts about the validity of the army contribution of the Netherlands to the European collective defense system, about their will to participate fully, about the equity of the cost sharing, and, in the final analysis, about the usefulness of the financial effort of the Netherlands to maintain an army component that in the 1976 budget cost them the considerable sum of 3,137 billion florins.[20] Under General Haig's vigorous stimulus and after long and difficult bargaining, it seems that a Netherlands brigade will soon be stationed in the Federal Republic of Germany.

A second measure relates to the standardization in Europe of conscript military service time. This principle has been recognized by the EDC treaty which stated in Article 72 that "personnel recruited by conscription to serve in the European Defense Forces shall perform the same period of active duty."

Since then, because of a less tense climate (for economic reasons, and particularly due to electoral motives which yield immediate results), the duty period has been considerably reduced to an absolutely unacceptable level, not only for the operational training of the young men called up, but also for performance of tasks and continuity.

A duty period of less than fifteen months is of doubtful value; the commitment of insufficiently trained young men to operations would be a crushing responsibility out of proportion to the electroal benefits counted on by a reduction in period of duty. Furthermore, it is inconceivable that, in a single country, the military service time should vary in different provinces and that eighteen months is served in the north, eight in the center, and eleven in the south. This, however, is the system used by the European member countries of the Alliance for a joint defense system. It would therefore be an urgent task for the future European parliament to examine the duty period of the conscript armies and to propose a *minimum of fifteen months*.

The measure will be unpopular. But public opinion must know that below a certain threshold the billions spent on defense have a *nil yield*; and that by giving in to the reduction in the cost of military service, it is severely mortgaging the future of the youth who will be called to fight and whose chances of survival are smaller because his training time is reduced.

Political courage will be needed to propose and ratify such a measure. We have no doubt that the European leaders, concerned for the security of their peoples, will give priority to this step in preference to the immediate problem of their future reelection. A choice must be made between the expenditure in time and money on the prevention of a conflict, and the expenditure in blood should we be engaged in an adventure with no way out, caused by our state of unpreparedness.

## "Popular Deterrence"; the Fourth Dimension of a European Strategy

It is now more than thirteen years since Raymond Aron wrote the following: "Reflection leads to the recognition of the practical effectiveness of territorial defense. This defense capability, if the heads of states or the population as a whole have the necessary courage, forces on the aggressor, armed with his giant bombs, the alternative of a *costly conquest or a vain destruction*."[21] And further on: "Whether an isolated state or an alliance is concerned, the territorial defense capabilities are *an essential factor in the strategy of deterrence*." (My emphasis.)

Since then, these obvious proposals have had clear results in various writings and were even the subject of a recommendation by the WEU assembly without however having been converted into fact regarding the "forward strategy."[22] Let us take a brief look at what could be the organization, equipment, and tasks of these "territorial deterrent forces" before making suggestions about their establishment.

### Organization

A book by Lieutenant Colonel Guy Brossollet has reopened the question of structures and combat procedures of the French active forces.[23] Noting the inadequacy of the financial resources as opposed to the operational requirements of the equipment for the combat units in the present structure system,[24] he proposes an original, imaginative, and not unrealistic solution from the budgetary as well as the maneuvering points of view which he calls "a modular system" capable of countering "the speed of the adversary, by the depth of our deployment; its size, by lightness; its numbers, by efficiency."

He means the creation around a nucleus of antitank weapons (medium-range missiles like the Milan, hand-held weapons of the recoilless gun type, mines), of teams of about fifteen men responsible for an area of action of some 20 sq. km. on an essentially regional basis. These modules form "the meshes of a vast net to be spread over the whole area where the enemy is liable to emerge." These meshes "do not stop, they catch, they retain, at least for a time. . . ." Indeed they ensnare and paralyze the adversary.

It is surprising to find that this idea has already been the subject of an article in the review *Stratégie*, written by three eminent members of the Los Alamos Scientific Laboratory, University of California.[25]

Let us note two or three significant passages from this remarkable article: "It has never been explained how the use of nuclear weapons could redress a military situation in the process of disintegration and this is probably the reason why the accent is put on our willingness to escalate. . . . The logic on which our theatre forces are at present organised thus appears to be based on doubtful assumptions which, we believe, will be completely obsolete if we had to face a brutal challenge."

And, moving on to the structure of the theater forces, the authors recommend "a substantial number of very mobile small units equipped with conventional weapons for the purpose of opposing attempted infiltration by enemy land or airborne units. The major part of these forces would consist of an organized militia, equipped and trained for this mission, a militia which could also play other roles, such as that of ensuring the defense of towns in the rear areas of the territory."

### The Tasks

In the same review, an article by Bernard Expedit on the "Russian Machine" informs us what might be the task of these units. "The mechanized adversary meeting such a force and penetrating it to a considerable extent is then liable to find itself enmeshed in a net becoming tighter and tighter as a result of the arrival of reinforcement of anti-tank weapons on its flanks and its rearguard, cutting it up, paralyzing it and dislocating it, allowing it no opportunity other than to be immobilized and exposed to contamination or to attempt costly, improvised linking-up maneuvers in force."

In support of his thesis, the author quotes the action of the Finnish light infantry at the end of December 1939 which decimated the Soviet divisions forced to remain on the roads among the forests and lakes of Suomossalmi.

He also chronicles the action in the Epirus mountains from November 4, 1940 to
January 9, 1941 when the Italian army lost most of its armored units in action
against a Greek army of mountain people who completely dominated the area.[26]

*Politically*, the idea found acceptance in the Western European Union assembly[27] which considered that:

> ... improved organisation, recruitment and training of the reserve forces
> would allow:
> (a) a considerable strengthening of the deterrent potential of the field
>     forces of the European armies;
> (b) European defense to be based to a substantial extent on recourse to
>     the widest possible mobilization of the people's energies in the
>     event of attack; recommends that the Council:
>  1. (a) together with the member states of the Atlantic Alliance
>         which are not members of WEU, specify the type of tasks
>         entrusted to the various components of the European
>         defense system: Nuclear forces, combat forces, internal
>         forces, internal defence forces;
>     (b) consequently define requirements in respect of internal
>         defence forces and combat forces with a view to harmoniz-
>         ing the concepts of European States in this field;
>  2. (a) to this end, set up a group of experts consisting of senior
>         defense officials to study measures likely to develop the
>         contributions by reserves to the internal defence of Euro-
>         pean territory and, inter alia, consider the possibility of:
>     (b) ... produc[ing] special equipment for reserves for internal
>         defense forces, combining power, simplicity, and robust-
>         ness, and ensure that it is made available immediately in
>         the event of mobilization. ...

The importance of the territorial reserves has been emphasized in a remarkable book by Horst Afheldt, *Verteidigung und Frieden*.[28] In this study scientific
exactitude is fully maintained in the depth of perception and, based on a
systematic analysis of present strategic conditions and above all on nuclear facts,
his ideas agree very closely with Brossollet's. Under his auspices, a team of
military and civilian experts (including Generals (retd.) Löser and Birnstiel)
working within the orbit of the Max Planck Institute of Starnberg is planning to
publish a vast synthesis of the "strategy of the 1990s."

On the other side of the Atlantic, there is also interest in a solution which (on
the basis of the considerable reserves of the European armies and more
particularly the Bundeswehr) might offer a valid answer to the problem of
overcoming the chronic weakness of the conventional forces and, at the same
time, ward off the temptation of a surprise attack.[29]

Based on the geographical fact that forty-five percent of the Federal Republic consists of forest or built-up areas, the Canby report stresses the advantages of territorial defense as *adjuncts* to the regular forces:

1. They can be more effective against surprise than prohibitively expensive readiness measures;
2. they can tie down large numbers of opposing forces if integrated into an overall scheme whereby these defense forces can play a meaningful complementary role with the regular forces;
3. they can relieve expensive regular formations, allowing the latter's concentration into an operational reserve;
4. they provide screening forces and territory to mask the positioning of reserves for launching flanking ripostes against Soviet thrust lines.[30]

The task would be to convert these new concepts into fact, concepts which seem to have gathered a large consensus in public opinion but which nevertheless have not given rise to positive initiatives.

We have already referred to the mass of German reservists (nearly two million) of which only a small proportion is incorporated into territorial formations whose main task is to ensure the protection of the rear area.

The operational arrangements for the establishment of light, mobile, and instantaneously mobilizable units already exist. These are the W.B.K. ("Wehrbereichskreis" which are incorporated in the FRG divisions as "Länder"), the backbone of German territorial defense. It appears that a period of trial and adjustment is essential; this could take place during the customery autumn large-scale allied maneuvers with troops in 1979.

The integration of the German territorial commands at various echelons into the allied operational commands would enable tasks to be allocated and the essential measures to be planned for coordination, logistics support, and reciprocal operational arrangements. Test units, consisting of reservists of the Bundeswehr, should take part in the maneuvers after joint plans have been drawn up.

This new approach to European defense would finally allow us to get out of the rut created by following Second World War procedures, which are extremely difficult to adapt to the nuclear environment. A second stage, should the results of this first experiment prove positive, would enable integration to be further advanced through periodic contacts, a common alert system, improvement in communication networks, integrated study periods, participation of allied reserve units established on a similar model, definition of desirable of weapons, and so forth.

The establishment of such a system would enable the effectiveness of the combat forces to be considerably increased, would "fill the gap in the battlefield," offer an immediate solution to the problem of protection of the rear against partisans and airborne troops, would guarantee the close support of the battle corps units, and would considerably increase the efficiency of intelligence. It would also introduce into the minds of those taking part the idea of interdependence on a European scale, and would, by that very fact, create an essential partnership between the populations and the armed forces.

Such a solution would take account of the qualities of initiative and high technological ability of the European soldier. It would shatter a paralytic hierarchy in an environment of mobile combat, in which the risks of losing contact is high, thus restoring the cohesiveness of the team, "participation" at all levels, and the offensive spirit.

It presupposes intensive training, adequate toughness, and a high sense of responsibility. I do not share the views of Brossollet when he proposes substituting his "modular system" for the armored and mechanized formations, which include specialists and experienced volunteers, that we now have available. For the defense of Europe, a minimum of power is required, centered on modern armored major units.

I do support Brossollet when he criticizes the inadequacy of our defense system and the deficiencies of our equipment. The law of numbers does not seem to be confirmed by present strategy. Accordingly, the combination of our present means with the meshed and modular system based on the immediate mobilization of trained reservists which he recommends seems to be the only viable way of getting out of the present deadlock and facing any attempt at a surprise attack.

The specter of nuclear apocalypse would be case aside and the concept of deterrence would be reenforced, thus diminishing the risks of a conflict we want to avoid at all costs.


## A European Nuclear Force

There is no lack of people who have said that a politically united Europe, resolved to take on responsibility for its own defense, should have an independent nuclear force.[31] The appropriateness of such a force is clearly defined by Andrew J. Pierre: "The goal should be a European nuclear role within the Atlantic Alliance which fortifies the European pillar and which serves as a step towards greater European political integration without damaging the partnership with the United States."[32]

The nucleus of this force would come from the French and the British nuclear arsenals which would merge into a European atomic pool, "the highest expression of sovereignty" according to General Beaufre. However logical and attractive this proposal may appear, how does it face up to reality?

We shall examine the political, technological, and operational *restrictions*, the *advantages*, and conclude with a series of desirable *aims* which may be less ambitious but are probably more realistic.

Major obstacles arise from the political point of view since the two national nuclear forces are each designed for their own specific purposes. France plans to use its nuclear force for strictly national ends, whereas the United Kingdom has resolved to assign its force to the Atlantic Alliance except if its vital national interests are involved. In this context, it seems that a European politico/strategic directorate would have no power to solve this difficulty in the absence of a closely linked and supranational political union.

Furthermore, it cannot be forgotten that the United Kingdom is linked with the United States by preferential agreements[33] whereas France has developed its nuclear capability alone with much greater financial effort. It has devoted 0.65 percent of its gross national product to it, as compared to 0.18 percent for the British.

It is here that an essential aspect of the problem arises—the attitude of the United States. We all know that the latter has always been extremely reticent about accepting the idea of an independent nuclear force. As long ago as 1962 McNamara said at Ann Arbor: "Limited nuclear capabilities, operating independently, are dangerous, expensive, prone to obsolescence and lacking credibility." And Ian Smart, in a probing study of the problem, clearly states the conditions which might encourage the United States to support such an undertaking: "Unless both France and Britain are prepared to associate their cooperation with NATO, and with the United States itself at the level of strategic policy, there seems to be no prospect of American agreement either to assist France technically or to authorize Britain to do so." ("Prospects for Anglo-French Nuclear Cooperation," Adelphi Papers, I.I.S.S.)

Finally, the position of Germany cannot be ignored since discrimination between nuclear and nonnuclear powers within a European political union would carry the germs of pernicious antagonism. Germany, the primary power interested in nuclear planning, should, in any case, take part in a European directorate responsible for decision on use.

This problem is, moreover, topical since it concerns the possible use of the "Pluton" tactical weapons sited in France, whose shells, in view of their limited range, would inevitably fall in Germany.

*Technology* is also a restriction, perhaps not insurmountable but very real in view of the differences in equipment and the asymmetry of development. The British appear to have a substantial lead in the computer field, in the range of the weapons, and in their megatonnage; on the other hand, the French have developed greater expertise in the use of solid fuels and guidance techniques.

The replacement or modernization of equipment will inevitably have to take place during the 1980s. In view of the time required for the development of new techniques, a decision on technological cooperation would have to be made within a relatively short time, since otherwise the developments of the two countries will inevitably diverge and the benefits of burdensharing, standardization of equipment, and the mutual use of the results of national research efforts will be lost.

From the *operational point of view*, it seems that there has been no coordination of tasks allocated to the strategic submarines or in targeting. The United Kingdom integrates its operational plans and targeting with NATO plans; France operates independently.

These are the contradictions between the only two European nuclear forces in existence. Despite contacts and declarations of intention at different levels, it appears that so far nothing concrete has been planned. This is brought out from the position taken by Lord Carrington:

> The Prime Minister has spoken of the possibility of an Anglo-French nuclear force held in trust for Europe.... There are substantive reasons why this is not an immediate issue. First and most obvious is the difference in France's defense philosophy and attitude to NATO; secondly our present generation of Polaris missiles derive from arrangements with the U.S. which place inhibitions on exchange of nuclear information; and finally the French are only just beginning to bring their nuclear submarines into service and ours have been in service for a comparatively short time.[34]

The advantages of a completely integrated European nuclear force are perhaps less evident than might appear at first sight. It seems realistic to think that the problem of the decision on use will not be solved for a good while and that possession of the supreme weapon will, ipso facto, carry the right to use it to the best advantage in the national interest.

Would such an embittered statement compromise or reduce the security of Europe? We do not think so. The multiplicity of decision centers creates an area of uncertainty which strengthens deterrence. Furthermore, would a European force be more speedily and more effectively brought into action on behalf of Germany, for example, than a French or British force as long as allied contingents are still present on FRG soil? ?

The whole thing is quite different from the technological and operational points of view. *Technologically*, the advantages of joint research and development on a weapon which demands considerable investment and the most advanced techniques are obvious. In this field, more than in any other, duplication of effort should be avoided and standardization of equipment can only be beneficial. In addition, as we have already mentioned, French and British "know-how" are complementary and each of the partners has a major interest in taking advantage of the experience gained by the other.

The attitude of the United States is a determining factor in this undertaking. As W. Joshua writes: "By strengthening France's nuclear program and expertise moreover, the United States would create the conditions in which Anglo-French nuclear cooperation would be possible."[35] Accordingly, if the indivisibility of joint defense at Atlantic level is not a meaningless expression, the United States should enable its European partner to benefit from the advantages of their discoveries in advanced nuclear technology. In this way, we would have an exact assessment of the solidarity and interdependence of the European and trans-atlantic partners, opening the path to cooperation which would finally be justified. Any delay or any reticence in this connection can no longer be justified by the arguments used in the past, since France and the United Kingdom have developed (one alone and the other in association) deterrent forces whose credibility, even if it is not on the same scale as that of the American arsenal, has nevertheless been officially recognized.

*Operationally*, it will be remembered that a strategic submarine is capable of carrying out four patrols of eight to ten weeks each year. The intervening periods are devoted to maintenance. Every three years each submarine undergoes a major refit, theoretically lasting six months, but perhaps lasting as long as a year.[36]

Accordingly, the "patrol" availability may be one submarine out of three. The following table shows the assumptions for the availability of strategic submarines.

| Number of vessels: | 1 : 2 : 3 : 4 : 5 : 6 : 7 : 8 : 9 : |
|---|---|
| Minimum number on patrol: | 0 : 0 : 1 : 2 : 2 : 3 : 4 : 4 : 5 : |

It can immediately be seen that Franco-British operational cooperation, using nine submarines, would enable five vessels to be permanently at sea, thus increasing the second strike capability and, as a result, strengthening the deterrence value of the two forces.

In conclusion, let us say that exchanges of information on the activities of Soviet submarines, guidance of the vessels, and particularly the allocation of targets could only be improved in such an environment of mutual cooperation. "In the nuclear age, there is no longer complete, nor even extensive, freedom of action whatever may be the statutory independence of forces. Within an alliance, very good cooperation is essential, both for general efficiency and in the direct interest of its members."[37]

The possible developments and rapprochements in the foreseeable future[38] may be considered from two points of view. Either, in a first stage, they are limited to coordination of deployment, maintenance, allocation of targets and possibly operational command and control; or else joint development of weapons systems is undertaken in accordance with a precise program drawn up many years before the present equipment is due for replacement.

According to P. Davis, five forms of cooperation may come into being:

1. Joint technological development;
2. Planned sharing of procurement and partial joint force allocation;

3. Shared deployment and patrolling but national control of planning and decisions as to use;
4. A joint planning mechanism for all purposes except decisions to fire;
5. Joint authority over threat exploitation or actual use.[39]

Alongside these desirable trends, which mainly concern France and the United Kingdom, it is certain that a coordinating body at European level would have to be set up. Germany would be an obligatory partner for the reasons already mentioned. This *"European nuclear planning group"* could also have other members among others possessing a European-manufactured tactical nuclear weapon.

It is doubtful whether complete nuclear integration at European level can be brought into effect for a considerable time. There is no urgency in the matter. On the contrary, it is feared that a premature reopening of the discussions might be harmful to the European allies who are deeply divided on the subject, and might compromise the chances of positive achievements in the most essential fields. One of these is the psychological aspect of European defense.

## THE EUROPEAN SPIRIT AND
## THE WILL TO DEFEND

"To think that Europe will save itself or lose itself because, without moreover changing anything, it has one division more here and one less there and that it will increase or diminish the percentage of GNP devoted to defense is to believe that the effects can really be changed without attacking the causes."[40]

The problem is clearly stated and it is true that a large part of public opinion is tired of a so-called Europe of "technocrats" and longs to see another Europe develop, perhaps more human, more tangible, and above all more directed toward concrete achievements rather than abstract constructions. Everything, or nearly everything, needs doing in this field, particularly regarding the security of a mass of more than 250 million inhabitants (the second economic power in the world), who find it quite normal to leave their defense problems to others.

We need to create in the masses that sense of urgency, solidarity in defense matters, idea of equity in cost-sharing, cooperation without reservation, *the European spirit* without which any joint undertaking would be meaningless. To begin with, we must seriously *inform* by the spoken and written word, using the mass media with a view to awakening public opinion to the vital necessity of defending what they have got. To many in the era of détente and the Helsinki conference, this will seem to be devoid of interest. Perhaps they will change their views when they become aware of the precariousness of our security. "For the lack of will, Europe will be a hostage. . . ."[41] This was a statement by General Steinhoff.

I cannot support the views of those who claim that Western public opinion is completely allergic to European defense problems. This is a question which is above party, which concerns everybody. The way in which we react will determine our destiny for a long time.

Information must be given at two levels:

> ... to *the public* who, in the final analysis, are the source of the defense budgets and have a right to know whether the budgets meet the requirements of minimum security (more frequent debates on television would probably enable an analysis to be given of all the aspects of the problem from both the national angle and its European context); ... and to *military personnel*, mainly the conscripts.[42] This internal information, in the form of periodical discussions, in which all opinions could be freely expressed, would ensure greater motivation, responsibility, and the essential feeling of participation. We are apparently very wide of the mark at present if we listen to the embittered opinions of those who consider military service useless or out of date or if we refer to the unbelievable ignorance of some people about defense, Europe, or the Atlantic Alliance.

We must *take action* through more frequent exchanges between contingents of various nationalities.

There is nothing to prevent a German, Belgian, or Dutch armored regiment from carrying out its periodical firing practices in the Oslo area in Norwegian "Leopard" tanks. Furthermore, we must remember that German units undergo training in Canada with prepositioned equipment. If the equipment is standardized, why not extend this solution within Europe?

As we have already said, the European spirit will develop from the lowest level upward. The armed forces represent a trial area with vast possibilities. We must not forget that it is within the Red Army that widely diverse ethnic groups of the huge Soviet empire are merged with convincing results.

The creation of a *European defense college* would enable various points of views for the defense of Europe to be compared. Organized on the model of the Institut des Hautes Etudes de Défense in Paris, it would be attended by military officers, industrialists, politicians, senior officials of the ministries of foreign affairs, as well as representatives of the media. It could be sited in Paris. This proposal was the subject of a recommendation by the WEU assembly to the Council of the organization.[43]

Some people will object to such an institution as a duplication of the NATO defense college in Rome. We do not think so. A European college would enable an identity of view to be created among those responsible for European defense; many problems must be tackled together in their European context if we want to get onto an equal footing with the United States in a rennovated Atlantic Alliance.

Rome would retain its role as a privileged meeting place between European and Atlantic allies working together.

## CONCLUSIONS

Analysis of the past and present have led us to propose solutions aimed at remedying the state of stagnation in European security. Certainly, other arrangements are conceivable. But it is essential to move on to concrete achievements wihout pause.

A frontal attack should be made in all three fields, political, military, and psychological. If public opinion becomes aware of the crucial importance of the problem, the governments will follow.

We shall try to discover our future destiny in the last chapter of this work.

# 12 The Uncertain Future: Conclusions

It is particularly difficult and perhaps not very wise to rush recklessly into what has been called "futurology." However, there is nothing to prevent an attempt at extrapolation to find what the future holds in store for us in terms of the security of Western Europe and preservation of a style of life and of spiritual values based on human freedom and dignity.

Between 1945 and the present time, deep changes have affected and perhaps impaired international relations. The number of actors has increased appreciably, and economic forces have apparently taken over from ideological proselytism or military power in the *strict sense*. (The last two factors could regain major importance if the circumstances of the moment were to give place to a radically changed scenario.)

The energy crisis has exposed the vulnerability and the dependence of Europe in a vital field and has forced recognition of its political weakness and the precariousness of an association based on economic interests rather than on European consensus and identity.

Europe has, for many years, been content with the American protection guaranteed by the monopoly of the ultimate weapon and the nuclear shield. This reassuring situation belongs to the past since thermonuclear parity has become a reality and brings with it immobility and reciprocal paralysis of the nuclear arsenals of the superpowers.

Accordingly, conventional forces regain their importance, and the crushing Soviet superiority resulting from a constant qualitative and quantitative improvement establishes a definite break in the balance of forces—the guarantee of a difficult peace in a climate in which competition between the two systems is continuing without truce despite a détente.

Opening up reassuring prospects theoretically excluding any possibility of open conflict, the détente can only have a soothing effect on a Western public opinion receptive to pacifism and little inclined to sacrifice the well-being and quality of life for unpopular security expenditures which are considered useless. Thus the imbalance can only increase, aggravated by erosion of the will to defend and by clever propaganda aimed at encouraging this tendency by all possible means.

On the basis of these fundamental differences, the increase in the Soviet military potential and the constant reduction in the West's defensive effort, what can we expect in the foreseeable future? Certainly we can only make conjectures but, at this stage, reasonable assumptions can be made without falling into the trap of extravagance or fiction.

## CONSTANTLY CHANGING POLITICAL PANORAMA

In our analysis of an offensive founded on speed and surprise and making maximum use of recent technological developments, we deliberately accepted that the situation in the West would be similar to what we know today. If anything is certain, it is that the course of events is constantly changing and we only need to look at history to be sure of this.

Who could have foreseen in 1943, at the height of the confrontation between Hitler's Germany and the Allies, that fifteen years later the United States and the United Kingdom would be competing to sell the Federal Republic of Germany the most modern weapons and that thirty years later, this same Germany would occupy a dominant position in a Europe moving towards unification? What enlightened prophet, in the middle of the cold war or during the Korean War, could have foreseen that economic agreements would link the United States and the Soviet Union to exploit the resources of Siberia with American technological support? In the euphoria of the reconstruction of Europe and of the German and Japanese miracles, who could have thought that this remarkable prosperity was going to prove fragile as a result of its dependence on black gold, held by Arab States as a monopoly and used as a decisive political weapon?

We could go on quoting examples, but the fact of living with them daily makes them less perceptible in their two dimensions and obscures their overall effect on a world in continuous development. It is therefore within the bounds of possibility that even more surprising changes will upset our present quietude and lead to major changes in history.

It is possible that a major economic recession will release deep social currents and prepare the way for regimes favorable to communism under the protection of the Soviet Union. Leftist governments may appear in Italy or France and Europe may have the impact of a European failure in the painful attempts at political union. Would a general economic crisis lead to a strengthening of European cohesion or, on the contrary, to a slide back to nationalist and despotic positions, each country trying to save itself with no concern for its weaker partners?

We also should wonder about the role of a strong Germany with an un-contestable economic power assuming the leadership in a divided Europe. Social disturbances, wildcat strikes, endemic violence, general underemployment, administrative disorder, and regional confrontations (perhaps exploited by adverse propaganda or internal subversion) could well succeed in shaking the fragile democratic structures. Finally, what will happen when Tito dies or if Leonid Brezhnev's successor were a dominating Soviet military personality?

So many questions leave room for a wide variety of scenarios whose extensive repercussions on the balance of the world and the geo-strategic situation of the major powers is almost impossible to forecast.

## STRENGTH AND WEAKNESS;
## THE TEMPTATION OF POWER

In twenty years' time, the population explosion will have made a major change in the present data concerning the problem. Centrifugal movements may perhaps have shaken the foundations of the communist world, and nuclear proliferation will have made areas of the world explosive where previously only limited conflicts seemed possible.

And during these twenty years, Western Europe may have failed in its attempt at unity and fallen under communist influence or domination, thus extending the enormous Eurasian continental mass towards the Atlantic, the open seas, and Africa. Such a situation can only result from a growing imbalance of forces facing each other.

But what answer could be given to the strategy of the "fait accompli" which puts almost the whole of West Germany in the hands of the Soviet Union as both a pledge and a hostage against unlikely reprisals likely to lead to total destruction? The blind pursuit of pacifism at all price, the constant reduction in the will and the effort to defend, and the temptation to give way to short-term electoral gains rather than to essential long-term interests all tend to make the risk greater.

The weaker one is, the greater the risk of a conflict one wants to avoid at all costs. In the last ten years or so, Canada has reduced its forces in Germany by fifty percent; Belgium has reduced its combat brigades by a third, has withdrawn half of what is left onto national territory, and is about to reduce its compulsory military service from twelve to six months. Denmark has considerably cut down its forces and its military service time; the Federal Republic is reducing the time from eighteen to twelve months. Italy is carrying out a "restructurization" which goes with an appreciable reduction in its potential and the United Kingdom plans to make substantial savings in its defense efforts. The Netherlands also has just proposed a massive reduction in its armed forces, and the United States is undergoing continuous political pressure in the Senate to start withdrawing troops stationed in Europe.

All this is going on despite the fact that no positive conclusion has been reached in Vienna during the talks on balanced reductions of forces facing each other, known as MBFR (Mutual Balanced Force Reductions). At the same time, the Soviets have not withdrawn a single battalion from East Germany; their forces have been considerably strengthened in tanks, artillery, and attack helicopters, and their military service time has now been increased from twenty-four to thirty months.

Why these different behaviors in the East and West if the Soviet Union sincerely desires to reduce tension and to avoid possible confrontations? Must we naively believe in the declared peaceful intentions when no significant gesture appears to lessen the formidable military potential which can go into action at a day's notice depending on the turn of events?

This continuous erosion of Europe's defense potential—which can only get worse if the present trend continues—will very likely lead us to the breaking point. Indeed, the geographical scenario is unchangeable. The 800 km. of frontier to be defended in Central Europe will be the same tomorrow, and the depth of the theater of operations will not change. On the other hand, the garrisons of troops on the spot will probably have been weakened; the intervention distances and the fronts to be defended by each division will increase to such a point that it is no longer logical or rational to envisage the possibility of coordinated defense.

We have reached a paradoxical situation. Below a certain limited threshold of conventional forces, it is no longer reasonable to agree to defense expenditures when it is known that it is no longer possible to use the forces under acceptable assumptions. It is no longer reasonable to maintain tanks without crews when it is known for a fact that any attempt at manning them will be overtaken by the speedy action of the adversary. The uninitiated must be aware that a defensive sector cannot be extended at will. A certain troop density in the field remains the prime condition for stopping the enemy and being in a position to use tactical nuclear weapons.

It is here that the skeptics ask (with disarming sincerity which shows deep ignorance of the restrictions and techniques involved) about the use of this vast deployment of troops whose role has become derisory or insignificant in comparison with the gigantic nuclear arsenals of the superpowers which make any war in Europe impossible because it would lead to the apocalypse and reciprocal destruction. This argument is so often invoked that it seems worth answering once and for all.

## THE CREDIBILITY OF THE NUCLEAR RESPONSE

In his work *Stratégie pour Demain*, General Beaufre considers that "nuclear deterrence stems from two essential but independent factors:

— the existence of an adequate and properly effective destruction capability;
— the *credibility* of the eventual use of this destruction capability.

Indeed, it is the *threat of use* of nuclear weapons which deters. It is the evaluation of this threat which measures the degree of deterrence effectively achieved."[1] (My emphasis.)

Under the assumption we have taken and developed, and in view of the speed of operations associated with the achievement of surprise, it seems impossible for the tactical nuclear weapons to be used even partially to support a land battle. It is possible, however, that the Allied air forces make use of their nuclear armament to destroy military targets belonging to the adversary. Such an action is *possible* but not *certain* since any use of the nuclear weapon, at whatever level it may be, would be subject to the prior approval of the president of the United States.

We have tried to demonstrate how difficult it would be to make this decision in an uncertain and even chaotic situation resulting from winning a territorial stake in a minimum of time, thus ensuring the success of the "fait accompli" strategy. We then wonder if the threat or the actual use of tactical nuclear weapons would force the Soviets to evacuate the conquered territories. Nothing is less certain if we examine the problem in an overall context in which we must necessarily take into account Western public opinion which is little prepared to undergo a nuclear holocaust.

Furthermore, we must also be reminded of the possible positive results of a nuclear counterattack from the moment when the targets of the surprise attack are reached: the temporary interruption of the Soviet lines of communication on the Vistula, the Oder, or the Elbe; the impact on the speed and success of operations already completed; and a firm warning before the escalation. But the United States would then have to resolve to go to extremes and use its strategic reprisal capabilities against the Soviet Union itself. Such a threat would be conceivable and would probably be followed by decisive effects if the United

States still had that atomic monopoly it held for years. Unfortunately, that earlier situation has completely changed and a decision of the kind would come up against the fear of reprisals on the sale scale—the possibility of the destruction of the United States by the Soviet Union's second strike force.

We feel that the stakes involved are too disproportionate for such an assumption to be taken seriously, since it involves an absolute determination, a prior consensus among the European Allies, and a disregard for the vital interests of the United States.

A limited reprisal against the Soviet troops in West Germany seems even more unlikely in view of the enormous losses which would be inflicted on the civilian population and the inevitable unfavorable reaction of public opinion. The fragility, if not the precariousness, of a flexible response nuclear strategy is immediately apparent as soon as the conventional forces required for such a strategy are not available. Their thinning out or disappearance makes it necessary to go to extremes, to the strategic and massive reprisals which are inconceivable because of thermonuclear parity. As a result we find another paradoxical consequence in the attitude of the pacifists—supporters of a unilateral reduction in the armed forces as goodwill toward an adversary who is thought to have only good intentions. *The raising of the nuclear threshold* is the direct result of such irrational behavior.

In other words, the trend which encourages the dismantling of our conventional forces and their chronic weakness results in a parallel increase in the risks of a nuclear conflagration at strategic level—the end of our civilization—and prevents recourse to a more subtle strategy concerned with not sinking into the irreparable and irreversible. It would probably be interesting to see if the reader could provide an answer to the terrible dilemma in which the president of the United States would find himself if he had to assume this vast responsibility.

An analysis of the answers might give an indication of the degree of confidence that the Europeans have in the "American atomic umbrella," and by that very fact provide a statistical measurement of the credibility of the nuclear response.

## THE AMBIVALENCE OF THE SOVIET UNION— STRATEGY AND TACTICS

It is difficult to present the aims of the Soviet Union's foreign policy. In the first chapter, we recalled that security and expansion were the foundations of the foreign policy of the great powers. According to some, the Soviet Union solely claims the first of these and its behavior is justified by the need to guarantee its security at all costs. This interpretation provides an explanation for putting the satellite states under Soviet protection since they are destined to serve as a barrier or buffer against aggression launched by the West. The obsession about encirclement will always be present in the minds of the Soviet leaders, and this is undoubtedly the reason for their incessant efforts to develop their naval forces and to extend their activities to all the seas of the world.

The building of the vast thermonuclear arsenal can only be seen as an appropriate answer to achieve and maintain strategic balance with the United States. The vulnerability of enormous frontiers, a latent threat on *two fronts*, is sufficient justification for this aggravated concern to guarantee security by all available means.

The weakness of NATO in conventional forces, the crushing imbalance of the capabilities facing each other, and the purely defensive nature of the Alliance exclude any direct danger from that side. Accordingly, the slogans about "German revanchism," "capitalist imperialism," and the "resurgence of a military clique" should be put on the shelf.

In the East it is clear that despite the Chinese demographic mass, there is no offensive capability for attack by the Chinese. They are certainly numerous but are incapable of launching an offensive into the vastness of Soviet territory because they cannot provide continuous logistic support and because of the low quality of their units.

Therefore there can be no plausible reason, based on potential threat against the security of the USSR, for maintaining and developing conventional forces which far exceed their needs. The same does *not* apply in the nuclear field. A major nuclear capability, although less than that of the Soviet Union, exists in Europe, and China has started a development program which, within ten years, will put it in the ranks of the medium-sized powers.

It is not easy to draw an absolutely clear line between the requirements of security and the tendency towards expansionism. While the first of these undoubtedly prevailed from 1945 to 1965, it seems certain that the second is now becoming more important.

Wondering about the possibility of future aggression against Western Europe, we have concluded in the negative *as far as the immediate future is concerned*. One of the characteristics of the power politics of the Soviet Union is its prudent and circumspect approach, as well as its reticence, about engaging *directly* in a conflict except if *its* direct interests are involved. Korea, Cuba, Vietnam, Angola, Ethiopia, and Shaba illustrate this concept. But this is not to say that it will always be the case.

Soviet strategy was clearly defined by Lenin; it proposes to dominate the world and to ensure final triumph over all other ideological systems. The tactics depend on the circumstances of the moment with a view to taking the maximum advantage of the weaknesses of the adversary and the contradictions of the capitalist world. The strategy is aimed at the top of the mountain. The tactics represent all the possible ways of reaching it; their routes may be winding or may move away from the final target, but in the long run will finish by reaching it.

The ambivalence of the Soviet Union appears again in this surprising paradox as the most convinced and aggravated feeling of nationalism in a power that claims kinship with orthodox internationalism and wants to be the uncontested leader. In any case, history has proved that although the national interests of the Soviet Union oppose those of the international, it is certainly these national interests which will take precedence. Herein lies a disconcerting evolution which has made the Soviet Union change from ideological proselytism to the expansionist ambitions of a superpower, following the most conventional rules of nationalism.

This ambiguous position enables it to carry on confrontation on two fronts and to use the apparatus of brother parties to follow, in the name of the common ideology, the struggle against capitalism and to undermine the democratic structures from inside. Here again tactics vary from the stiffest opposition to the most attractive offers of cooperation. Despite appearances, it is doubtful whether the final aim has been changed. Thus, whatever the future intentions of the Soviet Union, we can only make assumptions on this subject.

What guides nations, today just as much as yesterday, is the pursuit of their interests without any regard for the spectacular reversals of their past policies if the need arises. One only has to think of the Ribbentrop-Molotov pact, of the United States-Soviet Union rapprochement, of the abandonment of Taiwan by the United States, to quote examples in support of this argument.

Thus, intentions belong to the uncertain, the precarious. They depend on unforeseeable combinations of circumstances linked with the personalities of the political leaders. On the other hand, the instruments of power, whether they be economic or whether they constitute the essence of the military apparatus, are *certain data.*

We have tried to show that the Soviet Union has a sufficient capability to hold Europe as a hostage, under the most favorable circumstances, or to become its master if the occasion demanded without endangering the socialist edifice and its vital interests. This possibility, which no one can reasonably deny, brings with it the fundamental question of whether Europe can be satisfied with a state of masked subjection, of permanent dependence, and of a potential threat which hangs over its destiny and hampers its freedom of action.

## RESPONSIBILITIES AND THE
## JUDGMENT OF HISTORY

History abounds in examples in which, despite warnings, politicians have brought a whole nation to its knees or caused thousands and sometimes millions of deaths. I will only mention a few of the more significant cases; some refer to the failure to appreciate technological progress and others relate to surprise and the unbelievable blindness of men.

"In 1912, French soldiers always wore the blue cloak, the kepi and red trousers." Messimy, the minister of war, after visiting the Balkan front, observed that the dull color of the Bulgarians gave them a marked advantage in a war in which fire power and range of the weapons demanded that the soldier be made less visible. His proposal to abandon the red trousers came up against general opposition. Etienne, an earlier minister of war, cried out at the Palai Bourbon: "Do away with the red trousers? Never! Red trousers, that is France!"[2] "This blind and idiotic attachment to the most glaring of all colors was to have cruel consequences," Messimy wrote.

Let us also remember that the three-year law, voted in 1913 as a result of Poincaré's influence and despite socialist opposition, was threatened in July 1914 a few weeks before the war started.

A similar example may be found in General Beaufre's book, *The Drama of 1940* (*Le drame de 1940*). It is worth quoting in full.

> My first task enabled me to get to the heart of the problem immediately. I was asked for a study on the possibility of reducing military service to eight months. I did not understand: the service which was then one year was obviously insufficient when Hitler was already the Chancellor of Germany. . . .

> It was explained to me that the request came from the Marshal himself who wanted, it appeared, to give tokens to the left. Furthermore, a few days later he declared to the Army Commission that he opposed any increase in military service which without any doubt was contrary to our military requirements of the time.

> We were thus right in the middle of parliamentary maneuverings; the opposite of what public opinion, which had put its confidence in Doumergue and Marshal Pétain, was awaiting.

Here we find one of the constant factors of democratic regimes. Conscription and hence the duration of military service has always been the stake in an electoral policy aimed at currying favor with a public opinion concerned at seeing the cost of military service reduced. In this connection, troops numbers inevitably shrink as the years go by, units are incomplete, and military training covers only half or a third of the service time. In brief, the defense effort loses all its effectiveness and the costly equipment, which absorbs a major part of the budget, is only partially used. The nation must therefore accept what may be called a sterile investment.

There is nothing very new in all this. It is sufficient to quote Beaufre again to realize that (in 1975, as in the years before 1940) identical causes are giving rise to similar effects:

As a result of this system, the Army survived but did no more than rub along in a poor sort of a way. Everything I had gone through in Algeria was now explained: the skeleton forces weakened by fatigues and guard duties, the individual training completed in a slap-dash manner in four months and then all the available men being converted into "employees", i.e. cooks, messengers, secretaries, grooms, drivers, storekeepers, etc.—the batallions could never be trained in their wartime task. The officers and NCOs stagnated in administration or the basic training of recruits. Those called up too often had the impression, as Marshal de Lattre said later, of a military service which was no more than a sterile break just as they were becoming men. The army was using its substance to lie around in clothes too big for it.

It is particularly striking to note that, ten years earlier, General van Overstraeten expressed himself in similar terms:

Our military state of preparedness was then at its lowest. Since the armistice, Belgium had operated a Major Power foreign policy. It took a front seat at all the conferences which involved the application of the Treaty of Versailles; one of our army corps took part in the occupation of the Rhineland. But behind this pretentious façade, our franc had fallen under financial embarrassments, our regiments were wilting in the stagnant pool of a detestable militia law and public opinion was claiming a reduction in military expenditures. Acting counter to the wishes of the General Staff which was demanding military service of 20 months, parliament had reduced this service to 12 months, then to 10 months and had limited national servicemen to 49,500 men, 5,000 of which were unfit for anything but auxiliary employment, and had adopted the deplorable principle of recruiting the national servicemen half at a time at intervals of five months. Under this régime, the time spent on training was limited to the first five months. During the second half of their service, half the national servicemen acted as cooks, messengers, orderlies, workmen, etc. They forgot what they had learned and lost the spirit of discipline and drill. No unit got beyond the stage of recruit school. Companies and squadrons never reached the state of being trained, coherent, homogeneous units; this distressed the good officers, whereas the national serviceman felt that his call-up time tended to make him a fatigue-duty man rather than a fighting soldier; their families shared this feeling. As regards the unfit, they were no more than "hospital fodder". This disastrous system bore the fruits it deserved: the national regarded the army with horror. . . .[3]

It is hardly necessary to recall that a few years later Belgium and then France collapsed under the decisive blows of an army which had succeeded in forging a powerful military tool and in taking advantage of strategic surprise.

Must the lessons of history always be relearned at the cost of bloody losses and disastrous devastations or must it be admitted that, like the emigrés of the old regime, our political leaders have "nothing forgotten and nothing learned"?

We have pointed out the permanent lack of preparation and the precariousness of the defense and security effort, but it is in quite another field that a mistake is still more obvious.

Despite the most alarming signs and the clearest indications, surprise has nearly always succeeded in catching the adversary on the wrong foot. We need only remember Hitler's offensive against the Soviet Union in June 1941 and the obstinacy of Stalin, deaf to the warnings and alerts which reached him from all directions.

Pearl Harbor, followed by the destruction of part of the American fleet, is a sufficiently well-known historical fact. It only needs to be stressed that, before the event, it had appeared inconceivable that a Japanese fleet and its aircraft carriers could cover thousands of nautical miles without being detected to reach a position to attack the biggest naval base in the Pacific, and accomplish their task of destruction there without any significant reaction on the part of the American fleet and air force.

Another striking example is the landing in North Africa on November 8, 1942. Was it conceivable that a fleet of more than 800 ships converging on the coasts of Morocco and Algeria could succeed in reaching its targets without the Germans being able to suspect its final destination? Goering did not believe in a landing in North Africa and Hitler, who was concerned with Crete, only learned about the events at about three in the morning when the vast armada, which had spent two days almost within sight of Gibraltar and Algeciras, was already on the spot.[4]

More recently, the invasion of Czechoslovakia in August 1968 and the Arab offensive against Israel in October 1973 have demonstrated that surprise is the normal state of affairs and remains a vital factor in any offensive operation.

No one could predict with certainty when the Warsaw Pact forces would cross the Czechoslovakian frontier, reaching their assigned targets in record time. In October 1973, misled by preliminary deployments of the Arab forces, Israel only just escaped defeat, and the surprise effect had been achieved despite an intelligence service considered to be one of the best in the world. The Entebbe raid in 1976 astounded the world with the audacity of its concept and its execution.

All of these examples—and there are others—clearly show that an operation of the kind we have described is not only technically possible but carries with it the greatest chances of success. Chronic unpreparedness, linked with the lack of will to foresee the likely moment, location, and forces of an enemy who has the necessary tool for achieving strategic surprise, can only facilitate the preliminary conditions for an action.

If the assumption were one day to become reality, how would the responsibilities be established, and who would be called to task? It is likely that no one would be accused of incompetence or blindness for having followed "the spirit of the times" and having chosen to make immediate sacrifices rather than guarantee an uncertain future. In the interval, the dice would have been cast and history (which laughs at human errors) would have been made, endorsing a significant upheaval in the geo-strategic balance, with losses of human life and material destruction and perhaps an escalation to the extremes, putting at risk the very existence of our civilizations.

It seems unlikely that this long analysis of strategy, made possible by the parity in the nuclear weapons systems and the growing imbalance in conventional forces, will meet with enthusiastic acceptance and lead to concrete measures being taken to reduce, if not eliminate, the deep causes of the present insecurity and instability. It is certainly less difficult to follow the easy path, in contrast to making the effort, and it is certainly not the "voice crying in the wilderness" which will be able to alter this state of affairs.

But it is important to inform public opinion, which is too inclined to trust in the apparent signs of "peaceful coexistence" and is only too happy to believe that it can eliminate all sources of conflict and all occasions for confrontation. In the final analysis, what counts is the maintenance of peace.

In this world of constant evolution, each side claims for itself an unconditional pacifism whose arrangements are still obscure. The absurdity of war, the chain reaction catastrophes it unleashes, and the irreparable damage it might cause through the new power available to it, *should lead the responsible States* to reflect on the stupidity of using violence to settle differences. A general agreement banishing recourse to war would permit no further recourse to open conflict in order to settle arguments between the nations. Fear would be eliminated, and good faith and respect for undertakings would make it useless to maintain armed forces.

An international law organization would enable the quarrels between sovereign States to be settled by arbitration, substituting the rule of law for that of force.

For others, the best way of preventing a conflict which they want to avoid at all costs is recourse to deterrence, involving a policy of coherent defense matched by the necessary forces, both nuclear and *conventional*, to guarantee its credibility. The maintenance of sufficient forces and the human and financial effort involved are based on the lessons of history, on the constancy of human evolution, and on the impossibility of foreseeing the turn of political events.

These two schools of thought differ as to method but not aim. The first claims for itself a certain idealism, a logic of thought based on the absurdity of recourse to violence which, in the thermonuclear age, is liable to lead to escalation and the final cataclysm marking the end of civilization.

The other, more realistic, demonstrates a declared skepticism regarding the possibility of codifying international relations so that any risk of aggression may be avoided. It is based on experience of the past to support its argument, and on the fact that nations have always pursued their own interests. It also observes that any state of weakness or break in the balance of forces tends to encourage the aggressor, convinced that he will encounter no real opposition and will be able to achieve his warlike aims at relatively little cost.

It seems to us that the birth of the Atlantic Alliance was founded on these realistic observations. A quarter of a century of peace, the end of the cold war, and the announcement of détente characterized by a unilateral reduction in defense effort, have made our security precarious and our dependence more apparent than ever.

Comparison of the forces facing each other is unrealistic since it is limited to recording the relative values of static systems. Our present inferiority will go on growing if we do not react. The initiative we recognize as the prerogative of the adversary is a multiplying factor which further increases the disparity. This disconcerting situation could lead to formidable temptations for the Eastern Bloc to change the world geo-strategic balance in its favor.

Europe is feeling its way but it would be wrong for us to think that there is unlimited time available for us to reach our destiny. It seems to us that ensuring our security, as the equal partners of the Americans and with their assistance, is an aim which is both reasonable and achievable.

We have tried to demonstrate that the progressive deterioration of our military capabilities has been due to our inability to unite, to share armament research and production efforts, to harmonize tactical and strategic concepts, or to divide our defense burden on an equitable basis.

But the very basis of our weakness lies in the absence of political will. To establish the structure into which a coherent European defense will fit is not an insurmountable undertaking. But who will begin? Which political leader will go down in history as having taken up the European challenge and established a sound, effective, and homogeneous security system?

We feel that the enormous stake involved should be sufficient to provoke a reasonable effort on the part of the 250 million Europeans of the Nine to succeed in assuming responsibility for their own security, and no longer to depend exclusively on the United States in this vital area. If this effort were to be considered hopeless, the hope of a political Europe would fade away without any possibility of return.

As R. Woller has said: "If the answer is not found, the process of European unification no longer has any chance of being continued. What cannot be defended, in accordance with the classic definition of sovereignty, is not politically viable."[5]

Two worlds are facing each other: that of the "Gulag Archipelago" and that of freedom. Pray God that we may still have the possibility of making our choice and that our future will not depend on the plans of the Stavka and on the unforeseeable results of events which might take place on "that Sunday."

# Appendixes

# Appendix A

CONGRESSIONAL RECORD    JUNE 8, 1976

## Is NATO Militarily Viable?

Mr. TAFT, Mr. President, I noted in the RECORD of May 4 that I would, over the next few months, bring to the attention of my colleagues articles on the vital subject, "Is NATO Militarily Viable?" Accordingly, I ask unanimous consent that, at the conclusion of my remarks, an article from the Colorado Springs Sun "Slow Decisions Endanger NATO," by Mr. T.R. Milton, be printed in the Record.

The PRESIDING OFFICER. Without objection, it is so ordered.

Mr. TAFT, Mr. President, this article discusses the views of two reputable authorities on NATO, Brigadier Close of the Belgian Army and Gen. Johannes Steinhoff of the German Bundeswehr. Both of these authorities suggest that NATO is today very vulnerable to a surprise attack of the Warsaw Pact in Central Europe. Mr. Milton, in turn, raises two points which I think should be considered:

243

First. Forces intended to react to any surprise attack must be on the spot in Central Europe; they cannot be reinforcements intended to come from the United States. This means that these should largely be European, not American ground forces.

Second. U.S. participation in NATO should be conditioned on NATO being conventionally viable in central Europe. If NATO cannot resist a Soviet attack with conventional weapons, the United States is left "holding the bag", in that the situation will inevitably escalate to a strategic nuclear confrontation between the United States and the Soviet Union with the United States being the Nation under pressure to do the escalating.

I believe that it is possible for NATO to meet the Soviets successfully in a conventional conflict, providing certain changes are made. The prime responsibility, and perhaps ultimately the sole responsibility, for quick-reaction ground forces must be taken over by the Europeans. NATO'S forces must be concentrated in north Germany, where the main Soviet thrust will most probably come. New concepts, such as reorienting the direction of the fighting from an east-west to a north-south direction, must be explored. The United States must undertake to develop adequate naval capability to insure control of the Atlantic within a short time after the outbreak of hostilities.

As Mr. Milton notes, the reforms needed to make NATO militarily viable should perhaps be a condition for continued U.S. participation in the alliance. I strongly urge my colleagues to read this article, and to give serious thought to EXHIBIT I. SLOW DECISIONS ENDANGER NATO (By T.R. Milton).


## Slow Decisions Endanger NATO

A few weeks ago a Belgian, Brigadier Close, caused a major flap in Europe by his prediction that the Russians could reach the Rhine River in 48 hours while NATO was debating his moves.

Brigadier Close is Vice-Commandant of the NATO Defense College, in Rome, and his prediction was part of a study that apparently was intended for internal use only. Our allies follow their leader, the United States, in most things, and so the report leaked.

Naturally enough, the NATO officials denounced the study amid scattered cries for Brigadier Close's head.

Unhappily for those who had hoped the matter would now go away, a new book has just appeared arriving at much the same conclusion. It is called "Where Is Nato Drifting To?" or however the German translates, and it is by General Johannes Steinhoff.

Now General Steinhoff is not just your everyday military expert. He is a most distinguished figure who did a brilliant job of turning the modern German Air Force into one of NATO's principal assets and who served three years in NATO's highest post as Chairman of the Military Committee. I was his Deputy for a time, then worked closely with him for several more years as a member of the Committee.

In the course of those years we became friends, and I began to understand just how deeply Johannes Steinhoff feels about the need to preserve Western freedom, and how deep are his worries about Western resolve.

For this man, who shot down 175 airplanes in World War II and who suffered through more than 100 major operations to repair his burned and shattered face and body, is that rare species, a Free-World patriot who puts our collective freedom above national interests.

His book has attracted great attention in Europe because of the great respect he commands in all the NATO countries, even in those lands where Germans in general are not yet forgiven for the last war. General Steinhoff's worries about a declining NATO's ability to resist are vastly more difficult for NATO officials to discount than those of the Belgian Brigadier.

Briefly, General Steinhoff is concerned over the inability of NATO to react to a sudden Soviet Attack. He fears that political uncertainties between members of the Alliance would contribute to this inability. He goes on to cite the well-known deficiencies in NATO: lack of standardization, poor deployment and general lack of readiness of NATO units.

He is scornful, in his book, of the American promise of reinforcement by airlift. This comes as no surprise for he was scornful of this concept years ago when Secretary McNamara first unveiled it. Gen. Steinhoff, along with many Europeans, thought they saw in this notion the groundwork being laid for major American troop withdrawals from Europe. At any rate, Gen. Steinhoff thinks any such dependence on trans-Atlantic airlift a fatal strategy. The reaction forces to any Soviet attack must be on the spot in sufficient numbers, and ready.

It is increasingly hard for people to worry about things like this, even for Germans who can look across a minefield at the enemy himself. It is certainly difficult for Americans to worry about it.

Yet everything General Steinhoff is saying needs to be listened to carefully. It is a fact that the Alliance is going slowly downhill. In the old days of NATO, the capability of the European allies was not so important. What mattered was the U.S. and his nuclear weapons. Now that the Soviets have brought nuclear capability to a standing, the capability of NATO to respond in a non-nuclear way, at least at the start, is an essential part of its credibility as a military alliance. That credibility is what is now being questioned.

The fact is that NATO, our guarantor these past 26 years of a Europe free of Soviet domination, is in desperate need of an overhaul. The absolute democracy on which it was founded, in which Luxembourg, for instance, can veto a proposal to use nuclear weapons, or even to go to a higher state of alert, should be looked at in light of the new dangers NATO faces.

The Alliance now consists of a loose collection of national forces. There is no NATO unit as such. When the time comes, it is assumed the NATO politicians will gather and agree unanimously that the forces will be mobilized and turned over to international command. The Supreme Allied Commander in Europe, presently General Haig, must await unanimous decision before he has an Allied force in being. Meanwhile, say Brigadier Close and General Steinhoff, the Russians are at the Rhine.

These are things which must be thought about. The Soviet star is in the ascendancy these days. The lure of an adventurous thrust into Europe will become ever more enticing as the Soviets perceive a weakening and indecisive NATO. It is just as true now as it has been for NATO's creation that this Alliance is utterly dependent on United States leadership.

Leadership sometimes requires taking a tough line. The time for such a display of leadership has, it would seem, come. The things that need fixing are mainly in General Steinhoff's book. Since there is no point in the U.S. participating in an Alliance that cannot react to a Soviet attack—NATO's only real purpose— perhaps our next president should lay down some conditions for our continued participation.

# Appendix B

**EXCERPTS FROM A SPEECH DELIVERED BY
PRESIDENT CARTER BEFORE THE
FOREIGN POLICY ASSOCIATION IN NEW YORK
ON JUNE 23, 1976**

"We face a more immediate problem in the Atlantic Sector of our defense. The Soviet Union has in recent years strengthened its forces in Central Europe. The Warsaw Pact forces facing NATO today are substantially composed of Soviet combat troops, and these troops have been modernized and reinforced. In the event of war, they are postured for an all-out conflict of short duration and great intensity.

NATO's ground combat forces are largely European. The U.S. provides about one fifth of the combat element, as well as the strategic umbrella and without this American commitment Western Europe could not defend itself successfully.

In recent years, a new military technology has been developed by both sides, including precision-guided munitions, that are changing the nature of land warfare.

Unfortunately, NATO's arsenal, suffering from a lack of standardization, too often seems wedded to the past plans and concepts. We must not allow our Alliance to become an anachronism.

In all of this a major European and joint effort will be required, our people will not support unilateral American contributions in what must be truly mutual defense effort."

# Appendix C

## IMBALANCE OF SALES OF MILITARY EQUIPMENT BETWEEN THE UNITED STATES AND EUROPE[1]

### I. United States sales of military equipment to Western Europe

|  | United States Fiscal Year | | | | | | % of total military procurement |
|---|---|---|---|---|---|---|---|
|  | 1967 | 1968 | 1969 | 1970 | 1971 | 1972 | (1972) |
| Belgium | 9.3 | 6.4 | 0.6 | 7.9 | 6.2 | 7.4 | 5 |
| France | 15.7 | 12.6 | 25.1 | 12.4 | 15.8 | 3.7 | 1.5 |
| Italy | 29.3 | 50.1 | 50.4 | 50.4 | 50.2 | 41.6 | 6 |
| Netherlands | 5.7 | 18.2 | 12.6 | 6.4 | 10.2 | 7.5 | 2 |
| Federal Republic of Germany | 309.1 | 156.3 | 207.5 | 226.2 | 333.3 | 430.8 | 27 |
| United Kingdom | 156.9 | 270.5 | 369.5 | 221.5 | 118.6 | 79.9 | 3 |
| Totals in Western Europe[2] | 575.3 | 561.6 | 750.2 | 639.4 | 410.5 | 650.1 | 6 |
| % of total United States Sales throughout the world | 62.7 | 55.1 | 57.1 | 44.5 | 41.9 | 43.5 |  |

*Source:* United States Department of Defense, Security Assistance Agency, May, 1973.

*Notes:*

[1]WEU Document 689: "European and Atlantic Cooperation in the Field of Armaments" (Rapporteur: Mr. Lemmrich), December 1, 1975, Annex VI, page 32.

[2]All Western European countries except Greece and Turkey.

## II. European sales of military equipment in North America

The only producer country able to export a significant quantity of equipment to North America (directly or manufacturing under license) was the United Kingdom.

*United Kingdom sales for the period 1972-74* (in millions of U.S. dollars)

| | | |
|---|---|---|
| to Canada | 28.0 | (Blowpipe tactical missile) |
| to the United States | 111.8 | (Harrier V/STOL aircraft) |

# Appendix D

# F.A.S.

**FEDERATION OF AMERICAN SCIENTISTS**
307 Massachusetts Avenue, N.E.
Washington, D.C. 20002  (202) 546-3300

| George W. Rathjens | John T. Edsall | Jerome D Frank | Frank von Hippel | Jeremy J. Stone |
|---|---|---|---|---|
| *Chairman* | *Secretary* | *Vice-Chairman* | *Treasurer* | *Director* |

July 5, 1978

Maj. Gen. Robert Close
The Belgian Corps
c/o The Belgian Embassy
3330 Garfield Street, NW
Washington, DC  20008

Dear General Close:

First, my warm thanks for the insight into the preparedness of the Belgian Army and into NATO problems generally which was provided for our group from the Council on Foreign Relations.

As I said I would, I asked the Belgian Embassy for a copy in English of your book "Europe without Defense" and have examined it with great interest.

You make the case for the possibility of Soviet surprise attack with great power but, I think, lay stress on the less likely--though more dramatic--problem. I think the heart of the matter concerns the sounding of the alert. As you realize, your own calculations are extremely optimistic since the alert has never before been sounded (i.e., the process has never been exercised) and the NATO Council must, as I understand it, agree unanimously. It seems to me that a sounding of the alert, under these circumstances, before Soviet forces cross the border, is most unlikely.

But the worst and, I think, most likely case occurs when there is ambiguity about Soviet intentions or even an absence of ambiguity in favor of a benign interpretation such as the invasion of Czechoslovakia. Here NATO is unlikely to alert itself lest it "inflame" a situation in Eastern Europe while forces pile up on its own frontier. This would be asking for trouble but, I think, NATO is likely to do it. I make the case for this problem in the attached newsletter. Personally, I think the SHAPE commanders should have the authority to sound "military vigilance" and I am trying to get some attention to this view here in America.

In any case, General Close, I think your approach is nearer the truth than that of most of your NATO colleagues. I only wish I were sufficiently well informed on conventional warfare problems to make the case here as convincingly as you can.

With sincere regards,

Cordially,

*Jeremy J. Stone*

Jeremy J. Stone

# Notes and Bibliography

# Notes

## CHAPTER 1

1. Alexis de Tocqueville, *La démocratie in Amérique*, introduction.
2. Bourquin, *Les Aspirations Federalistes. La Sainte Alliance*, chapter 4.
3. "The OECD Observer," 1975 Ed. 11th year, No. 74, March-April 1975.
4. In the United Kingdom at the end of 1970, a quarter of the electorate, i.e. 10.5 million adults, had no experience of the events of the Second World War or the beginning of the cold war. (G.L. Williams and A.L. Williams, *Crisis in European Defence* [London: London and Tonbridge, 1974] p. 69.)
5. Général Beaufre, *Stratégie pour domain*.
6. Address before the Economic Club of Detroit, November 24, 1975 (U.S. Information Service).
7. Guy de Carmoy, *Fortune de l'Europe* (Paris: Domat, 1953), p. 260.
8. *Le Monde*, December 25, 1952, quoted by Guy de Carmoy (see n.5 supra), p. 272.

# CHAPTER 2

1. "U.S. Foreign Policy for the 1970s: Building for Peace," Report to Congress, February 25, 1971.
2. Donald E. Naechterlein, "The Influence of Domestic Politics on American Foreign Policy." (Paper prepared for the Political Studies Association's Annual Conference at Nottingham University, March 22-24, 1976, p. 9.)
3. This "disengagement" of the American option with regard to Europe was stressed by the American participants in the 179th Conference at Wilton Park (March 26-April 10, 1976).
4. See "Copy of the Plan for European Domination" left by Peter the Great to his successors on the throne of Russia. Part was copied at Peterhoff by Chevalier d'Eonde Beaumont and given to the Duc de Choisenl in 1760. Quoted in 1812 in "Table of Progress of Russian Power," ed. Lesur, p. 177. See also "Chevalier d'Eons Memoires" (1836), 3:169.
5. The Austrian minister Achrenthal had supported this project in exchange for Russian agreement to the annexation of Bosnia-Herzegovina by Austria.
6. Note also the Russian intervention, supporting the Austrian armies, to put an end to any desire for independence on the part of Kossuth's revolutionary government in Hungary; and the repression of two Polish revolutions in 1849 and 1863.
7. G. Kennan, *Russia, the Atom and the West* (1958) p. 35, quoted by W. Knapp, *A History of War and Peace 1939-1965* (Oxford University Press, 1967) p. 446.
8. As was the case during the 1956 uprisings in Poland and Hungary. See n.7 supra, p. 363.
9. Knapp (see n.7 supra), p. 136.
10. With the exception of the Nordic countries (Denmark and Norway) which do not accept the presence of nuclear weapons on their soil, and of Luxembourg, Iceland, and Portugal. The restrictions on their use by the other allies stem from the double key procedure.
11. Let us try to imagine how, in May 1940 after the Sedan breakthrough, France could have effectively used nuclear weapons against Rommel's armored brigades pursuing their rush to the sea and mingling with the French civilian population and the logistic rear areas of the armies. *Express*, No. 1298, 24-30 May 1976, Readers' Letters, Letter from General Close.
12. See Hélène Carrère d'Encausse, "La politique soviétique au Moyen-Orient 1955-1975," *Presse de la Fondation Nationale des Sciences Politiques*, Paris 1976.
13. Pierre Hassner, "L'Equilibre international à l'heuredes SALT," *Revue francaise de Science Politique*, August 1973, quoted by Guy de Carmoy in "Force de Frappe et défense européene," *Revue Politique et Parlementaire*, No. 847, December 1973.

14. Lt. Colonel Guy Doly (author of *Stratégie France-Europe*), "Neutron Bombs: For or Against?," *Le Quotidien De Paris*, April 19, 1978.
15. Marc Geneste, "Un concept de défense crédible pour l'Occident: Les Murailles de la Cité," *Orbis* XIX (1975) No. 2; and *Stratégie*, 45 (1976).
16. André Fontaine, "L'Avoir ou pas? Se préparer pour l'imprévisible," *Le Monde*, August 21, 1973.
17. The "German White Paper on Defense" (1975-1976) is an excellent source of information in this connection (pp. 32-37). See also "The Military Balance" and its statistics regularly published by the International Institute for Strategic Studies, London.
18. See "Le déploiement stratégique des forces soviétiques," *L'Express* (1294) April 26-May 2, 1976.
19. "German White Paper" (see n.17 supra), p. 35.
20. de Carmoy (see Ch. 1, n.5 supra), p. 10.
21. "German White Paper" (see n.17 supra), p. 31.
22. Address by General George S. Brown, Chairman of the Joint Chiefs of Staff, Pensacola Area Chamber of Commerce, Pensacola, Florida, March 15, 1976 (U.S. Information Service, U.S. Embassy, Rome-Anno VI, March 16, 1976), p. 15.
23. *Le Monde*, June 2, 1976. Analyse de l'ouvrage d'Hélène Carrère d'Encausse, "La politique soviétique au Moyen-Orient 1955-1975."
24. When Churchill went to Moscow on October 9, 1944, an agreement was reached with Stalin on the sharing of their respective interests in the Balkans: Rumania: 90 percent Russia, 10 percent the others; Greece: 10 percent, 90 percent (Great Britain); Yugoslavia: 50 percent-50 percent; Hungary: 50 percent-50 percent; Bulgaria: 75 percent Russia, 25 percent the others (W. Knapp, ch. 2, n.7 supra, p. 61).

## CHAPTER 3

1. On June 11, 1948 Senator Vandenberg had a resolution passed by the Senate (64-4), addressed to the president of the United States, and expressing the senate's desire to see a continuation of the "progressive development of individual and collective defense measures in accordance with the aims, principles and clauses of the United Nations Charter." It requested that the United States should "through constitutional channels, be associated with these regional or collective measures based on individual, mutual, effective and continuous aid."
2. Jean Legaret and E. Martin-Dumesnil, *La Communauté européene de Défense*. Analytical study of the Treaty of May 27, 1952. (Paris: Vrin, 1953).
3. "Additional protocol to the North Atlantic Treaty relating to the assistance

commitments of the parties to the North Atlantic Treaty towards the member states of the European Defense Community" dated May 27, 1952, and "Protocol relating to the assistance commitments of the member states of the European Defense Community towards the member states of the North Atlantic Treaty."

4. André de Smet, *La Communauté Européene de Défense. Experience et leçons*, Heule (Belg.) Editions U.G.A., 1966, p. 32.
5. "Radical Congress at Bordeaux: Congress of the UDSR at Clermont-Ferrand," see n.2 supra.
6. Henry Frenay, *The European Defense Community (EDC)–Reply to General de Gaulle* (Paris: Presses de la C.I.T., March 1953).
7. de Carmoy (see Ch. 1, n.7 supra).

# CHAPTER 4

1. "The Sinews of Peace" (1946), pp. 198-202, quoted in Knapp (see Ch. 2 n.7 supra).
2. de Carmoy (see Ch. 1 n.5 supra), pp. 335-336.
3. On April 13, 1954, a convention was signed under which the United Kingdom undertook to nominate a representative of ministerial rank to attend the meetings of the council of ministers of the EDC where problems of cooperation between the community and the U.K. were discussed. See Knapp, Ch. 2 n.7, p. 301.
4. According to his memoirs, this idea came to him when he was having a bath. Knapp, Ch. 2, n.7 supra, p. 305.
5. The Israeli-Arab conflict and the embargo on Arab oil, the dock strike in London and Liverpool, and the slowing down of exports.
6. *No. 1 group* controlled nine Vulcan B-2 squadrons and *No. 3 group* six Victor BK-1 and B-2 squadrons, plus Victor and Canberra reconnaissance squadrons. (Neville Brown, European Security 1972-1980, A.V.S.I., April 1972, p. 63.)
7. *Hansard Parliamentary Debates*, Mr. Wall and Mr. Paget, March 1967.
8. *Ibid.*
9. House of Commons, Written Answers, April 17, and November 22, 1967 (Mr. Emrys Hughes).
10. Marshal of the RAF, Sir John Slessor, *Times* (London), June 1962.
11. £554 million in 1975-1976 (including £86 million on research alone). Statement on the Defense Estimates 1975, March 1975 Cmnd. 5976, p. 82.
12. Cmnd. 4290, Statement on Defense Estimates 1970, para. 40.
13. Cmnd. 2902, p. 30.
14. Statement on the Defense Estimates (see n.11 supra), p. 12, fig. 4.
15. *Ibid.*, p. 9, para. 25.

16. *Le Monde* (see Ch. 1 n.6 supra), August 19, 1978, p. 9.
17. Statement on the Defense Estimates (see n.11 supra), p. 9, para. 25.
18. "The indispensable foundation for more effective European cooperation on procurement and logistics is of course closer identity of views on the strategy and tactics which determine our operational requirements" (speech by the Secretary of State for Defense Denis Healey, at an American Chamber of Commerce luncheon in London, April 16, 1969). See also n.12 supra, p. 8, para. 39.

# CHAPTER 5

1. Guy de Carmoy, *Les politiques étrangères de la France (1944-1966)*, ed. de la Table Ronde (Paris, 1967), p. 71.
2. Paul Stehlin, *Retour à zéro. L'Europe et sa défense dans le compte à rebours* (Paris: Laffont, 1968), pp. 177 and 178.
3. de Carmoy (see n.1 supra), p. 247.
4. de Carmoy (see n.1 supra), p. 329.
5. H. Kissinger, *Transatlantic Misunderstandings* (Paris: Denoël, 1967), p. 29.
6. de Carmoy (see n.1 supra), p. 331.
7. James Bellini, *French Defense Policy* (London: R.V.S.I., 1974), p. 32; and Charles Aillert, *L'aventure atomique française* (Paris: Grasset, 1968), p. 143.
8. Ailleret (see n.7 supra), p. 143.
9. Bellini (see n.7 supra), p. 31.
10. Bellini (see n.7 supra), p. 33.
11. *Times*, July 25, 1960.
12. Bellini (see n.7 supra), p. 49.
13. Documents on American Foreign Relations, 1962, p. 245, quoted by Knapp, Ch. 2, n.7 supra, p. 464.
14. *White Book on National Defense*, 1 (1972): 63.
15. Ailleret (see n.7 supra), pp. 142-175.
16. Bellini (see n.7 supra), p. 49.
17. *Revue des Forces Aériennes Françaises*, October 6, 1964, No. 207, p. 446.
18. *Times*, April 30, 1963.
19. Quoted by Major General W.G.H. Beach, "The Springs of Policy," a study which appeared in *European Military Institutions—A Reconnaissance*, Universities Services Study Group, Scotland, p. 35.
20. Raymond Aron, *Le grand débat—Paix et guerre entre les nations*, 4th ed. (Paris: Calman Levy, 1966), p. 112.
21. *Revue de Défense Nationale* (Paris, May 1969), p. 207.
22. Fourth Fighter Group of two squadrons of Mirage III E at Luxeuil and the Seventh Group of two squadrons of "Jaguars" based at Saint-Dizier, a total

of sixty aircraft (Bellini, see n.7 supra, p. 56).

23. François de Rose, "Nuclear Weapons and the Alliance," *Foreign Affairs* (April 1963); *Survival* (July/August 1963): 151-161.

24. Declaration on the Atlantic relations (para. 6), approved by the North Atlantic Council at Ottawa (June 19, 1974) and signed by the NATO heads of government, Brussels, June 24, 1974.

25. Aron (see n.20 supra), p. 133.

26. *Le Monde* (see Ch. 1, no.6 supra), July 11, 1974 and July 6, 1974.

27. Article by Jean-Laurens Delpech, "Armaments," December 1975. See *Le Figaro*, June 30, 1970.

28. Aron (see n.20 supra), p. 119.

29. François de Rose, *La France et la Defense de l'Europe* (Paris: Seuil, 1976), pp. 10 and 13.

30. *Le Monde* (see Ch. 1, n.6 supra), p. 14.


# CHAPTER 6

1. 1970 White Paper on the security of the FRG and the situation of the Federal armed forces, Federal Government Press and Information Office, p. 40.

2. Western European Union Assembly, Twenty-First ordinary session, Doc. 663, April 2, 1975. Preface by Mr. Dankert.

3. See Appendix A. Permanent positions of the land forces in the Central Europe region on April 1, 1974 (from WEU Assembly, n.2 supra).

4. WEU Assembly (see n.2 supra), p. 17.

5. WEU Assembly (see n.2 supra), p. 27 and Appendix 1 (map).

6. More than fifty percent of land forces of Central Europe have to cover more than 100 km. to reach their combat positions (Johannes Steinhoff, *Wohin treibt die Nato? Probleme der Verteidigung Westeuropas* [Hamburg: Hoffman und Campe, 1976] ), p. 57.

7. WEU Assembly (see n.2 supra), p. 12.

8. Assessment (1974). These figures need to be increased to take inflation into account (see n.2 supra), p. 33.

9. WEU Assembly (see n.2 supra), p. 39.

10. Despite Senator Hubert Humphrey's criticisms of the "lamentably deficient state of preparation of American troops in Europe" (report not published by the General Accounting Office). Statement reprinted by the Belgian press (*Stendard, Dernière Heure, Le Peuple*, July 10, 1976). See also the article printed in *Krasnaia Zvezda* (journal of the Soviet armed forces, September 21, 1976) which, quoting a Pentagon report, mentions that in the depots in Europe, there are only thirty percent of the necessary quantities of medium tanks, that there are only 420 armored troop carriers

instead of the 1,029 needed, 147 guns instead of 294, and that there is a shortage of 2,400 radio sets (note by author: the latter obviously applies to the *American* forces in Europe).

11. White Paper (1970) on the security of the FRG and on the situation of the Federal Armed Forces (p. 10, para. 11).

12. Fifty ATK missile systems instead of thirteen for armored brigades and eighty-six instead of eight for the mechanized brigade (1975-1976 White Paper, p. 111).

13. "Surprise Attack Could Make Nuclear Weapons Useless," *The* (London) *Times*, March 15, 1976, p. 1.

14. "Consequences of War and Prevention of War," quoted by *Süddentsche Zeitung*, December 16, 1970, and by Beach (see Ch. 5, n.19 supra), p. 40.

15. WEU Assembly (see Ch. 6, n.2 supra), p. 47.


# CHAPTER 7


1. Prolonged neutrality or the fundamentally peaceful nature of the populations? As long ago as 1891, Belgian participation in the military effort was well below that of its neighbors. Per head of population it was 7.64 francs in Belgium, 16.22 in Holland, 16.64 in Germany, 22.53 in France, and 21.9 in England.

2. We should remember that the tank battalion of former times had *4* squadrons of 3 platoons of 5 tanks which, with the tanks of the headquarters, gave a total of 72 tanks. The present battalions have 3 squadrons of 4 platoons of 3 tanks, i.e. a total of 40 tanks. During the same period, the number of tanks of the Soviet mechanized division rose from 188 to 266, i.e. an increase of 41.4 percent. See John Erickson, *Soviet Theatre Forces and NATO Modernization* (Edinburgh: University of Edinburgh, 1976), p. 20.

3. Eighteen months of service time in April 1954 when a liberal/socialist coalition came to power (the bill had been submitted by the socialist leaders on February 4, 1953); reduction to fifteen months by Royal Decree of October 17, 1957 in view of the electoral campaign then in progress; twelve months service by Royal Decree of August 8, 1959, which came into force on September 27, 1959.

4. Mutual Defense Aid Programs. Since 1949, this has undergone major changes. Practically nothing to begin with, this aid very quickly rose to some 20 billion francs in 1952 and 1953. After that, it steadily decreased (1.5 billion in 1959 and 400 million in 1961), finally ceasing altogether in 1964.

5. On this subject see Johannes Steinhoff, *Wohin treibt die NATO? Probleme der Verteidigung Westeuropas* (Hamburg: Hoffmann und Campe, 1976), pp. 94-95.

6. Steinhoff (see n.5 supra), p. 116.
7. By themselves, Greece and Turkey represent a land mass of some 2,200 km. from east to west and 800 km. from north to south (see WEU Assembly, Doc. 671, p. 23).
8. *The Military Balance, 1975-76*, International Institute for Strategic Studies, September 1975, p. 17.
9. 48,000 men including 29,000 conscripts; 292 combat aircraft (The Military Balance, see n.8 supra, p. 26).
10. The NATO infrastructure projects in the Greece-Turkey area are assessed at $1.2 billion, i.e. twenty percent of all SHAPE infrastructure projects (WEU Assembly, see n.7 supra), p. 23.
11. Bitsios, Kissinger agreement. NATO Press Service, July 7, 1976.
12. WEU Doc. 671 (see n.7 supra), p. 24.
13. *The Military Balance*, 1975-1976 (see n.8 supra), p. 76. This percentage puts Italy at the bottom of the list of the Atlantic partners together with Luxembourg and Canada.
14. Twenty-one for the army, according to Steinhoff (see n.5 supra), p. 99.
15. Steinhoff (see n.5 supra), p. 99.
16. In order to get a better appreciation of the vastness of this sum, it must be compared with the total indebtedness of the Third World, assessed for 1976 at $54 billion (according to the Club of Rome) or with the debt of Eastern Europe to the West, which, at the end of 1975, had reached the enormous sum of $32 billion (according to Jean-François Revel, *L'Express*, July 26-August 1, 1976, p. 45).
17. Speech to Congress by Harry Bergold, assistant principal secretary of state for defense, on the importance of the new agreement reached between the United States and Spain (*Atlantic News*, no. 842, June 25, 1976, p. 2).

## CHAPTER 8

1. "Increases in the Unit Cost of Various Types of Military Equipment," from: Mary Kaldor, *European Defence Industries. National and International Implications* (Brighton: University of Sussex, England, 1972), p. 53.
2. *Ibid.*, p. 9.
3. International Institute for Strategic Studies, London, *The Military Balance 1968-69; 1971-72; 1975-76.*
4. "Indices of NATO Defence Expenditure, Current and *Constant* Prices (in local currency, 1970 = 100)," see *The Military Balance 1975-76*, n.4 supra.
5. President Ford's speech to the New England Council outlining the national security posture and policy of the United States (United States Information Service, Embassy of the U.S.A., Rome, November 10, 1975).

6. Tables on the "Federal budget and defence budget" and "evolution of defence budget proportion of the Federal budget from 1962 to 1974" are taken from *White Papper 1973-1974*. "The Security of the Federal Republic of Germany and the Evolution of the Federal Armed Forces," (Federal Defense Ministry, January 1974), p. 224.

7. Statistics taken from *The Military Balance* of 1960 to 1976 (International Institute for Strategic Studies, London).

8. House Armed Services Committee Hearings on Cost and Escalation in Defense Procurement Contracts (1973). Explanation by Department of Defense Deputy Comptroller for Program/Budget (Callaghan, see n.3 supra), p. 85.

9. Aron (see Ch.5, no.20 supra), p. 498.

10. "For Your File," NATO Bulletin for Commanders and Public Information Officers 11 (1975):3.

11. The passages are taken from the revised edition of the report, updated by articles, congressional testimony, lectures, and so forth; copies can be obtained from the Center for Strategic and International Studies, Georgetown University, 1800 K Street, N.W., Washington, D.C. 20006 (Callaghan, see n.3 supra).

12. WEU Doc. 689; "European and Atlantic Cooperation in the Field of Armaments," reported by Mr. Lemmrich, December 1, 1975, p. 16 and Appendix 6, p. 32.

13. Callaghan (see n.3 supra), p. 44.


## CHAPTER 9

1. "The rivalry, if not the confrontation, between the two political, economic and social systems reigning in the industrial societies remains the law of the international environment and, although to some extent the policy of détente may have changed its vocabulary, it has in no way altered the Communist credo, since even the Chinese statesmen who exhort the West not to relax their military efforts at all count on the future collapse of our system (de Rose, see Ch. 5, n.23 supra), p. 14.

2. Alexander Haig, Jr., "NATO and the Security of the West," *NATO Review*, no. 4, August 1978, pp. 8-11.

3. Gerhard Hubatscheck and Dieter Farwick. *Entscheidung in Deutschland*, (Berg am See: Kurt Vourneckel-Verlag, KG, 1978).

4. Haig (see n.2 supra).

5. At the end of 1975, this debt amounted to $32 billion of which $8 billion was owed to West Germany alone (quoted by Jean-François Revel in *Express*, July/August 1976, p. 45).

6. This opinion is similar to that expressed by R. Garthoff ("Soviet Concept

of Limited War," Centre d'Enseignement Supérieur Aérien, October 1958, p. 43).

7. On this subject see André Fontaine, "Défense de l'Occident," *Le Monde*, October 5, 1976, p. 21.

8. The 31 divisions of Eastern Europe are category 1 forces, i.e. fully manned with troops and equipment. The tank divisions are equipped with 325 medium tanks; the mechanized divisions have between 200 and 266. *The Military Balance, 1975-76* (see Ch. 7, n.8 supra), p. 9.

9. Philip A. Karber, "The Tactical Revolution in Soviet Military Doctrine," BDM Corporation, March 2, 1977. It also appeared in "Europäische Wehrkunde," June 1977.

10. General Steinhoff, former chairman of the NATO military committee, whose authority on the subject is beyond all questions, treats this assumption as certain under present conditions. See his book *Wohin treibt die Nato?* (Ch. 6, n.6 supra), p. 133.

11. O. Heilbrunn, *Conventional Warfare in the Nuclear Age* (London: George Allen and Unwin Ltd., 1965), p. 127.

12. de Rose (see Ch.5, n.23 supra), p. 37.

13. de Rose (see Ch. 5, n.23 supra), pp. 66-78.

14. de Rose (see Ch. 5, n.23 supra), p. 51.

15. Extract from the *Annual Defense Department Report*, section on "General Purpose Forces," February 5, 1975, issued by Secretary of Defense Schlesinger to Congress.

16. Quoted by *Military Review*, No. 6, June 1970, p. 73.

17. A. Beaufre, "Considérations sur la stratégie opérationnelle," *Strategie*, January/February/March 1970, p. 9.

18. This argument has been brought up on several occasions by the press and television to refute the author's thesis. It has been dealt with by, among others, the Central Europe Command, certain NATO authorities, and civilian publications (*Le Peuple*, *Het Volk*, *Le Drapeau Ronge* of March 23, 1976 and AFP of the same date).

## CHAPTER 10

1. *The Military Balance, 1975-76* (see Ch. 7, n.8 supra), p. 10.

2. This assumption is particularly mentioned in the *White Paper 1975-1976*. "The Security of the Federal Republic of Germany and the Development of the Federal Armed Forces," (Federal Defense Ministry, February 1976), p. 18, paragraph 33.

3. Aron (see Ch. 5, n.20 supra).

4. Steinhoff (see Ch. 7, n.5 supra).

5. T.R. Milton, "Slow Decisions Endanger NATO," *Colorado Springs Sun*, May 1976.

6. The text, as it appeared in the *Congressional Record* of June 8, 1976, is reprinted here in the Appendix.

# CHAPTER 11

1. See Aron (Ch. 5, n.20 supra).
2. OECD-Main economic indicators, September 1975. UN, *Monthly Bulletin of Statistics*, July 1975.
3. Source: EEC–*National Accounts 1973*.
4. Export, merchant fleet, steel, and vehicle figures from UN, *Statistical Yearbook*, October 1975.
5. *The Military Balance, 1975-76* (see Ch. 7, n.8 supra), pp. 10; 18-24.
6. "Western Europe and the Evolution of the Atlantic Alliance," report submitted on behalf of the General Affairs Committee by Mr. Leynen, WEU Assembly, Doc. 680, p. 3.
7. See Aron (Ch. 5, n.20 supra).
8. Mr. Van Eslande, Belgian foreign minister, referring to the future of the EDC, said that "it caused the loss of a quarter of a century in the organization of Europe as regards defense."
9. Recommendations (232) and written questions (129) until 1972. Quoted by Jacques Westhof, "The Western European Union before and after the enlargement of the European Communities," *European Yearbook* 22 (1977), published under the auspices of the Council of Europe.
10. See WEU Assembly, Doc. 554, "The Brussels Treaty and the European Institutions," report submitted on behalf of the General Affairs Commission by Lord Gladwin, November 4, 1971, p. 3.
11. Ambassador de Staercke, 1970 address at the Belgian War College.
12. "The Eurogroup within the North Atlantic Alliance," FRG Government Press and Printing Office, July 1972.
13. "European Union," report by the Commission of the European Communities. Cover letter dated June 26, 1975 from François-Xavier Ortoli, to the president in the office of the European Council.
14. In this connection, see the excellent report submitted on behalf of the General Affairs Commission of WEU by Mr. Leynen, "Western Europe and the Evolution of the Atlantic Alliance–Examination of Present Problems," Doc. 680, October 23, 1975, pp. 3-13.
15. Leo Tindemans, "The European Union," report to the European Council, Brussels, December 1975.
16. This happened as a result of the statement made at the 1961 European summit conference. Quoted by Burrows and Irwin, *The Security of Western Europe* (London: Knight & Co., 1972), p. 140.
17. A particularly valuable source on this subject is WEU Doc. 663 (see Ch. 6, n.2 supra).

18. J.A. Kielmannsegg, "The Feasibility of Defending Western Europe," lecture given at the University of London, May 6, 1969.

19. "It may be in the highest degree improbable that Soviet tanks will cross the West German/Warsaw Pact border. The degree of improbability, however, is exactly proportionate to the tank strength on our side and the political determination behind it." (London) *Times*, August 7, 1969.

20. Tweede Kamer der Staten-Generaal, Zitting 1975-76, 13600 hoofdstuk X, Nr. 1, p. 4.

21. Aron (see Ch. 5, n.20 supra), Ch. 6.

22. Recommendation no. 290 on reserve forces, WEU Assembly proceedings, 22nd ordinary session, first part, June 1976, p. 45.

23. Guy Brossollet, *Essai sur la non-bataille* (Paris: Belin, 1975).

24. See also the article by Major B.E.M. Briquemont, "Reflexion sur le livre di Guy Brosollet," *Revue Infanterie* 45 (1976): 51-65.

25. W.S. Bennet, R.R. Sandoval, and E.G. Shreffler, "Securite Nationale des Etats-Unis et armes nucléaires," *Stratégie*, Institut Français d'Etudes Stratégiques, 40 (1974): 24-25; 31.

26. Bernard Expedit article, *Stratégie* (see n.25 supra), pp. 56-57.

27. Recommendation 290 on reserve forces following the report by the committee on defense questions and armaments and the draft recommendation, Doc. 707, reported by Mr. Delorme, France. This draft recommendation was unanimously adopted.

28. Horst Afheldt, *Verteidigung und Frieden* (Munich: Carl Hanser-Verlag, 1977).

29. Steven L. Canby, *Short (and Long) War Responses: Restructuring Border Defense and Reserve Mobilization for Armored Warfare: Final Report, March 1978*. Ref. TSC-W2707A159. See Ch. 5, pp. 57-70: "Territorial Defense Countering Surprise and Obtaining Border and In-Depth Defense."

30. Canby (see n.29 supra), p. 55.

31. Mr. Strauss, former minister of defense and then of finance of the FRG, considered that a Franco-British nuclear pool could be the first step toward the creation of a European political union with its own defense force (statement made in London, May 1969). This opinion is shared by Dr. A. Albonetti, in *The Role of Nuclear Weapons and Problems of Atlantic and European Defense* (Rome: NATO Defense College, May 21, 1976).

32. A.J. Pierre, *Nuclear Politics* (New York: Oxford University Press, 1971), p. 342.

33. Anglo-American Agreement for Cooperation on the Uses of Atomic Energy for Mutual Defense Purposes (July 3, 1958).

34. Lord Carrington, British Defense Policy, RVSI, September 1973, p. 6.

35. W. Joshua, "A Strategic Concept for the Defense of Europe," *ORBIS*, Summer 1973, p. 455.

36. Ian Smart, "Prospects for Anglo-French Nuclear Cooperation," Adelphi Papers, I.I.S.S., p. 10.

37. A. Beaufre, *Discussion et stratégie* (Paris: Armand Colin, 1964), p. 113.
38. Kapitein G. Schiltz, "Ein Kernmacht voor West-Europa," Belgische Krijg-school, Div. 90, March 1975, p. 60.
39. P. Davis, "A European Nuclear Force: Utility and Prospects," *ORBIS*, Spring 1973, pp. 110-131, quoted by Schiltz (n.38 supra), p. 61.
40. Fontaine (see Ch. 9, n.7 supra), p. 22.
41. *Le Monde*, October 5, 1976, p. 22.
42. The Federal Republic of Germany may serve as an example in this connection. The Bundeswehr has set up an objective and complete information service for the purpose of informing its military personnel; opinion polls have verified the beneficial effect of this policy.
43. WEU Assembly, 22nd session, June 1976, Doc. 707, reported by D. Delorme on behalf of the committee on defense questions and armaments, May 19, 1976, p. 157.

## CHAPTER 12

1. A. Beaufre, *Stratégie pour demain* (Paris: Plon, 1972), p. 28.
2. From Barbara W. Tuchman, *August 14* (original title: *The Guns of August*) (Paris: Les Presses de la Cité, 1971), pp. 43-44.
3. General van Overstraeten, *Albert I, Leopold III—20 years of Belgian Military Policy: 1920-1940* (Albert Ier, Lépold III—Vingt ans de politique militaire belge 1920-1940). Brussels: Editions Desclaé de Brouwer, 1946), p. 32.
4. See *D Day in Africa* (Jour J en Afrique) by Jacques Robichon (Paris: Ed. Robert Laffont, 1964), p. 139.
5. R. Woller, *Der Unwahrscheinliche Krieg* (Stuttgart: Seewald Verlag, 1970), p. 136.

# Bibliography

## BOOKS

Afheldt, Horst. *Verteidigung und Frieden*. Munich: Carl Hansen-Verlag, 1977.

Ailleret, Charles. *L'aventure atomique française*. Paris: Grasset, 1968.

Aron, Raymond. *Le grand débat—Paix et guerre entre les nations*. 4th ed., Paris: Calman Lévy, 1966. *Republique Imperiale*. Paris: Calman Lévy, 1962.

Aron, Raymond, and Lerner, Daniel. *France Defeats EDC*. New York: Praeger, 1957.

Beaufre, A. *L'OTAN et l'Europe*. Paris: Calman Lévy, 1966.

Beaufre, A. *Dissuasion et stratégie*. Paris: Armand Colin, 1964.

Beaufre, A. *Stratégie pour demain*. Paris: Plon, 1972.

Bellini, James. *French Defense Policy*. London: R.U.S.I., 1974.

Bloes, R. *Le "Plan Fouchet" et le problème de l'Europe politique*. Bruges: Collège d'Europe, 1970.

Brossollet, Guy. *Essai sur la non-bataille*. Paris: Belin, 1975.

Buchan, Alastair. *Europe's Futures, Europe's Choices*. London: Chatto and Windus, 1969.

Burrows, Sir Bernard, and Irwin, Christopher. *The Security of Western Europe*. London: Charles Knight and Co., 1972.

269

Callaghan, Jr., Thomas A. *US/European Economic Cooperation in Military and Civil Technology.* 2d ed. Washington, D.C.: The Center for Strategic and International Studies, Georgetown University, 1978.

Canby, Steven L. *Short (and Long) War Responses: Restructuring Border Defense and Reserve Mobilization for Armored Warfare.* Final Report. Silver Spring, Maryland: Technology Service Corporation, March 1978.

Carrère d'Encausse, Hélène. *La politique soviétique au Moyen Orient: 1955-1975.* Paris: Presse de la Fondation Nationale des Sciences Politiques, 1976.

de Carmoy, Guy. *Fortune de l'Europe.* Paris: Domar, 1953.

de Carmoy, Guy. *Les politiques étrangères de la France (1944-1966).* Paris: Edition de la Table Ronde, 1967.

de L'Ecotais, Yann. *L'Europe sabotée.* Brussels: Rossel, 1976.

de Rose, François. *La France et la défense de l'Europe.* Paris: Seuil, 1976.

de Smet, André. *La Communauté Européene de Défense–Expériences et leçons.* Belgium: Heule, Editions U.G.A., 1966.

Doly, Guy. *Stratégie France-Europe.* Paris: Les Editions Media, 1977.

Erickson, John. *Soviet Military Power.* London: Royal United Services Institute for Defence Studies, 1971.

Foch, R. *L'Europe et la technologie.* Paris: Les Editions Media, 1977.

Gillessen, Günther. *Sieben Argumente für Europa.* Bonn: Europa Union-Verlag, 1976.

Hubatscheck, Gerhard, and Farwick Dieter. *Entscheidung in Deutschland.* Berg am See: Kurt Vowinckel-Verlag, KG, 1978.

Kissinger, Henry. *Les malentendus transatlantiques.* Paris: Denoël, 1965.

Knapp, Wilfrid. *A History of War and Peace: 1939-1965.* Oxford: Oxford University Press, 1967.

Legaret, Jean, and Martin-Dumesnil, E. *La Communauté européenne de Défense.* Paris: VRIN, 1953.

Luquet, Charles. *L'Europe satellisée ou l'agression permanente.* Tournai (Belgium): Casterman, 1970.

Northedge, F.S. *The Foreign Policies of the Powers.* London: Faber and Faber, 1968.

Northedge, F.S. *East-West Relations–Détente and After.* Lagos: Nigeria University of Ife Press, Caxton Press (West Africa), 1975.

Revel, François. *La tentation totalitaire.* Paris: Laffont, 1976.

Schelling, Thomas C. *The Strategy of Conflict.* Oxford: Oxford University Press, 1973.

Schütze, Walter. *Coopération européenne et Alliance Atlantique.* Paris: Institut Atlantique, 1969.

Stehlin, Paul. *Retour à zéro–L'Europe et sa défense dans le compte à rebours.* Paris: Laffont, 1968.

Steinhoff, Johannes. *Wohin treibt die NATO? Probleme der Verteidigung Westeuropas.* Hamburg: Hoffmann und Campe, 1976.

Tatu, Michel. *Le triangle Washington-Moscou-Pékin et les deux Europes*. Tournai (Belgium): Casterman, 1972.

Taylor, A.J.P. *The Struggle for Mastery in Europe: 1848-1919*. Oxford: Clarendon Press, 1969.

Taylor, Maxwell. *The Uncertain Trumpet*. London: Stevens and Sons Limitted, 1959.

Tuchman, Barbara W. *The Guns of August*. New York: Dell Publishing Co., 1971.

Williams, Geoffrey Lee, and Williams, Alan Lee. *Crises in European Defence*. London: London and Tonbridge, 1974.

## DOCUMENTS

Assembly of the Western European Union.

*Official Records of the 22nd Ordinary Session*. Paris: June 1976.

Document 554: *Brussels Treaty and the European Institutions (Perspectives Offered to the Western European Union)*. (Reporter: Lord Gladwin), November 4, 1971.

Document 557: *Organization of Future Western Defense*. (Reporter: Mr. Boyden), November 16, 1971.

Document 663: *Rational Deployment of Forces on the Central Front*. (Study by General Ulrich de Maizière), April 2, 1975.

Document 671: *State of European Security*. (Chairman: Mr. Critchley, Reporters: Mr. Dankert, Mr. Duvieusart, Mr. Wall, and Mr. Lemmrich), April 29, 1975.

Document 680: *Western Europe and the Evolution of the Atlantic Alliance – Examination of Present Problems*. (Reporter: Mr. Leynen), October 23, 1975.

Document 682: *Development in the Iberian Peninsula and the Atlantic Alliance*. (Reporter: Mr. Critchley), November 10, 1975.

Document 689: *European and Atlantic Cooperation in the Field of Armaments*. (Reporter: Mr. Lemmrich), December 1, 1975.

Document 690: *The Air Forces on the Central Front*. (Reporter: Mr. Roper), December 1, 1975.

Document 707: *Reserve Forces*. (Reporter: Mr. Delorme), May 19, 1976.

*Report of the Commission of the European Communities*, Brussels, June 27, 1975.

*Congressional Record*, June 8, 1976.

*Congressional Record*, September 13, 1976.

*First and Second Chamber of the General Defense Staff national budget* (Department of Defense), Session 1975-1976. The Hague, The Netherlands.

*Handout on Danish Armed Forces*. Denmark: Chief of Defence, September 1975.

*White Paper 1975-1976.* "The Security of the Federal Republic of Germany and the Development of the Federal Armed Forces," Bonn: Minister of Defense, February 1976.

*White Paper 1973-1974.* "The Security of the Federal Republic of Germany and the Evolution of the Federal Armed Forces," Bonn: Minister of Defense, January 1974.

*NATO Final Communiqués* (1949-1974). Brussels: Information Service of NATO, 1974.

*Rapport au Conseil Européen par Monsieur Léo Tindemans, Premier Ministre.* Brussels: L'Union Européenne, December 1975.

*Report of the Activities of the Sub-Committee on European Defense Cooperation.* North Atlantic Assembly, September 1975.

*Traité instituant la Communauté Européenne de Défense et Documents annexes.* Paris: La Documentation française, 1952.

## ARTICLES

Aron, A., Staar, R.F., de Raeymaeker, O., Vivario, G., Schwarz, U., and van der Beugel, E.H. "Politique de défense des petites puissances." Ecole de Guerre —Congrès (1870-1970), Brussels, September 28-29, 1970.

Atlantic Treaty Organization Publications. "The Soviets and Northern Europe." Paris, September 1971. "The Security of North Sea Oil and the Over-all Soviet Naval Threat." Paris, December 1975.

Beach, W.G.H. "The Springs of Policy." *Scotland Universities Study Group,* 1971.

Brown, Neville. "European Security: 1972-1980." *R.U.S.I.,* April 1972, p. 63.

Callaghan, J. "Britain and NATO." *NATO Review* 4 (1974): p. 13.

Calleo, D.P. "The European Coalition in a Fragmenting World." *Foreign Affairs,* October 1975, p. 98.

Chirac, Jacques. Excerpts of a statement, *Atlantic News* 4 (1974), p. 35.

Critchley, Julien. "Défense de l'Europe ou défense européene." *Revue de l'OTAN* 1 (1976): p. 13.

Debré, M. "Défense de l'Europe et sécurité en Europe." *Revue de Défense Nationale,* December 1972, pp. 1779-1804.

de Carmoy, Guy. "Les attitudes des Européens ` l'égard des Etats-Unis." *Revue de l'OTAN* 5 (1975): p. 27.

Geneste, Marc. "Un concept de défense crédible pour l'Occident: Les Murailles de la Cité." *ORBIS* 19 (Summer 1975), p. 477.

Gladwin, Lord. "The Defence of Western Europe." *Foreign Affairs,* April 1973, pp. 589-597.

Haig, General Alexander M. "NATO and the Security of the West." *NATO Review* 4 (August 1978): pp. 8-11.

Hunt, Kenneth. "The Alliance and Europe. Part II, Defence with Fewer Men." *Adelphi Papers* 98 (Summer 1973): p. 73.

Joshua, W. "A Strategic Concept for the Defence of Europe." *ORBIS* 17 (Summer 1973): pp. 448-482.

Kaldor, Mary. "European Defence Industries—National and International Implications." Institute for the Study of International Organization, University of Sussex, England, 1972, p. 53.

Karber, Philip A. "The Tactical Revolution in Soviet Military Doctrine." BDN Corporation, March 2, 1977.

Kielmannsegg, J.A. "The Feasibility of Defending Western Europe." University of London, May 6, 1969.

Löwenthal, Richard. "Has Détente Failed?" *Encounter*, May 1976, p. 55.

Mason, R. "The Eurogroup in 1975." *NATO Review*, April 1975, p. 6.

Naechterlein, Donald E. "The Influence of Domestic Politics on American Foreign Policy." Paper prepared for the Political Studies Association's Annual Conference at Nottingham University, March 22-24, 1976, p. 9.

Nixon, Richard. "U.S. Foreign Policy for the 1970s: Building for Peace." Report to Congress, February 25, 1971.

Pierre, A.J. "Nuclear Diplomacy: Britain, France and America." *Foreign Affairs*, 49 (1971): pp. 283-307.

Schmidt, Helmut. Excerpts from a statement on NATO, *NATO Review* 4 (1974): p. 34.

Schütz, Walter, "Perspektiven der französichen Wehrpolitik." *Europa-Archiv*, 1972, 22, p. 41.

Smart, Ian. "Future Conditional: The Prospect for Anglo-French Nuclear Cooperation." *Adelphi Papers*, 1971, p. 40.

Stehlin, Paul. "Défense de l'Europe et l'Alliance atlantique." *Revue Militaire Générale*, September 1968, p. 57.

Westhof, Jacques. "L'Union de l'Europe occidentale avant et après l'élargissement des Communautés européennes." London: *European Yearbook 1977* (published under the auspices of the Council of Europe), p. 22.

# Name Index

Acheson, D., 44, 46
Adenauer, K., 44
Ailleret, C., 79, 80
Aron, R., 137, 216

Beaufre, A., 35, 166, 220, 231, 235
Bellini, J., 79
Bennecke, J., 214
Bergold, H., 122
Berlinguer, E., 119, 120
Birnstiel, F., 218
Bourges, Y., 87
Bowden, B.V., 62
Brandt, W., 184
Brentano, H. von, 44
Brezhnev, L., 22, 41, 229
Brossollet, G., 216, 218, 220

Brown, G.S., 39
Brzezinski, Z., 35

Callaghan, T.A., 139, 140, 144, 149
Canby, S.L., 219
Carrington, P.A., 222
Carter, J., 33, 68, 120
Castex, W., 170
Chaban-Delmas, J., 65
Chirac, J., 86
Churchill, W.L.S., 58, 63

Davignon, E., 204
de Carmoy, G., 53
de Chardin, T., 4
de Gaulle, C., 52, 53, 72, 75, 76, 77,
    78, 79, 83, 166, 201

# About the Author

General Robert Close, born in Brussels in 1922, attended the Ecole des Cadets and the Ecole Royale Militaire. He took part in the May 1940 campaign at Dunkirk, where he was taken prisoner and sent to Germany. After being released, he returned to Belgium to join the Resistance, and was later arrested by the Gestapo.

After the war he was recalled to active service, filling a succession of posts within the army. In 1959, he was appointed Chief of Staff of the 7th Infantry Brigade, where he remained until joining the Supreme Headquarters of the Allied Powers in Europe in 1961. He served as military, naval, and air attaché at the Belgian Embassy in London from 1966-1970. In 1971, he took command of the 17th Armoured Brigade, holding this post until 1974, when he was made Deputy Commander and Director of Studies to the NATO Defense College in Rome. Two years later, he was appointed Major General, and made Commander of the 16th Armoured Division of NATO Forces in Germany. He is currently Chairman of the Board of the Commission for National Defense in Brussels.

General Close holds degrees from the Free University of Brussels and the Liège University. He has received numerous awards for his distinguished service, including *Grand Officer de l'Ordre de la Couronne* and the *Croix de Guerre avec palme.*

# Pergamon Policy Studies